"This commentary is distinctive in of Samuel in the fundamental storyline of Scripture, which climaxes in the death and resurrection of Jesus Christ. It deals faithfully with the text and unlike many commentaries is replete with application to the world in front of the text. The book is rich with insight and practical application, but avoids moralizing, always seeking to show the events in the lives of the key figures in the biblical books in the light of the gospel. It is ideal for pastors and leaders who are trying to preach the Old Testament faithfully but having a difficult time doing it. Hard texts are not avoided but are given careful treatment. It is an honor for me to recommend this commentary."

Stephen G. Dempster, professor of religious studies, Crandall University, Moncton, New Brunswick, Canada

"J. D. Greear and Heath Thomas give pastors what we most need. Beginning with clear exposition of biblical passages, they show us how these Old Testament stories fit within God's larger work of revelation in Scripture. Every page points to the practical significance these stories have for our lives in the West today. More than that, the authors write an Old Testament commentary free from the modern habits of proof texting, therapeutic sentimentalism, and narrow moralizing. In the end, Greear and Thomas have gifted us with a masterful book that will draw us into the stories of Israel's kings and carry us along as this story unfolds expectantly and magnificently in the life and work of Jesus Christ, the true king of Israel.

"This is pastoral scholarly commentary at its finest. Indeed Greear and Thomas give us a rare example of writing where erudite academic insights meet the everyday life of today's Christian reader. Their meticulously researched work never burdens the reader with abstract academic jargon. Instead, *1–2 Samuel* demonstrates over and over, with clarity and conviction, the power of these books to capture our hearts and reshape our lives.

"The move in this commentary from scholarly grounded research to grist for preaching and personal application never seeks to impress, never confuses, and never disappoints. Their writing flows out of patient and careful study of Scripture and lives deeply grounded in the faith they nurture in their readers."

Ryan P. O'Dowd, PhD, pastor of Bread of Life Anglican Church, Ithaca, New York; adjunct professor of biblical studies, Gordon College

"Rarely does one find a commentary with strong, biblical theological foundations that reads so accessibly and makes so many relevant points to our lives today. Greear and Thomas excel in showing how the message of Samuel points to Christ and remains vitally important for the Church today."

Trevin Wax, Bible and Reference publisher at LifeWay Christian Resources, author of *Gospel-Centered Teaching* and *Counterfeit Gospels*

CHRIST-CENTERED

Exposition

OT / COMMENTARY   FEATURING

AUTHORS **Heath Thomas and J. D. Greear**

SERIES EDITORS **David Platt, Daniel L. Akin, and Tony Merida**

CHRIST-CENTERED

Exposition

EXALTING JESUS IN

1 & 2 SAMUEL

HOLMAN®

REFERENCE

NASHVILLE, TENNESSEE

SERIES DEDICATION

Dedicated to Adrian Rogers and John Piper. They have taught us to love the gospel of Jesus Christ, to preach the Bible as the inerrant Word of God, to pastor the church for which our Savior died, and to have a passion to see all nations gladly worship the Lamb.

—David Platt, Tony Merida, and Danny Akin
March 2013

AUTHORS' DEDICATIONS

To Doug and Kristy Warden and the rest of our Summit Small group
(Potters, Lillys, Bogles, Murphys, Zambranos, Ragains,
Papas, Will, Chris, Boyds, Nina, and John).
I am grateful for your friendship.
Together we have seen King Jesus.
—Heath

To the incredible pastoral team God has blessed me with.
I couldn't do anything without you.
I am a blessed man.
—J. D.

CONTENTS

ACKNOWLEDGMENTS

We want to thank Jeremy Howard and his stellar team at B&H for making this book—and this series—a possibility. Thanks to our editor, David Stabnow, for a fantastic job. Jeremy and his team believe in the vision behind this series and have put tremendous energy into making that vision a reality. We are thrilled with the result. Thanks too to the series editors Danny Akin, David Platt, and Tony Merida. Your vision to see a Christ-honoring preaching commentary is salutary and we pray it will serve our Savior and his Church well.

I (J. D.) would like to thank Chris Pappalardo, who is more invaluable to my speaking and writing ministry than I can express. And many, many thanks to the people of The Summit Church, who patiently put up with me as I attempted to work through 1–2 Samuel (and many other books of the Bible) together. They are a very forgiving people. The greatest earthly joy I have is preaching the Word of God to them each week. I would rather preach weekly at the Summit than I would preach anywhere else in the world, no matter how big the crowd. Thank you for, by God's grace, doing the most important work—believing (John 6:29).

I (Heath) would like to thank J. D. for the privilege of writing this volume with him. It is a joy to serve with my (former) pastor in this way. Serving as a small group leader and elder at the Summit for the years that I was there was a challenge and a real delight. We saw so many lives changed! Although now serving in Oklahoma, I pray God's continued blessing, anointing, and protection as the Summit reaches a lost world with the light of Jesus Christ. To the congregations at The Summit Church, Duke Memorial Baptist Church (NC), and New Covenant Church (TX), it was an honor to preach and teach through 1–2 Samuel with you. This volume is the fruit of us laboring together to hear the voice of the Lord Christ in and through the Scriptures. My prayer is that this volume will help the future ministers and preachers that we train through the Hobbs College of Theology and Ministry at Oklahoma Baptist University.

J. D. Greear and Heath A. Thomas
Durham, North Carolina, and Shawnee, Oklahoma
Summer 2016

SERIES INTRODUCTION

Augustine said, "Where Scripture speaks, God speaks." The editors of the Christ-Centered Exposition Commentary series believe that where God speaks, the pastor must speak. God speaks through His written Word. We must speak from that Word. We believe the Bible is God breathed, authoritative, inerrant, sufficient, understandable, necessary, and timeless. We also affirm that the Bible is a Christ-centered book; that is, it contains a unified story of redemptive history of which Jesus is the hero. Because of this Christ-centered trajectory that runs from Genesis 1 through Revelation 22, we believe the Bible has a corresponding global-missions thrust. From beginning to end, we see God's mission as one of making worshipers of Christ from every tribe and tongue worked out through this redemptive drama in Scripture. To that end we must preach the Word.

In addition to these distinct convictions, the Christ-Centered Exposition Commentary series has some distinguishing characteristics. First, this series seeks to display exegetical accuracy. What the Bible says is what we want to say. While not every volume in the series will be a verse-by-verse commentary, we nevertheless desire to handle the text carefully and explain it rightly. Those who teach and preach bear the heavy responsibility of saying what God has said in His Word and declaring what God has done in Christ. We desire to handle God's Word faithfully, knowing that we must give an account for how we have fulfilled this holy calling (Jas 3:1).

Second, the Christ-Centered Exposition Commentary series has pastors in view. While we hope others will read this series, such as parents, teachers, small-group leaders, and student ministers, we desire to provide a commentary busy pastors will use for weekly preparation of biblically faithful and gospel-saturated sermons. This series is not academic in nature. Our aim is to present a readable and pastoral style of commentaries. We believe this aim will serve the church of the Lord Jesus Christ.

Third, we want the Christ-Centered Exposition Commentary series to be known for the inclusion of helpful illustrations and theologically driven applications. Many commentaries offer no help in illustrations, and few offer any kind of help in application. Often those that do offer illustrative material and application unfortunately give little serious attention to the text. While giving ourselves primarily to explanation, we also hope to serve readers by providing inspiring and illuminating illustrations coupled with timely and timeless application.

Finally, as the name suggests, the editors seek to exalt Jesus from every book of the Bible. In saying this, we are not commending wild allegory or fanciful typology. We certainly believe we must be constrained to the meaning intended by the divine Author Himself, the Holy Spirit of God. However, we also believe the Bible has a messianic focus, and our hope is that the individual authors will exalt Christ from particular texts. Luke 24:25-27,44-47 and John 5:39,46 inform both our hermeneutics and our homiletics. Not every author will do this the same way or have the same degree of Christ-centered emphasis. That is fine with us. We believe faithful exposition that is Christ centered is not monolithic. We do believe, however, that we must read the whole Bible as Christian Scripture. Therefore, our aim is both to honor the historical particularity of each biblical passage and to highlight its intrinsic connection to the Redeemer.

The editors are indebted to the contributors of each volume. The reader will detect a unique style from each writer, and we celebrate these unique gifts and traits. While distinctive in their approaches, the authors share a common characteristic in that they are pastoral theologians. They love the church, and they regularly preach and teach God's Word to God's people. Further, many of these contributors are younger voices. We think these new, fresh voices can serve the church well, especially among a rising generation that has the task of proclaiming the Word of Christ and the Christ of the Word to the lost world.

We hope and pray this series will serve the body of Christ well in these ways until our Savior returns in glory. If it does, we will have succeeded in our assignment.

David Platt
Daniel L. Akin
Tony Merida
Series Editors
February 2013

1 and 2 Samuel

Introduction

To read the Old Testament is to read about the God who created the world, who saw His creatures commit treason against their Maker, and who enacted a rescue mission to "reconcile everything to Himself by making peace" through the blood of His one and only Son, Jesus the Messiah (Col 1:20). Jesus is the King. He is the secret of heaven and earth, the secret of Scripture, the clue that unlocks the confusion of our lives. To know and love God, to know and love ourselves, to know and love our fellow humans, and to know and love our world, we must first know this King, Jesus the Messiah. There are many beautiful but troubling things about the theology of Karl Barth, but on this point he gets things right about Jesus:

> This man is the secret of heaven and earth, of the cosmos
> created by God. To know Him is to know heaven and earth

in their diversity, unity and createdness, and to know God as their Creator. The Old Testament insight into this matter can thus be understood as meaningful and practicable only if it is understood as the promise, or prototype, of the knowledge of the Messiah. (Barth, *Church Dogmatics*, III/1: 21–22)

To read Scripture in this way means we must learn to read the Bible front-to-back and back-to-front. Both practices are vitally important. Reading the Bible front-to-back means beginning at the beginning (Gen 1) and then going to the end (Revelation). As we do, we will discover a God who created everything and who has redeemed everything in His Son, Jesus. As we read front-to-back, we discover God, the One on whom everything depends and the One who deserves all allegiance and worship. We discover His virtues and values. We discover all the major stories, images, and themes present in Israel's history, the roles each major person in Israel's history plays, and how the stories of Israel find their fulfillment in Jesus. We see how Jesus really is the culmination and crest of Scripture.

But this way of reading is still not complete. We must learn to read the Bible back-to-front as well. This means that once we see Jesus in the New Testament, we then turn back to the stories of the Old Testament in the light of Jesus and find that He was always there. He is there at creation, and everything is made through Him and for Him. He is the exodus from slavery to freedom. He is the deliverance at the waters of the Red Sea. He is the promised rest for Israel. He is the judge, prophet, priest, and king. Jesus is the temple and the sacrifice. Jesus is the all in all, the beginning and the end, the secret of heaven and earth. Both movements are necessary for a truly evangelical (sometimes called "Gospel-centered" or "Christ-centered") reading of Scripture. As we read in this way, we will find Christ exalted in the Scriptures, and we will proclaim Christ from them! As we read in this way, we will discover God's plan for the coming and reigning King.

As a unified narrative, 1–2 Samuel reveals God's plan for this King. We cannot avoid this fact, and we must understand the significance of the King's story. The coming of Israel's king to the world stage marks a watershed moment in history.

The monumental nature of this moment is not due to the nobility, wisdom, or greatness of the kings of Israel, especially when one compares them to other kings in history. In many (perhaps most) ways, the kings of Israel played marginal roles in the political and national goings on in the ancient world. Israel's kings found themselves caught between major players on the world stage: the hammer of Egypt and the anvil of the Tigris-Euphrates river valley nation-states. Babylon was known for law. Egypt was known for wisdom. Assyria was known for brutal power. The gleam of Egyptian pharaohs, Babylonian warlords, and Assyrian kings shone more brightly in history than did the dim light of the kings of the people of Israel. Yet appearances can be deceiving.

As we will see in this commentary; while nations prize visible strength and great wealth, true power comes from the hand of God. The greatness of Israel's kings has little to do with human greatness at all. What makes the advent of Israel's king so significant in world history is what God would do with and through him. And this is the story 1–2 Samuel tells.

Readers will notice that in their (English) Bibles, 1–2 Samuel appears to be two books. However 1–2 Samuel is not really two separate books but one book. That is not to say it is seamless and was composed at one time. Clearly there are different portions of the book. Still, these different parts have come together and been incorporated into a unified whole.

In ancient times our two books appear together on one scroll, and they tell one story of major transitions in the life of God's people. It tells of the transition of Israelite worship at God's shrine in Shiloh to His worship in Jerusalem, at the central sanctuary. It tells the story of the transition to kingship under Saul, the first king of Israel. It proclaims the transition from Saul's reign to the reign of David, God's appointed king. And it shows the story of the transition from Israelite tribal confederacy (as in the book of Judges) to a monarchy. But each of these transitions occurs in one unified and unfolding story. So in this commentary we will be using the language the "book" of Samuel or "1–2 Samuel" to describe the entire account.

Taking stock of the full story of 1–2 Samuel is important for reading and preaching the book. If we exalt Christ in 1–2 Samuel, we should not be content to pick out a story here or there, or a verse here or there, and show how it connects to Jesus, His life, and ministry. Rather, the whole freight of 1–2 Samuel draws us to Jesus, helps us see His beauty and glory, and helps us fit into His story.

1–2 Samuel as Mirror

In so many ways 1–2 Samuel is like a mirror to the modern world. It shows us a society with serious trouble. Among other things this text puts on display

men abusing women,

wives betrayed by husbands,

children gone wild,

corrupt religious leaders,

conspiracy to murder,

deceitful politicians,

power struggles,

and the horrors of war.

Does any of this sound familiar? It should. The realities in 1–2 Samuel remind us of the modern world because we see them over and over again in our neighborhoods and friendships! You see, we all share the common problem of sin. Sin is, at its root, rebellion against God. It is our way of saying to our Creator that we know more than He does, and as a result we can live as we want rather than living according to His best plan. This was true for ancient Israel, and it is true for us today. So 1–2 Samuel mirrors the modern world.

And as a mirror 1–2 Samuel reveals something else profound: as people turn their backs on God and His ways, the results are catastrophic. What was true for their day is true for ours. Except for God's gracious help, our sin would swallow us whole.

This point on the persistence and consequences of sin in the book of Samuel stands out because it reminds us of the realism of the biblical books. The actions of the leaders of Israel in the book of Samuel often are atrocious and immoral, and they help expose the foibles of our own leaders. Families, too, appear as dysfunctional as modern families. In the light of the earthiness and messiness of the biblical texts, we should not try to read or preach them by making them more palatable for a religious audience. Nor should we whitewash the problems of the characters presented therein so that we get a sanitized picture of life.

Reading the book of Samuel, we see life in all its gory detail. And as a result, readers who become familiar with the horrors of Scripture discover the vocabulary to speak about the horrors of our own world. God did not give 1–2 Samuel to show us the perfect world or even the best world. That is more the realm of science fiction or utopian novels.

First and Second Samuel expose for careful readers the horrors and hope of the real world.

1–2 Samuel and Story

Eugene Peterson reminds us that 1–2 Samuel presents a story with realism and power but that we should not underestimate its power as a story:

> Story doesn't just tell us something and leave it there, it invites our participation. A good storyteller gathers us into the story. We feel the emotions, get caught up in the drama, identify with the characters, see into nooks and crannies of life that we had overlooked, realize there is more to this business of being human than we had yet explored. If the storyteller is good, doors and windows open. The Hebrews were good storytellers, good in both the artistic and moral senses. (*First and Second Samuel*, 2)

Peterson hits the nail on the head. We would take his point one step further: how the author tells the story of 1–2 Samuel is as important as the fact that it is a good story! So, how does this book present the story? We touch on two dialectics: specificity and detail, story and divine redemption.

Specificity and Detail

The author of Samuel presents the narrative with a certain specificity of detail. By using the term *specificity*, we do not mean that the author gives us all the details. Rather, the author gives only details that carry the story forward to present the message the author wants to convey.

It is similar to the way the Gospels present their stories of Jesus. The apostle John concludes his Gospel by saying,

> *And there are also many other things that Jesus did, which, if they were written one by one, I suppose not even the world itself could contain the books that would be written.* (John 21:25)

The point is that John selected only the details that would give the story of Jesus that was necessary to get across his message to the readers of the Gospel. Other things could have been added, to be sure, but the goal was not to give a blow-by-blow report of all Jesus did; the goal was to show how Jesus—the Word of God and Son of God, the Savior of the world, the King of Israel and King of creation—came to live a perfect life, die a sinless death, and rise from the grave so that those who call on His name might be saved and find life eternal.

Similarly, other details could have been added in 1–2 Samuel, but it does not give a blow-by-blow record of all the events in the history of Israel. It is a story with specific details that get across a specific point. So the details that appear in the story are sparse but specific, concise but concrete. Often this means that some details are left out, leaving readers wondering what else was going on in the story! But that is not a bad thing. Peterson argues that the "reticence" to give all the details of the story opens a space for the reader to enter in, join the story, and figure out how (or whether) he or she fits! Biblical authors

> show us a spacious world in which God creates and saves and blesses. First through our imaginations and then through our faith—imagination and faith are close kin here—they offer us a place in the story, invite us into this large story that takes place under the broad skies of God's purposes, in contrast to the gossipy anecdotes that we cook up in the stuffy closet of the self. (Peterson, *First and Second Samuel,* 2)

Story and Divine Redemption

The major actor in the story of Samuel is none other than Yahweh, the God of Israel. It is His story rather than merely Israel's story. As a result, the One issuing the call in the book of Samuel is Yahweh. He extends His invitation to come and see what He is doing in His redemption.

Readers catch a glimpse of God's invitation as the actors in the book respond to Him. Take, for instance, the praise prayers of Hannah (1 Sam 2) and David (2 Sam 22). These songs capture the magnitude of God and His invitation. In each song the singers proclaim the praise of their God. They proclaim that this is the God of redemption:

- He saves, delivers, and protects (1 Sam 2:1; 2 Sam 22:2-3).
- He judges the wicked and vindicates the righteous (1 Sam 2:3,9; 2 Sam 22:8-16,21-25).
- He raises up the lowly and humbles the proud (1 Sam 2:1,3; 2 Sam 22:26-28).
- He provides life to the barren (1 Sam 2:5).
- He raises up the poor (1 Sam 2:8).
- He created the world for His glory (1 Sam 2:8).

- He strengthens the weak but overpowers the strong (1 Sam 2:4; 2 Sam 22:17-20).
- He brings life out of death (1 Sam 2:6; 2 Sam 22:6-7).
- He gives power to His Son, the King of Israel (1 Sam 2:10; 2 Sam 22:44-51).

Because the story is framed in praise, we are invited to sing the song of our great Redeemer as well. The story of Samuel draws us in: Do we want to know this God? Do we want to receive His invitation to know Him and be known by Him? Reading His story in Samuel takes us on a journey to see who He is, what are His virtues and values, and what He is doing in redemption through Jesus.

Major Characters

Although Israel's God, Yahweh, is the central character, other characters remain fundamental to the story. Other than Yahweh, 1–2 Samuel presents four major characters:

1. Hannah (1 Sam 1–2)
2. Samuel (1 Sam 2–12)
3. Saul (1 Sam 13–31)
4. David (1 Sam 13–2 Sam 24)

The plot of the narrative revolves around these characters and those who associate with them. This emphasis will be important in this commentary because it will focus more on these characters than the other characters who serve as agents that propel the story of Hannah, Samuel, Saul, and David. When we look at the book from the opening presentation of Hannah, each character links forward and backward to the other, creating a forward momentum to the narrative.

Hannah gives birth to Samuel.
   ↘ Samuel anoints Saul as king.
      ↘ Saul's faulty kingship gives way to David.
         ↘ David's kingship proceeds despite setbacks.

The challenging, scandalous, and unfolding realism presented in Samuel reminds the careful expositor that one cannot teach or preach the parts of Samuel without an eye to the whole. If we want to preach the story of David and Goliath, yet ignore David's faults with Bathsheba, his terrible faults as a father, or his selfishness in his interaction with his people and with God, then we present an untrue portrait of Israel's greatest king. A focus on the whole story of the book of Samuel is an urgent need for the church in her preaching and teaching (Brueggemann, *First and Second Samuel*, 6).

Structure

And the whole story of Samuel is organized along a structure. Authors create books in the Bible to present various messages, and the structure(s) of the books help carry those messages forward. Unfortunately, there is no existing manual from the biblical period—written by Moses or David or anyone else for that matter—that tells us in advance what the structures of biblical books actually are! So, as readers, we are left on an adventure of discovery to figure out the structure(s) of books and how they present the messages the authors want to convey.

When it comes to 1–2 Samuel, a number of possibilities appear for its structure. Peter Leithart helpfully presents the following structure of the book, where repeated elements across both halves draw us to the central concern of the whole (Leithart, *A Son to Me*, 31):

A – Birth of Samuel (1 Sam 1:1–2:11) / (Hannah's Song: 1 Sam 2:1-10)
 B – Corruption of Eli's House (1 Sam 2:12–3:21)
  C – Exile and Return of the Ark (1 Sam 4:1–7:17)
   D – Saul's Rise (1 Sam 8:1–12:25)
    E – Saul's Fall (1 Sam 13:1–15:33)
     F – David in Saul's House (1 Sam 15:34–20:42)
      G – Saul versus David (1 Sam 21:1–27:12)
       H – Saul's Death (1 Sam 28:1–2 Sam 1:27)
      G´– House of Saul vs. House of David (2 Sam 2:1–4:12)
     F´ – David as King (2 Sam 5:1–9:13)
    E´– David's Fall (2 Sam 10:1–12:31)
   D´– Absalom's Rise (2 Sam 13:1–15:12)
  C´– Exile and Return of David (2 Sam 15:13–19:43)
 B´– Rebellion of Sheba (2 Sam 20:1-26)
A´– The true King (2 Sam 21:1–24:25) / (David's Poems: 2 Sam 22:1–23:7)
This structure recognizes the repeated elements within the narrative and is known as a "chiastic" structure. Such structures appear throughout Old Testament narratives, and Leithart's analysis is sound as it relates to 1–2 Samuel. Following on this structure, the careful expositor will note a few things:

First, poetry frames the entirety of Samuel in Hannah's and David's songs (A parallels A´). Poetry also lies at the center of the story (H, where David sings a lament over Saul and Jonathan in 2 Sam 1:19-27). The death of the sinful king of Israel (Saul) opens the way for the new king of Israel (David). The imminent death of the new king (David) then opens the way for the true king of Israel (Jesus). In this way the death of Saul is the hinge on which the plot of Samuel moves.

Second, in the parallel between C and C´, one sees the exile and return of the central tabernacle element (ark) and the new king (David). This parallel is important thematically as it links tabernacle and king. Jesus is the One in whom both the Davidic king and Israelite worship find their ultimate fulfillment and meaning. Jesus is the King of Israel and the place where God's people find forgiveness from sin.

Third, this structure reveals the eerie parallels between David and Saul (D, E and E´, D´). Saul rises and falls and David rises and falls. The difference between the two lies in their inversion: God raises the Davidic line up once again while the Saulide dynasty is no more after his fall. This reminds the careful exegete that David, for all his greatness, is just a man with all the vicissitudes and foibles of humanity.

David is a type and a shadow of the true King who will come: Jesus the Messiah. David rises again to power because God is faithful to His promises (2 Sam 7); and this foreshadows the fact that God will be faithful to His promises in and through the true King, Jesus the Messiah. Although He will die at the hands of sinful people, God will raise Him up in power.

Plot

One can understand the structure of 1–2 Samuel as organized along a series of plot movements, centered on major figures in the book: Samuel, Saul, and David. Samuel is the prophet, priest, and judge of God's people who transitions them from the leadership of judges to that of kings. Saul is the first king of Israel, the king of Israel's choosing but rebellious against the ways of the Lord. David is the second king of Israel but the king of God's own choosing, a king after God's heart. We should not be too idealistic with David, however. He is a king who commits murder and adultery, and he is a man with hands full of blood. He is not a perfect person, and so, in his imperfection, he points us to the perfect King, Jesus Christ.

1 Samuel 1–7	The Rise of Samuel and the Kingship of Yahweh
1 Samuel 8–15	The Rise and Fall of Saul, King of Israel
1 Samuel 16–2 Samuel 4	The Rise of David, King of Israel
2 Samuel 5–24	The Reign of David, King of Israel

Within this basic plot line, some points that emerge remain important for preaching and teaching 1–2 Samuel.

First, the story of David is part and parcel of a larger testimony of God's message in the book. It is tempting to focus sermons and teaching from 1–2 Samuel (almost) solely on David, his life, and his times. This is not altogether inappropriate and can be done well (see Boda, *After God's Own Heart*). But if we want to attend to the story of David, we must attend to the message God communicates in the *book* of Samuel. The life of David in the book remains secondary to the message of the book itself. Faithful interpretation attends to the message of the *book* of Samuel.

Second, the transitions in the book highlight a common theme in Scripture: the interweaving of divine judgment and salvation. While God judges Eli's household because of their sin in 1 Samuel 1–3, He simultaneously plans and promises salvation through Samuel in 1 Samuel 1–7 (and as we will see, ultimately, through Jesus). While God judges Saul for his failure to follow God's requirements as king in 1 Samuel 10–15, He simultaneously plans and promises (and fulfills) a future king after His own heart through David in 1 Samuel 16 (and as we will see, ultimately, through Jesus).

Judgment and salvation are part of the two-step rhythm of Scripture. God judges wickedness and sin, yet His love and compassion in salvation extend higher, wider, farther, and deeper than we could ever imagine. Exodus 34 beautifully captures the connection between divine judgment and salvation:

> *Yahweh—Yahweh is a compassionate and gracious God, slow to anger and rich in faithful love and truth, maintaining faithful love to a thousand generations, forgiving wrongdoing, rebellion, and sin. But He will not leave the guilty unpunished, bringing the consequences of the fathers' wrongdoing on the children and grandchildren to the third and fourth generation.* (Exod 34:6-7)

Judgment and salvation together reveal the character of Israel's God, Yahweh. God's judgment is sure (to the third and fourth generation) and just. Yet note the grand extent of God's faithful love and forgiveness: "to a thousand generations." The point of this text is not to give us a calendar for how long judgment or salvation ensues, as if we could say, "Whew! I'm in the fifth generation. I suppose God's judgment does not extend to me!" Or alternatively, "Oh no! I'm in the thousand-and-first generation. God's faithful love does not extend to me!" No. These timelines are there to illustrate the judgment and salvific mercy of God. While His judgment is sure, God's faithful love and forgiveness extend beyond His judgment to His people. This really is good news, and we see it in 1–2 Samuel. Although He judges His people, His priests, and His kings (even David!) because of their sin, His faithful love extends beyond judgment to preserve His people, provide faithful priests, and present us with a future Davidic king, Jesus the Messiah, who will save the world from sin.

Third, the final emphasis of the book is on the God of Israel who leads us to Jesus. Both of us (J. D. and Heath) grew up in churches where it was common to hear a teaching about the people in Scripture whom Christians should emulate. In interpretation this process is known as a "character study" on a biblical person. So, for 1–2 Samuel, we learn about Samuel or David, their character, and emulate their "heart" so that we can have a heart like them. Only then will God bless us. This is, in fact, the thesis of the highly popular study of 1 Samuel by the popular pastor Warren Wiersbe, particularly focused on David (*Be Successful*). David certainly was a man after God's own heart. And we do want to learn from him. But the question that needs to haunt us as we look at the whole of the book is this: if we are going to do a character study, which character should we study as most important?

For 1–2 Samuel, the primary actor who takes center stage, the One from whom we learn and whose voice we strain to hear, is God Himself. Israel's God, Yahweh, remains always and ever the One who raises up Samuel, Saul, and then David. He is the One who brings down Eli and Saul, and He is the One who is praised in the opening and closing of the book of Samuel (1 Sam 2 and 2 Sam 22–23).

The goal of reading 1–2 Samuel is to hear what this God might say to us from the book. The stories of 1–2 Samuel (like most of the narratives of the Old Testament) are there for our instruction (Rom 15:4; 1 Cor 10:1-14) so that we might grow in the grace and knowledge of our Lord Jesus Christ. Growth in Christ means that we learn who God is, what God values, and what God is doing with His people in the book of

Samuel. Still, when we learn to read the book to hear God's address, a number of challenges present themselves, creating obstacles to hearing God's word well.

Challenges for Interpretation and Preaching

Different Time, Different Culture

Despite the fact that we have said the story of 1–2 Samuel is a mirror to the modern world, we must be honest and affirm that much of the book seems far distant from us today, especially the Western world (North America and continental Europe). This is because it is culturally distant from the modern world. The stories of kings and priests as well as prophets and witches seem strange to "enlightened" people with smart phones, advances in modern science, and a globalized culture. These tales from Samuel take us back to "the dark ages"! For example, the "witch" of Endor from 1 Samuel 28:3-25 will catch a modern reader's attention. We have found that many Christian readers in our American contexts don't know what to do with this story. What political leader today would put a witch on his or her official cabinet as a paid advisor? But this is the practice of King Saul, at least almost. He consults a witch to make a decision. A witch is his advisor, though she is not in his royal court. I (Heath) remember teaching 1–2 Samuel in class one day when a student boldly declared that I should stop talking about witches because they are "unbiblical." Clearly he had not read 1 Samuel 28! A strange story indeed. For those who live in the Western world, these realities seem like the stuff of legend.

But for those who live and work in majority world contexts, kings and prophets, priests and witches are not the stuff of legend but part of the normal order of things. The careful reader needs to become familiar with the customs and social structures reflected in the Old Testament to get a bearing on what is going on in the text of 1–2 Samuel. A couple of good resources we have found are by Chalmers (*Exploring the Religion*), Matthews and Benjamin (*The Social World of Ancient Israel*), and King and Stager (*Life in Biblical Israel*).

Individual and Community

Another thing we can mention about the strangeness of 1–2 Samuel has to do with how it speaks to the *community* of God's people primarily and then secondarily to *individual* readers or hearers. The question for 1–2 Samuel is not, what does this text mean to *me*? The question it answers is, what does this text mean for *us*? The book's viewpoint is oriented more to the *collective group* than to the *individual*. What this means in practice is that the stories are oriented more to God's work with the group rather than with the individual.

When we read Samuel, we should not be thinking it addresses God's will for *my life exclusively*, but rather it speaks to what God is doing with *our lives together*. Again this perspective is decidedly non-Western, where the value is the individual over and above all others. So those who live and work in non-Western or majority world contexts likely will find familiar ground in Samuel's stories while the rest of us have to work to get there.

Honor and Shame

The book of Samuel arises out of an honor-shame structure of society, which is inherently foreign to Western readers. In the biblical world, honor was the ability of a household to care for its own members and the ability to take care of a neighboring household when it faced dire circumstances such as drought, death, or war (Matthews and Benjamin, *The Social World of Ancient Israel*, 142–44).

Individuals in a household would act in such a way that brought it honor and avoid behavior that brought it shame. Shame was the inability for a household to provide for its members or its covenant partners. In the Old Testament honor and shame were closely tied to a family's fidelity to Israel's God.

Honor and shame dynamics appear throughout the narrative of 1–2 Samuel. For example, note the following elements in the book:

- The grievous sins of Hophni and Phinehas, Eli's sons, not only bring shame on his father and the priesthood, but they shame the God they serve. Or, as the text reads: "They had no regard for the LORD" (1 Sam 2:12) and treated the Lord's sacrifice "with contempt" (1 Sam 2:17). Their infidelity to God brought shame on their household rather than honor.
- David takes great care to honor Saul as the anointed king of Israel (1 Sam 26:8-25). David cares for Saul's household, as he is the anointed king and he does not want to bring shame on his God or his king by harming the anointed of God.
- The name of "Ish-bosheth," Saul's son (2 Sam 2–4), means "man of shame." As he attempts to succeed Saul as king over

Israel, his name casts an ominous shadow over his attempt to rule.

- Amnon's rape of Tamar is not merely unethical, but it brings great shame on Tamar. Amnon does not care for his household but creates tension and strife within it. The rape not only is an affront to God, but Tamar also frames the horrific violation in terms of honor and shame. The rape "humiliates" (2 Sam 13:12) and brings "disgrace" (v. 13).

- Absalom's murder of Amnon for raping Tamar is an exercise of honor killing (2 Sam 13:32-33). Western readers likely see it purely in terms of vengeful murder. The honor-shame dynamic likely does not enter into their interpretation.

- Absalom's revolt against David, his father, in 2 Samuel 15–16 is not merely unethical. Even more so, it brings dishonor, or shame, to his father. It exposes David as unable to provide for or protect his household. This is one of the major reasons Absalom has sexual intercourse with each of David's concubines after running his father out of the capital. Absalom engages in this act in the sight of all Israel to publicly shame David and solidify his authority before the people and denigrate David's authority as king and head of his own household (see 2 Sam 16:21-22).

The actions of those in the book of Samuel are governed not only by what we would term "ethics." They are inherently informed by what would bring honor or shame to the larger social group in which the offender lives.

For this reason we need to take care not to impose Western values onto an ancient Near Eastern society out of which 1–2 Samuel originated. So, for instance, it might seem ridiculous that David would want to go out and destroy Nabal's entire household (1 Sam 25:1-44) because Nabal essentially disrespected him. But in that culture an action that brought shame on David—especially considering the narrative reveals that he is the anointed of God—necessitates action to preserve the honor of the Davidic house. Nabal's faithful wife, Abigail, recognizes who David is, steps in, and ameliorates her husband's dishonor by bringing greater honor to David. As a result, David does not go through with his plan.

Does all this sound strange (and perhaps unethical)? Perhaps to Western ears but not to those in majority world contexts! The alert reader must attune his or her interpretive ears to the different music that comes from an honor-shame culture.

Sex and Family

Another thing that makes this book strange for Western readers is the sexual and family structure. In 1–2 Samuel, polygamy is common: King David had at least seven wives, and probably eight, not counting concubines.[1] One should not apologize or try to downplay this reality in the text. However, just because the text *describes* David's polygamy does not mean God *prescribes* such family and sexual norms!

When one reads the rest of the story, multiple wives and the sordid family of David turn out to be a problem, not an ideal. The narrative *shows* the problem of dysfunctional and illicit sexual and family structures rather than *telling* it overtly. That is the point. As readers, we are invited to see the problems of David and his family and, using our sanctified imaginations, we have the opportunity to respond: "What a tragedy! What a dysfunctional family. I know my family is not perfect to be sure, but that's not the kind of family model we want to emulate!"

Of course, the world Church often engages the issue of polygamy because those they reach with the gospel are sometimes part of families with more than one wife! For instance, while teaching in Ethiopia, I (Heath) learned of how the church wrestled mightily with how to address polygamy once those who engaged in it converted to Christ. Their reactions varied. Some churches demanded immediate divorce for all wives except the one who was first married to the husband. However, this put terrible strain and social shame on the divorced wives and their children. Other churches allowed converted polygamous families to be baptized and normalized in the life of the church as a concession but taught that polygamy was not the ideal. Polygamous men were excluded from eldership and leadership as well. The church taught monogamous marriage to the second generation in the family and held it as the ideal (grounded in Gen 1–2), with the firm belief that polygamy would recede from the life of the church. Indeed, those who read Scripture with non-Western eyes perhaps can grasp the nettle of sex and sexuality in Samuel better than Western readers!

We argue that monogamous marriage remains the norm and ideal, not least on the foundational teaching of Genesis 2:24 and Matthew 19:5.

---

[1] For David's spouses, see 2 Sam 5:13; 6:23; 15:16; cf. 1 Kgs 1:3-4; 1 Chr 3:1-8. Concubines are females whose relationship to their sexual partner is other than primary wife. See Day, "Concubines," in *Eerdmans Dictionary*, 273. For a good study of sex and sexuality in the Old Testament, see Lamb, *Prostitutes and Polygamists*, esp. 59–86.

But for Western eyes illicit sex and different family structures (multiple wives and concubines) seem odd because these are so commonplace in 1–2 Samuel, and they just don't mesh with Western values. (Well, maybe the illicit sexuality does mesh, and the polygamous relationships do not, but who knows? Modern American culture is ever shifting away from God's norms.) Again, just because the text *describes* this kind of activity does not mean it *prescribes* such family and sexual norms.

Teachers and preachers of the book of Samuel must wrestle with each of these challenges (and probably more!) as they engage the text. This commentary will address these issues along the way as we work through the narrative. We hope our wrestling with these issues gives a helpful model for how expositors might handle them in their own preaching or teaching contexts.

1–2 Samuel in the Story of Scripture

There is another challenge to bring up in this introduction. The book of Samuel is not an isolated story in the Bible. It is part of a bigger story that extends from Genesis through 2 Kings on the one hand and from Genesis through Revelation on the other. We should not forget this as we read and preach 1–2 Samuel. Although the Bible is a coat of many colors, it is still one coat! We will look at both of these in turn.

Scholars often call the section of Scripture from Genesis through 2 Kings the "Primary History." To understand the book of Samuel well, we need to place it against the broader canvas of the Primary History, which tells the true story of the world:

1. God's creation of the world (Gen 1–2)
2. Humanity's fall into sin (Gen 3–4)
3. God's purification of the world from its wickedness (Gen 6–9)
4. God's plan for the healing of the world through Abraham's family, Israel (Gen 12–22)
5. God's calling of Israel to be a light to the nations in the land of Canaan, with their responsibilities (Exodus–Deuteronomy)
6. Israel's entrance into the land and general problem with sin (Joshua–Judges)
7. Israel's transition from a tribal confederacy to a nation under the Davidic King (1–2 Samuel)
8. The sin and exile of the Davidic monarchy and the people of God (1–2 Kings)

When we look at the Primary History, it raises important questions. These questions remain crucial for our answering:

Where are we? We are in God's created world, with an important role to play in His creation. There is a God who creates: He is loving, powerful, and infinitely good. He creates a world that thrives and flourishes and lives. This world is ordered, symmetrical, and good according to Genesis 1. Everything has its place and rests under the loving care of its Creator.

Who are we? We are human beings, created in the image of the Creator God, and His vice-regents on the earth. We are creatures in God's creation. We are not gods, but God has made humanity to be in relationship with Him, our fellow humans, and His created world.

Why are we here? We are created to be fruitful in God's world, to multiply, to order and rule the world in a way that imitates God's creative and orderly creation of the world. We cannot do what God has done, but we can create culture and work in a way that imitates God's loving care. Work, then, is part of what it means to be human as we relate to God, one another, and the world (Gen 1–2).

What has gone wrong? The Primary History tells us that our frustration, disappointment, and pain in life arise as a direct result of human sin. It tells us that human sin is the *internal desires* and *external actions* that lead us to live outside of God's good order for His world. So we think we can live outside the lines of God's care. We think we know better than Him, and therefore we live like it. Unfortunately, sin corrupts the primary relationships for which God creates humanity: relationship with God, relationship with our fellow human, and relationship with the world. As a result, our relationships and our work—indeed our very lives—are stained and twisted by sin, leading to rivalry, frustration, domination, and horrors (Gen 3).

What happened next? In the face of corrupting sin, God does not junk the world He made because God does not make junk! Rather, God goes on a rescue mission to bring back the broken world to Himself. This act of bringing what is lost and broken back to Himself is called "redemption." God's mission is to "redeem" the world back to Himself, and He does this in and through a specific family, the family of Israel. The father of the family, Abraham, is given special promises (Gen 12; 15; 17; and 22). These promises are that God will grant Abraham and his family a name, a land, and children (Gen 12:2-3). This family is later called the people of Israel (Gen 24–50), and through this family all the nations on the earth will experience God's blessing (Gen 12:2-3). So Abraham's family will be the channel through which God's blessings will flow. But to be this channel of blessing, God's people must put away sin and follow Him only (Exod 19:4-6). As they follow their God, all the nations on the earth will see the light of God and be drawn to Him (Exod 19:4-6; Deut 4). Israel, however, has a perennial problem with following God. Sometimes they do, but often they do not. This is true early on (Exodus–Numbers) in their relationship with Him but also deep into their story in the land He gives them (Deuteronomy–Kings). It is true when they have a leader like Moses (Exodus–Deuteronomy), and it is true when they have charismatic leaders to lead them after Moses (Joshua–Judges). It is true when they have kings who rule over them as well (Samuel–Kings). By the end of the book of Kings, God exiles His people from the land because of their sin. What will happen to God's redemption of the world? How will God's promises end up? What will happen now? The remainder of the Scriptures through the book of Revelation tell the rest of the story.

In the face of Israel's sin, God remained faithful to His promises. In 1–2 Samuel, God promises salvation through the royal line of David, Israel's anointed king. The book of Psalms and the prophet Isaiah in particular show that this Davidic King is the ruler of Israel and all nations, the Son of God, and the One through whom all the nations will be blessed. The prophecy of Isaiah shows that this Davidic King will renew Israel and restore creation but not through a victorious battle over enemy nations. Rather, the Davidic King will renew and restore all by suffering on behalf of the sins of others. In His suffering and death, the Davidic King will provide the solution to the sin problem (forgiveness of sins: Isa 53) and will be the key that unlocks the healing of creation (the kingdom of God: Isa 60–65).

The New Testament tells us that this Davidic King, the Son of God and the descendant of Abraham, is none other than the man Jesus the Messiah. He was born of a virgin, preached the coming of the kingdom of God, suffered unjustly under Jewish and Gentile (Roman) officials, and died a cruel death on a cross.

The miracle of all is that His suffering and death on a cross brought forgiveness of sins and the healing of creation. Jesus died, but He did not stay dead. God raised Him up from the grave on the third day after His crucifixion. His resurrection proves that Jesus is the suffering and

saving Messiah pictured in Isaiah and the Psalms, and He is the fulfillment of all God promised to Abraham and David.

Moreover, in Jesus the problem of human sin finds its solution
for those who believe in His work and live under His lordship and
care. The New Testament also pictures the future rule of Jesus, the
Davidic Messiah. As He puts death, sin, and corruption under His
feet, Jesus makes all things new (Rev 21:5). Those who believe in
Christ Jesus become princesses and princes in God's world, utterly
reconciled back to God as His daughters and sons (2 Cor 6:18, drawing on 2 Sam 7:14). The apostle Paul boldly affirms that those who
have faith in Christ now are in the family of God, the family of David.
The Church, then, in Christ becomes the agent through which
Davidic blessings flow!

The book of Samuel introduces readers to King Jesus: He is from
the family of David, God's anointed and appointed ruler for Israel. Jesus
is the fulfillment of the story of Israel and the fulfillment of the hope
of the Davidic king. He is the true King of Israel and the Lord over all
creation.

This point is revealed clearly in the opening lines of the New
Testament. The Gospel of Matthew opens by stating, "The historical
record of Jesus Christ, the Son of David, the Son of Abraham" (Matt
1:1). Why is Jesus identified first as the Son of David rather than the Son
of Abraham? Historically, of course, Abraham came first! The reason is
that Matthew emphasizes the Davidic kingship of Jesus.

The closing lines of the Gospel of Matthew affirm this point and
take it further. In Matthew 28, the Davidic King is recognized as the crucified and risen Savior, the King of all things. Jesus has suffered, died for
sin on a cruel cross, was buried, rose again from the grave validating His
royal and divine power, and appeared to many. God the Father grants
all authority to Jesus. Possessing all authority over the whole of creation
("in heaven and on earth"), King Jesus commissions those who are in
His family to go into the entire world and proclaim the good news: He
has died for the forgiveness of sin. He has risen, defeating death and
vindicating life. He is King of all things! So the conclusion of Matthew's
Gospel reads,

> *Then Jesus came near and said to them, "All authority has been given
> to Me in heaven and on earth. Go, therefore, and make disciples of
> all nations, baptizing them in the name of the Father and of the Son*

*and of the Holy Spirit, teaching them to observe everything I have
commanded you. And remember, I am with you always, to the end of
the age.* (Matt 28:18-20)

**The book of Samuel helps us see a key component in the way God
achieves His project of redemption: from Israel, the royal line of David
will be key in providing the King who will heal the brokenness of the
entire world.**

Theological Themes in 1–2 Samuel

Israel's God and King

Samuel presents to its readers "Yahweh," the covenant God of Israel
(1 Sam 17:45; 2 Sam 6:2). The name *Yahweh* is the name God gives in
Exodus 3:14-15, when Moses asks for it. Yahweh is the personal name for
God, worthy to be praised and honored as the Holy One of Israel, who
expects Israel to be holy as He is holy. As Moses and the Israelites sang
of Yahweh in the "Song of the Sea" in Exodus 15:

*Who is like You
    among the gods, O Yahweh?
Who is like You,
    glorious in holiness,
    awesome in praise,
    doing wonders?* (Exod 15:11, authors' translation)

Yahweh is high and mighty, holy beyond compare, awesome and worthy of praise, beautiful, and a miracle-working God! He is worthy of all
honor and fidelity that is due Him. If God's people do not follow Him,
then they walk away at their peril. Yahweh is the giver of life to those who
follow Him, yet He by no means clears the guilty but punishes iniquity
and sin (see Exod 34:6-7). He is high and holy, the source of all love,
faithfulness, and salvation. So Hannah sings in 1 Samuel 2:2:

*There is no one holy like the LORD [Yahweh].
There is no one besides You!
And there is no rock like our God.*

Further, Yahweh is King. As scholar David Firth rightly argues, the
book of Samuel reminds us that any and all

human authority exists under Yahweh's reign, a theme that comes to prominence under David's closing songs (2 Sam 22:1–23:7). Apart from Yahweh, Israel's kings have no authority. (*1 & 2 Samuel*, 43)

We are reminded of Jesus' final words in the Great Commission, that God has granted Jesus all authority in heaven and on earth (Matt 28:18). Jesus' authority as King was given by the Father, and He rules as one who lives to do the will of the One who sent Him. As Jesus says,

> *"I can do nothing on My own. I judge only as I hear, and My judgment is righteous, because I do not seek My own will, but the will of Him who sent Me."* (John 5:30)

As we see in Hannah's song, although utterly holy and wholly other, Yahweh, the divine King, is the One who enters into a deep and abiding relationship with His people. He cares for them as a parent cares for a child. He strengthens the weak, lifts up the lowly, and hears the cries of the suffering! King Yahweh is the heavenly Father.

Yahweh desires to relate with His people. This is no grey-haired Zeus who stands far above, only watching the affairs of his people but never getting involved with them. Yahweh is no deist blind watchmaker. Rather, the God of Israel, Yahweh, is the One with whom Israel must deal, the One with whom Israel has the joy of relating. The name Yahweh occurs no fewer than 6,700 times in the Old Testament, by one scholar's count, highlighting the importance of understanding God in the Old Testament as Yahweh, the holy Creator-God and intimate covenant Lord (Anderson, *Contours of Old Testament Theology*, 41).

Covenant

Yahweh is revealed in the covenants He makes with His people. Covenants in the Old Testament are not contracts as we understand them today. If two parties enter into a business contract (such as a cellular phone contract), then both parties must abide by the contract. If one party breaches the terms of the contract, then the contract is null and void, and the business relationship is off.

However, covenants in the Old Testament are not like that, especially if we are speaking of divine covenants Yahweh establishes by His own prerogative. The Old Testament has six such divine covenants. Significantly, one of them appears in 2 Samuel 7. These covenants make up the backbone of the story line of Scripture.[2] Six covenants appear in the Old Testament:

1. *God's covenant with creation (Gen 1–2; 9).* In the covenant with creation, God establishes a world that is good and thriving. God sees His world, and it is very good. In His world God creates humanity to serve as His vice-regents. Humanity is made to relate to God, to fellow humans, and to the created world. God creates humanity to cultivate His world so that it thrives, a good place for the good of all.

2. *God's covenant with Noah (Gen 6–9).* Humanity rebelled against their Maker, thinking themselves to be like their God (Gen 3). So Adam and Eve fell into sin, and every human after them has fallen into the same pattern. The text describes the activity of humanity as "corrupt" in Genesis 6:3 and goes further to say that "every scheme his mind thought of was nothing but evil all the time" (Gen 6:5). But God purified the world with a flood that covered the earth. The waters purified the world of human sin, and God preserved one family, the family of Noah, through whom He would repopulate the earth and bring blessing to the world. God establishes His covenant with Noah in Genesis 8–9 and promises never again to flood the earth with water; rather, Noah and his family will be the channel of blessing through whom God will bless the world.

3. *God's covenant with Abraham (Gen 12; 15; 17; 22).* Noah's descendants carry the line of divine blessing, particularly through the lineage of Noah's son Shem, whose descendant is a man named Abram (God later changes his name to Abraham, meaning "father of many nations"). God promises Abraham a great name, a land, and descendants. Through the line of Abraham, all the families of the earth will find God's blessing. Abraham has a large family, true to God's promise, and his descendants constitute the 12 tribes, which are called Israel.

4. *God's covenant with Israel (Exod 19–23; Deuteronomy).* God establishes a covenant with Israel to make them His chosen possession. They are to be a kingdom of priests and a holy nation (Exod 19:4-6; Deut 7:6-11). God's people are to be a lighthouse

---

[2] The most extensive works on the nature of the covenants in Scripture are Dumbrell, *Covenant and Creation,* and Hahn, *Kinship by Covenant.*

in the land where He plants them so they might shine His light out to all nations, so they in turn will know Israel's God. Israel, then, is a missional people set among the nations.[3] God establishes a covenant with the family of Abraham because of neither their righteousness nor their power (Deut 7:6-11; 9:4-6). Rather He establishes a covenant with them *out of His divine grace* and *on the basis of His former promise to Abraham.* Thus, God *will* accomplish His purpose of blessing the whole world and reconciling it back to Himself, and He *will* accomplish this through the family of Abraham and His covenant with Israel.

5. *God's covenant with David (2 Sam 7).* The covenant with Israel is narrowed down to the royal family line in the reign of David, the true king of Israel. God promises to be a "father" to David and his royal line, and Israel's Davidic king will be a "son" of God. Yahweh promises a great name, a dynastic house, and land. These promises are similar to the Abrahamic promises (see the parallel in the exegesis of 2 Samuel 7 in the commentary below). This covenant is important because the Davidic king represents the people and mediates for the people. As a result, as goes the king in Israel, so go the people! If the king stays faithful to God, then the people will remain faithful as well. If the king strays, then the people will wander from fidelity to Yahweh too.

6. *God's new covenant (Jer 31–33).* All the covenants are partially fulfilled and *un*fulfilled in the Old Testament. That is because the covenants anticipate something greater: a new covenant. This covenant is only called "new" in Jeremiah 31–33, but it is pictured in a number of other Old Testament texts. What is the new covenant? It is the fulfillment of *all* the covenants. God's people will dwell securely in God's land under God's rule (Jer 31:31-40; 33:25-26; a fulfillment of the Abrahamic and Israelite covenants). His divinely appointed Davidic King will reign eternally (Jer 33:14-18; a fulfillment of the Davidic covenant). God's covenant with creation and Noah will be fulfilled as well, as the entire created world is reaffirmed, and sin and death are no more (Jer 31:35-37; 33:25-26). Divine forgiveness for human sin

---

[3] Two works that explain this beautifully are Wright, *The Mission of God*, and Goheen, *A Light to the Nations.*

is secured, and atonement is secured, forever. God says in the new covenant, "I will forgive their wrongdoing and never again remember their sin" (Jer 31:34). In the new covenant Yahweh proclaims,

> *They will be My people, and I will be their God. I will give them one heart and one way so that for their good and for the good of their descendants after them, they will fear Me always. I will make an everlasting covenant with them: I will never turn away from doing good to them.* (Jer 32:38-40)

These covenants are not contracts. Because God initiates them in each case, God will see them through even if the covenant partner fails to obey the terms of the covenant. In short God's covenant plan will not fail in the face of human sin. Rather, God *will* achieve His purposes. We know from the Old Testament that all the covenants *will be fulfilled* in the new covenant. We know that the time of the new covenant will mean an end to sin, and forgiveness will be complete. The new covenant, then, is the climax of all the covenants.

But Jeremiah never stipulates the mechanism by which this new covenant will come about, only that it will be accomplished at the initiative of Yahweh. Other prophetic texts (Isaiah and the Psalms, for example) do stipulate that the Davidic King, who is Messiah, will bear the sins of many and be raised victorious. They do not, however, clearly link this action of this Davidic Messiah to the new covenant. Because of this, connections between Isaiah's Suffering Servant (Isa 53), the Psalms' Davidic King (Pss 1–2), and the new covenant in Jeremiah sit rather loosely together.

What is loosely connected or dimly portrayed in the Old Testament, however, finds brilliant and radiant illumination in the ministry of God's Son, Jesus. According to the New Testament writings, Jesus is the firstborn over all creation, the hope of salvation, the seed of Abraham, the faithful Mosaic teacher, the Davidic King, the true and faithful Israelite, the perfect priest, the teacher of all righteousness, the temple, the sacrificial lamb, the true prophet, the wise teacher, and the instigator of the new covenant. Jesus is the One who brings about the new covenant that is anticipated in the Old Testament texts. So the writer of Hebrews says,

> *Therefore, He is the mediator of a new covenant, so that those who are called might receive the promise of the eternal inheritance, because*

a death has taken place for the redemption from the transgressions
committed under the first covenant. . . .

But now He has appeared one time, at the end of the ages, for the
removal of sin by the sacrifice of Himself. And just as it is appointed
for people to die once—and after this, judgment—so also the Messiah,
having been offered once to bear the sins of many, will appear a second
time, not to bear sin, but to bring salvation to those who are waiting
for Him. (Heb 9:15,26b-29)

Jesus brings about the forgiveness of sin and restoration of all things to
which the new covenant testifies! His sacrifice for sin on the cross bears
sin once for all, and His victorious resurrection provides the guarantee
of new life for all who believe.

Leadership

The book of Samuel reveals the significance of leadership among God's
people. Good leaders love the Lord wholeheartedly and lead God's
people to do the same. Good leaders draw God's people to appropriate
worship, which is a theme described more fully below.

However, leadership in Samuel often fits the description of the
offices of leadership presented in Deuteronomy 16–18: judge, prophet,
priest, and king.

Judge. There are two offices of "judge" in the Old Testament. The first
is what we find in Deuteronomy 16:18–17:13—the role of an appointed
official who operates without partiality or corruption to settle disputes
among God's people. This is one who gives "righteous judgments" to
God's people as he adjudicates. The second office of "judge" in the Old
Testament comes in the book of Judges—a charismatic leader anointed
and appointed by God to lead God's people, to settle disputes (Deborah,
for example, is described as a judge and prophet in Judg 4:4), and to
deliver God's people from oppressors. In the book of 1–2 Samuel, Eli
(1 Sam 4:18) and Samuel (1 Sam 7:15) are judges in this latter sense of
the word: leaders who settled disputes and led all God's people.

Priest. The role and office of Levitical priest is found in Deuteronomy
18:1-8. The Levites were those who received sacrifices from God's people and mediated between God and the people. They also had the role
of teaching God's people His law. Eli is a priest in 1 Samuel 1–2, where
we find that Eli and his household are not mediating between God and
Israel faithfully. The failure of priestly leadership is the reason God will

raise up a "faithful priest" who will do all that is in God's heart and mind. He will faithfully mediate between Yahweh and Israel. In the narrative we know that this priest is Samuel (1 Sam 2:18; cf. Exod 28:4), but ultimately Samuel and the Scriptures show that the priest is Jesus (Heb 8).

Prophet. The role and office of prophet remains significant in the book of 1–2 Samuel. Samuel is clearly a prophet (1 Sam 3:18-21), and David has prophets in his court (Nathan, 2 Sam 12; Gad, 2 Sam 22–24). What is a prophet? Biblical prophecy originates with God, who gives messages to a prophet. A prophet, then, is a spokesperson for God, who declares God's ways and words to a particular people. In the Bible prophets can be both men and women, and we find this in the New Testament as well. Male prophets we know more often, perhaps, because they have books that bear their names: Isaiah, Jeremiah, Ezekiel, and Habakkuk, for example. But there is clear evidence of female prophets as well: Miriam (Exod 15:20-21), Deborah (Judg 4–5), Isaiah's mother (Isa 8:3), and Huldah (2 Kgs 22:14), for example. Prophets could come from any portion of the society, whether in the royal house (Isaiah), in priestly families (Haggai, Zechariah, and perhaps Habakkuk), or from the farming community (Amos and Elisha). According to the teaching of Deuteronomy, prophets speak only what God gives them to speak, nothing more and nothing less (see Deut 13 and 18). With this in mind, it might be tempting to think God gave prophets spontaneous speeches to the people when they were under some form of trance or divine possession. However, that is not usually the way prophetic speech works. While prophets were "carried along by the Holy Spirit" (2 Pet 1:21 ESV), they used a traditional set of speech patterns to communicate God's messages. This makes one think prophetic preaching is a learned form of communication, although the individual personalities and creative styles shine through as well.[4] Eli, David, and Saul are not prophets, though Saul is a curious case where people wondered whether he was "among the prophets" (1 Sam 19:24).

King. Saul and David are anointed and appointed as king in the book of Samuel.

Saul: 1 Samuel 8:9-18; 9:18-22; 10

David: 1 Samuel 16:1-13; 2 Samuel 2; 5; 7

---

[4] For more information on prophecy, see Thomas, *Faith amid the Ruins*, especially chapter 2, "Prophecy in the Bible."

Neither Eli nor Samuel is called "king." The appeal of God's people at Ramah for Samuel to "appoint a king to judge us the same as all the other nations have" (1 Sam 8:5) is interpreted as an act of rebellion against God, their true King. So Samuel would not lead them at all beyond the role of a judge. It is extraordinarily telling that God predicted His people would ask for a king like all the other nations had. Deuteronomy 17:14 reveals that God knew the people would want a king like all the other nations. But God wanted a king after His own heart.

Kingship is not a bad thing, and the Scriptures anticipate kingship at a number of points throughout the first five books of the Old Testament. However, the appeal by God's people for a king "the same as all the other nations have" exposes their wayward hearts. The law of the king in Deuteronomy 17:14-20 forbids

1. Israel from setting a foreign king over them, restricting it to a fellow Israelite (Deut 17:15);
2. the king from gaining a large number of horses for a cavalry or chariot force, effectively circumscribing the military power of the king (Deut 17:16); and
3. the king from amassing great wealth through taxation of the people or incursions into foreign kingdoms to amass plunder (Deut 17:17).

Effectively, the king's power is balanced or kept in check by the Lord, His law, and the authority of the Levitical priests, who teach God's law (Deut 17:18-20). The king, then, is to be the leader who loves the Lord and loves his neighbor, both his fellow Israelite and the foreigner. So long as the king loved God, followed His word, and led the people to do the same, the king would remain in power, and all would be well.

The leadership offices are important for 1–2 Samuel. They highlight the importance of Samuel, who was prophet, priest, judge, and almost king. And they highlight the importance of David, who was anointed and appointed by God and served Him as one who lived his life after God's own heart (1 Sam 13:14; Acts 13:22). However, the book of Samuel reveals that neither Saul nor David lived up to the standard and failed ultimately in this regard.

But the failures of Israel's leaders in 1–2 Samuel show how Israel still searches for the true leader, the true prophet, the true priest, and the true king! The New Testament confirms that this long-sought-after figure was none other than Jesus.

Jesus is the Judge. He is the One who adjudicates and leads His people. In the New Testament, Jesus is the One who arbitrates among many nations and casts out the wicked and vindicates the righteous. This is done in the last days, so it is apparent what is in black and white in the persons of Eli and Samuel comes to full color in the person of Jesus. In fact, Jesus will be the Judge who adjudicates all things (Acts 10:42; 17:31; 2 Cor 5:10). In Revelation 19:11, the notion of Jesus as the Judge who delivers from oppression takes hold as well: "Then I saw heaven opened, and there was a white horse. Its rider is called Faithful and True, and He judges and makes war in righteousness."

Jesus is the Prophet. Over and over again characters in the Gospels characterize Jesus as a "prophet" (Matt 14:5; 16:14; 21:46; Mark 6:15; 8:28; Luke 7:16; 9:8,19; 24:19; John 4:19; 7:40; 9:17). Jesus self-identifies as a prophet while indicating that God's prophets (such as He) will not receive honor in their hometowns (Luke 4:24). As a prophet, Jesus performed many of the miracles one finds performed by Old Testament prophets (esp. Elijah), such as raising the dead, multiplying food, and healing (Witherington, *Jesus the Seer*, 333; Brodie, *The Crucial Bridge*). He also spoke the word of the Lord, as one would expect from the true prophet of God. Jesus is filled with the Spirit of God to speak God's word, particularly about the kingdom of God. In this latter act Jesus is the eschatological Prophet of the new covenant. His prophetic word then deals with God's appointed time of judgment and salvation for the people of God, which would usher in God's reign.

Jesus is the Priest. The writer of Hebrews teaches that Jesus is a greater priest than all who have gone before Him. But this is difficult because Jesus does not derive from a priestly family according to His genealogy (e.g., Matt 1:1-17). Jesus comes from a royal family (from the Davidic line and the tribe of Judah) but not a priestly family like the tribe of Levi. No matter. Hebrews tells us that Jesus was a priest in the order of an earlier priestly family, namely, that of Melchizedek (from Gen 14:18-20). Melchizedek's priesthood is an eternal priesthood and, therefore, better than that of the Levites (cf. Ps 110:4). Jesus, then, is able to mediate eternally on behalf of those who come to Him to be reconciled to God.

Jesus is the King. Kingship remains central to His identity. The term *messiah* is a claim about Jesus' divine anointing and appointing to do the work of salvation that would belong only to the Davidic king (Isa 53; 61). Jesus was killed as the "king of the Jews" (Matt 27:37), a mocking title the Romans gave Him, which actually spoke the truth they did not know or understand. Jesus the King preached the arrival of the kingdom of God, and the early church confirmed that Jesus was the true King (Acts 17). Jesus is the "Son of David" in the genealogy of Matthew 1, confirming that Jesus is the One through whom the promises of 2 Samuel 7 come to absolute fruition.

True Worship

Worship frames the book of Samuel, as we see in the structure of the book, above (A and A´). The opening of Samuel begins with Hannah's prayer and praise to God at the temple (1 Sam 1–2). The conclusion of the book of Samuel contains David's praise and prayer (2 Sam 22:1–23:7) and focuses on David's plan to build a temple for Yahweh where all peoples can worship Him (2 Sam 24:18-25). So we see that a focus on worship serves as bookends to the book of Samuel.

Many readers of the Old Testament may not know that the worship of God in Jerusalem, at the temple, was not always the norm in Israelite faith. The book of Samuel presents a movement from the worship of God at the tabernacle in Shiloh to the worship of God in Jerusalem, the new place of Davidic rule. Although David cannot build the temple, the narrative of Samuel reveals that his son (Solomon) can and will (see 1 Kgs 6–8).

First Samuel opens with a focus on worship at Shiloh, which was corrupt. This is not so because of Hannah—she is faithful! But it is so because of the lack of vision, discernment, and faithfulness of the priesthood at Shiloh. At the shrine in Shiloh, the high priest Eli and his sons (Hophni and Phinehas) minister before the Lord. But this family reveals itself to be faulty and wicked. The sins of the sons will be discussed in the commentary, but note the characterization of Eli in 1 Samuel 1–3:

- He can't differentiate prayer from drunkenness in 1 Samuel 1 (lack of discernment).
- He loves a good meal more than his God in 1 Samuel 2 (lack of discipline).
- He neither sees God nor hears God's voice in 1 Samuel 3 (lack of spiritual vision).

As a result of the failure of the father and his sons, God will raise up a priest for His people, and this priest is Samuel: "Then I will raise up a faithful priest for Myself. He will do whatever is in My heart and mind"

(1 Sam 2:35). Because of the problem with the priests and the need for a true priest, the opening chapters of the book expose the problem of true worship among God's people, especially God's leaders.

What does the book of Samuel teach about true worship? The secret to true worship is aligning inward devotion and outward obedience out of our love of God and His gospel. God does not demand only interior devotion in the heart; that is a common myth perpetuated by purveyors of empty piety who say, "God only cares about our hearts but not our lives!" No. God cares about a healthy and holy alignment of heart and life, inner and outer, soul and body. The book of Samuel shows that true piety and true worship are expressed in an alignment between heart and life.

For example, when Saul fails to do what God tells him to do in destroying everything in 1 Samuel 15, Saul responds by saying that what he kept he was going to give to the Lord in worship. However, his is not true piety or worship; it is a misalignment of devotion and obedience. Saul's inner love for God should be marked by outward obedience to God's commands. Instead he tries to appease God with a show of outward piety (offerings and sacrifices) without real devotion to God in his deepest self. This lack of alignment between the inner life and the outward expression exposes the problem of false worship. Samuel's well-known words spoken to Saul ring in our ears:

> Does the LORD take pleasure in burnt offerings and sacrifices
>   as much as in obeying the LORD?
> Look: to obey is better than sacrifice,
>   to pay attention is better than the fat of rams. (1 Sam 15:22)

Sin and Punishment

We stated above that judgment and salvation form the two-step rhythm of Scripture. This point holds true in Samuel, and for a moment we want to focus on the first step in that rhythm: judgment. Divine judgment comes as punishment for sin.

This is too often a point missed not in Scripture but in modern culture. If we mention sin at all, it is usually someone else's sin! With evocative and troubling detail, the narratives of Samuel present the pervasive problem of human sin. The narratives never offer the guilty party a rock to hide behind; they do not allow the characters in the story or the readers of the story to point the finger of blame toward someone else. The problem of sin lies at the doorstep of the one who has committed the affront to God or one's fellow human. For example, when Saul blames someone else because of his sin, it reveals his own moral ineptitude and culpability rather than his innocence. When David attempts to hide behind his own righteousness and to conceal his sin with Bathsheba and Uriah, God exposes him terribly.

In each of these cases and more, the narratives of Samuel demonstrate in a wonderfully human way the problem of sin. The faults of Saul or David (or Absalom or Eli!) may as well be the same faults we share. After all, who does not attempt to avoid blame when caught in sin? By giving the horrible truth about sin—its pervasiveness, its problems, and the horrors of human response to sin—the narratives hold up a mirror to the modern world.

These texts of terror are wonderfully productive in instructing readers on the subtleties of sin in human hearts, negative examples of sinners and those who cast blame, and diverse ways for readers to reflect on our own proclivity to rebel against God and harm our fellow man. But we should reflect carefully: God punishes human sin, and the searchlight of God's holiness shines no matter the shadowy underside of human hearts or actions. And sin brings punishment.

Hope and Messiah

The hope of the book of Samuel lies in the goodness of Israel's God to provide life out of death and to provide justice on the earth. Hannah's song affirms both theological points:

Life out of death: *The LORD brings death and gives life; He sends some to Sheol, and He raises others up.* (1 Sam 2:6)

Justice on the earth: *Those who oppose the LORD will be shattered; He will thunder in the heavens against them. The LORD will judge the ends of the earth.* (1 Sam 2:10)

Hope for life and justice do not derive from any source other than Israel's God. Yahweh, Israel's God and King, is the wellspring of vitality and equity in the world. An entire book could be written on the source of hope in our world (Zimmerli, *Man and His Hope*; Drinkard and Dick, *The God of Hope*).

But in 1–2 Samuel, the specific shape for hope in God takes a rather human form, surprisingly: Israel's God brings life and justice by way of

His anointed and appointed king. Another way to say it is like this: God's messiah is the divine agent of hope for the world.

The structure of the book of Samuel bears this out. As we look at the structure of the book (see p. 10), we see that the hinge of the book is found in "H–Saul's Death (1 Sam 28:1–2 Sam 1:27)." This means the dynasty of Saul does not embody the ultimate divine anointing or appointing to "judge the ends of the earth" through God's "power" (1 Sam 2:10). Rather, it will come through another anointed and appointed leader.

God's anointed and appointed leader is the Davidic king. The word *messiah* comes from the Hebrew word that means "to anoint." So to speak of God's anointed leader is to speak of God's Messiah. As the plot of 1–2 Samuel carries forward, David's rise as the messiah and Saul's fall become apparent. David enjoyed divine anointing, but Saul's anointing left him. David was a man after God's heart, but Saul was a man after his own heart. So Saul is not the king God would use to bring hope to the world, but the Davidic king is that hope.

The link between Israel's God, life, justice, and the Davidic king appears in David's final poems in 2 Samuel 22–23. In these poems God delivers the Davidic king from all terrors and perils and enemies (2 Sam 22:8-31). God empowers the Davidic king to quash those who oppose God's plans and to provide justice in the earth (2 Sam 22:32-43). God empowers the Davidic king to reign over all nations with justice and equity, providing peace (2 Sam 22:44-49). David becomes God's agent of justice and life for all peoples so that God says over the Davidic king,

> "The one who rules the people with justice, who rules in the fear
> of God, is like the morning light when the sun rises on a cloudless
> morning, the glisten of rain on sprouting grass." (2 Sam 23:3-4)

God pronounces this affirmation over the Davidic king, His anointed and appointed agent of justice and peace. So David rhetorically says of God's pronouncement over him, "Is it not true my house is with God? For He has established an everlasting covenant with me, ordered and secured in every detail" (2 Sam 23:5).

So we can ask of the book of Samuel: *Where* is hope found?

And the answer comes: *Hope is found in Israel's God!*

But this answer raises the question: *How* does God bring hope?

And the answer comes: *Through God's Davidic Messiah!*

David knows this truth. Hope is found in his royal dynastic line, anointed and appointed by God to give life and justice to Israel and the nations. So he concludes his song with these words:

> *Therefore I will praise You, LORD,*
> *among the nations;*
> *I will sing about Your name.*
> *He is a tower of salvation for His king;*
> *He shows loyalty to His anointed,*
> *to David and his descendants forever.* (2 Sam 22:50-51)

But by the end of 2 Samuel, we have seen David's fall into sin (E´ in the structure, above, which is recorded in 2 Sam 10:1–12:31), and we know that David, too, is soon to die. So although the Davidic messiah is God's agent of hope, life, and justice, we do not know when the true Messiah will come.

But because of the faithfulness of Yahweh, the true Messiah will come, and this fact is certain. Second Samuel 22–23 in particular reveals God's plan with the Davidic Messiah: He will bring life, hope, and justice in the world. But at that point we do not know *when* He will come, only *that* He will come. Still, what a day that will be!

Long Live the King!

1 SAMUEL 1

Main Idea: Yahweh, the great King, raises up Samuel to be His priest and prophet in the midst of pain, praise, and prayer.

I. **Hannah's Hopelessness**
II. **Romance as the Savior?**
III. **Hannah's Salvation**
IV. **Hannah, David, and Jesus**
V. **Hannah, David, Jesus,** *and Us*
    A. Most of our hurt and disappointment comes from seeking another "king" besides God.
    B. God is better than "many sons" or a king.
    C. Bitterness does not mean God-forsakenness.
    D. God loves people the world casts away.

David—the man most famous for killing a giant—is himself one of the greatest giants of the Bible. Besides the story of his life, he is mentioned 182 times in the Old Testament and 59 times in the New (Howard, "David," 41). He was a man of many talents—a shepherd, musician, poet, warrior, and the king by which all Israelite kings would be judged (ibid., 41, 46). Nearly half of the book of Psalms bears his inscription, and the Dead Sea Scrolls attribute another 4,050 psalms to his name ("David," in *Dictionary of Judaism*, 151)! In understanding the Old Testament—or the Bible as a whole—it is difficult to overestimate the importance of David. As Old Testament scholar Walter Brueggemann has written, "David is the dominant figure in Israel's narrative" (*David's Truth*, 13).

David came onto the scene at a crucial time in Israel's history. Israel had settled into the promised land of Canaan, and after many years of turmoil (caused by their disobedience), they asked God for a king. They saw this as the answer to their national woes. All the neighboring nations had kings, which seemed to serve them well enough. A king, they believed, would guarantee prosperity, give them national stability, and protect them from harm. A king was the key to success.

In many ways the book of Samuel presents the story of Israel's search for that king. After all, in 1–2 Samuel, David would be the ideal king when compared with Saul—and just what Israel thought they were searching for. Readers of the book are struck, however, by how tragically David disappointed everyone in the end, as we saw in the introduction of this commentary. His story ends with an uncomfortable question mark. The reader is left asking (with Israel), "Is that it? David is the best king we could have hoped for, and look what happened to him. Is there no hope?"

If David's reign represents life as good as it gets, then we are indeed left with hopelessness. This alerts us to the fact that the hero of Scripture is Israel's true King, Yahweh Himself. As Psalm 95:3 proclaims, "For the Lord is a great God, a great King above all gods." Psalms 95–100, rightly understood as the theological "heart" of the book of Psalms, affirm that Yahweh reigns, and that is truly good news (McCann, *A Theological Introduction*, 44). So as great as David is, he pales in comparison to Yahweh, who reigns with equity, justice, and righteousness. He is the hope of Israel and the nations.

David's story connects Yahweh's kingship to the Lord's anointed and appointed Israelite king, particularly in 2 Samuel 7. So Yahweh reigns through the Israelite king whom He installs as His "prince" (from the Hebrew word *nagid* in 2 Sam 7:8) over His people. So Israel's king does not have ultimate authority; he only has authority in so far as he rules in a way that accords with Yahweh's rule over all things.

The story of David, once it is taken in the whole of Scripture from Old to New Testament, shows us that no mere human king would rule as God saw fit. So in the fullness of time, God would send His own Son, Jesus the Messiah, to be the true King over Israel and over all creation. Rather than a mere "prince," Jesus rules perfectly and is indeed God incarnate. In this way the David story is in the Bible to point us forward to the coming King who would not only be *from* God but would be *God Himself*. David's story points us to Jesus, and Jesus was both Davidic and divine. He is the Lord of lords and King of kings. He is Israel's covenantal and Davidic King who would rule God's people but also the Creator and cosmic King who would rule the universe.[5] Jesus,

---

[5] For more on this point, see Hurtado, *Lord Jesus Christ*, and idem, *How on Earth Did Jesus Become a God?*

then, is the King of all kings and the King that Israel—and we—are searching for.

This is where David's story applies to us today. All of us, like Israel, are "searching for a king." We want someone to guarantee to us our prosperity, stability, and safety. Each of us in our own way chooses someone or something to be our king. For some it may be marriage. Perhaps we think that if we could just get married, then our life would be fulfilling and rich. We imagine that we could handle any other trouble in the world, provided we were happily married. When we think this way, we've made marriage our king.

For others of us, success at work may be our hope. If we can get to a point where we are successful at our job, then we will have significance and security. Or perhaps it is just the money we long for. As long as we are financially stable, we feel that we can tackle any other obstacle that comes our way.

Still others might place family on the throne. If our family is healthy, in close proximity, and harmonious, then life is good. We see family as the surest foundation for stability and happiness. Family is our king.

Whatever we desire to give us stability, prosperity, and happiness, that is our king! David's life shows us that God is the only King that can ever truly satisfy those longings. Everything else will only disappoint. All other kings promise great things, but they are incapable of delivering on their promises.

As we explore the story of David, we will also learn many ways David's life can serve as an example for us. As Paul notes, God intended for Old Testament characters to serve as an example to us, both good and bad (1 Cor 10:11). Many aspects of David's life are worth our imitation. But we must keep in mind that the entire trajectory of David's life is meant not to point to himself but to point us to Jesus. David, like all earthly kings, disappointed; Jesus did not disappoint, nor will He ever. The story of David, like all Old Testament stories, is not meant to give us a hero to emulate but a Savior to hope in.

The story of David begins with a vignette that, on the surface, seems to have no connection at all to David! As we will see, however, the author of 1 and 2 Samuel placed Hannah's story here deliberately. Hannah's story and the story of David are intricately connected: Hannah sought on a personal level what Israel sought on a national one.

Hannah's Hopelessness
1 SAMUEL 1:2-7

[Elkanah] had two wives, the first named Hannah and the second Peninnah. Peninnah had children, but Hannah was childless. This man would go up from his town every year to worship and to sacrifice to the LORD of Hosts at Shiloh. . . . Whenever Elkanah offered a sacrifice, he always gave portions of the meat to his wife Peninnah and to each of her sons and daughters. But he gave a double portion to Hannah, for he loved her even though the LORD had kept her from conceiving. Her rival would taunt her severely just to provoke her, because the LORD had kept Hannah from conceiving. Whenever she went up to the LORD's house, her rival taunted her in this way every year. Hannah wept and would not eat. (1 Sam 1:2-7)

Hannah was a woman who, to put it plainly, was really down on her luck. Hannah's problem was that she was incapable of bearing children (v. 2). She was barren. As devastating as that is today, in those days it was even more distressing. According to the Jewish Talmud, a person without children was considered "as good as dead." Barrenness was even a legitimate grounds for divorce ("Barrenness," in *The New Encyclopedia of Judaism*, 108–9)! Why was it so crucial that families have a lot of children? The Israelites saw children as an essential part of the good life for three main reasons:

First, Israel's society was agrarian, which meant that the more sons a person had, the more potential laborers there were to work the land. The more workers, the greater the crop's yield. The greater the yield, the greater the income. The greater the income, the higher the status. So children—particularly sons—guaranteed that a family would be financially stable and occupy a higher status in society (Johnson and Earle, *The Evolution of Human Societies*, 362).

Second, Hannah lived in an age before social security and a 401(k)! Children were the retirement plan of the ancient world. The more children a couple had, the more likely that couple was to be taken care of in their old age (ibid., 361).

Third, having children was necessary for the survival of the nation. The economy and military were completely dependent on having a large number of children born. Bearing children was a life-or-death issue not only for individual families but for the country as a whole (Borowski, *Daily Life*, 22).

Women who bore a lot of children were, therefore, treated with honor. They were heroes. Women who were unable to bear children felt useless; they experienced shame rather than honor and were looked on with pity rather than respect. In biblical narratives this theme comes up a lot. Barrenness "is an effective metaphor of hopelessness. There is no foreseeable future. There is no human power to invent a future" (Brueggemann, *Genesis*, 116). Not many people think about children in this way today. We tend to put more value on the kind of job a person has, where a person went to school, or how a person looks. But think of this from Hannah's perspective: in a culture that puts all of a woman's significance and security in her children, she can't have kids! Practically speaking, she has no significance, no life, and no hope!

To make matters worse, Elkanah's other wife, Peninnah, had a lot of children. Daily, Hannah was confronted with her failure by a rival who was all too willing to rub it in her face. Verse 6 says that Peninnah "provoked" her, which is a creative rendering of a rather unusual Hebrew expression. The Hebrew word used here literally means "to thunder" or "to roar," like a storm. This is the sort of word that would be used to describe being caught in a hurricane. In fact, as Tim Keller notes in a sermon on this passage, this is the only place in the Bible that the word is used to describe anything other than an actual storm (*The Prayer for David*; Firth, *1 & 2 Samuel*, 51).

In other words, Hannah's emotions were thundering and roaring like a hurricane. The text even tells us that Peninnah's harassment was continual. There was no relief for Hannah from the relentless reminders of her barrenness. To say that Hannah was a deeply distressed individual is an understatement. Verse 7 indicates that her depression was so intense that she even refused to eat. Hannah must have lain awake many nights in despair, feeling like a broken, hopeless failure.

Romance as the Savior?
1 SAMUEL 1:8

> *"Hannah, why are you crying?" her husband Elkanah asked. "Why won't you eat? Why are you troubled? Am I not better to you than 10 sons?"* (1 Sam 1:8)

You have to hand it to Elkanah, the husband—he's trying to be a good guy. And there's something engaging about this man's self-confidence, even if he's not very tactful. "Hannah, baby, you may not amount to much, but I love you, and my love should be better than 10 sons!" Verse 5 indicates that as a sign of his affection, Elkanah would give Hannah a double portion of food. (Admittedly, this is an odd way of showing affection, isn't it? Imagine Elkanah sitting there with his two wives, and reaching over to Hannah's plate, winking, as he gives her two scoops of mashed potatoes. Ladies, feel free to swoon.)

Elkanah tried to offer Hannah romantic salvation, telling her that through his love he would be able to fill the void in her soul. But Elkanah's romantic solution failed to address Hannah's hurt. Year after year they would all continue to go up for the sacrifice, and Elkanah's double portion couldn't still the storms of Hannah's heart.

This is the primary solution our culture offers to life's problems. Like Hannah we find ourselves surrounded by Peninnahs who tell us we will never be valuable unless we do or achieve certain things. We need to have a high quality education or a large house or a husband who really cares. So when we fail to live up to these expectations, we feel worthless, jealous, and dissatisfied.

So we seek fulfillment, meaning, and significance in romance. Atheist scientist Ernest Becker put it this way:

> The love partner becomes the divine ideal within which to fulfill one's life. . . . What is it that we want when we elevate the love partner to this position? We want redemption—nothing less. We want to be rid of our faults, of our feeling of nothingness. (*The Denial of Death*, 160, 167)

We might think good romance and exciting sex will be "better to us than 10 sons." This is, after all, the consistent message that we receive from Hollywood and pop music stations: love is all you need. The end, however, is tragedy. As Becker notes, "No human relationship can bear the burden of godhood" (*The Denial of Death*, 166).

Others of us try to dull the pain through drugs and alcohol. Still others simply adopt an attitude of cynicism and retreat into loathing. Deep within us we know that no human romance can fulfill us, that no drug can satisfy us that no cynicism can protect us. We cling to saviors that have no power because we feel like these are the best options we have. Hannah's story—her pain and the vain attempts to mask that pain—is replicated in each one of us in our own unique way.

Hannah's Salvation
1 SAMUEL 1:9-11,18

Hannah got up after they ate and drank at Shiloh. . . . Making a vow, she pleaded, "LORD of Hosts, if You will take notice of Your servant's affliction, remember and not forget me, and give Your servant a son, I will give him to the LORD all the days of his life, and his hair will never be cut." (1 Sam 1:9,11)

Verse 9 contains the turning point of Hannah's story, but it is a subtle turning point. In fact, a casual reader is liable to miss it altogether: "Hannah got up." This is not merely a superfluous detail, as if the author were saying Hannah finished her meal and got up to walk into the living room. No, the Hebrew word for "got up" indicates decisive action (Tsumara, *The First Book of Samuel*, 115, 117). Hannah stood up resolved and made a choice. Something had changed.

What had just changed? What had Hannah resolved to do? We are given her new resolution in the vow she utters. Two features of her prayer are particularly important. The first is that by pleading with God to "remember me," Hannah indicates that she perceives that God cares for the plight of a rural, barren farm woman who everyone else says is a failure. She reveals a belief that the Lord of Hosts is the sort of God who cares for small, broken, failed people. God is so compassionate and good that He cares even for Hannah. This is faith in God's goodness and grace: that He is a God full of compassion and an ever-present help for the weak (Exod 34:6). This is the kind of faith that pleases God (Heb 11:6).

Second, notice that Hannah offers to give back to God any son He gives to her. The detail about no razor touching the boy's head shows that Hannah is invoking what the Israelites called a "Nazirite" vow. Her son would leave the family to serve in the temple of God.

The Nazirite vow was a special provision for those in the nation of Israel who wanted to serve God like a priest. Normally only those sons born into the house of Levi, the priestly tribe, were allowed to serve in the temple. If a person outside of the Levite tribe desired to serve in God's presence, he could take the Nazirite vow to consecrate himself.

Numbers 6 explains the requirements and details for taking a temporary Nazirite vow as a form of worship. This vow was effective for a certain period of time. Paul took such a vow (Acts 18:18). However, what Hannah is doing here is consecrating her son for his entire life. This is similar to what Samson's parents did when they were instructed by the angel to consecrate him for his whole life for service as a warrior (Judg 13:4-5). As we know, Samson violated his oath. John the Baptist was also a lifelong Nazirite (Luke 1:15).

When Hannah takes this vow, it means she is giving up all claims to her son in order to let him live in the temple and serve God. The Nazirite vow effectively moved a person out of one's family. In other words, when Hannah makes this Nazirite vow for her son, she renounces everything that would have been valuable about having a son! Her son would not grow up in her house. He would not be an emotional support for her. He would not be available to take care of her in her old age. He would have no land inheritance, just as the Levites had no land allotment in Israel. Hannah prayed for a son but laid aside every benefit a son could have given her.

Yet Hannah "went her way and ate, and her face was no longer sad" (v. 18 ESV). She rejoiced before she received a son, despite knowing that if she did receive one she had renounced everything she had previously hoped for in him. Hannah's joy is no longer dependent on obtaining a son. Hannah's joy is now found in God, the God of her salvation (2:1). This discovery anchors her soul to a rock that quiets the storms of her heart (2:2).

We might expect the order here to be

1. Hannah prays.
2. Hannah gets pregnant.
3. Hannah is joyful, and the storms of her life dissipate.

But something different appears in the story. Instead of the order listed above, we find

1. Hannah prays.
2. Hannah is joyful.
3. Hannah gets pregnant.

The order of events is not empty! Hannah found joy and deep faith as she found her deepest needs met in God. Faith-filled Hannah has found a source of joy and security greater than her hope of sons: God Himself!

Can you feel the excitement she pours forth in her prayer in chapter 2? Hannah says, "My heart rejoices in the LORD. . . . There is no one holy like the LORD . . . there is no Rock like our God" (2:1-2 NIV).

Faith means rejoicing in God when our dreams are still unfulfilled and resting on God when life is still falling apart all around us. In the following verses of this prayer, Hannah goes on to talk about God's unfathomable wisdom, His great strength, His perfect beauty, His compassion for small, broken, and sinful people. This, she says, is the ultimate treasure; and because she has found a God like that, she no longer looks to children to provide her with value and worth. This was the moment of Hannah's repentance and salvation. She found her life, her security, her identity, and her significance in God. She was finally set free from her bondage to the idolatry of family.

Hannah still prays for a son, but her tone is altogether different: "God, I'm still asking You for a son, as I have hundreds of times before. But all my life I've asked for You to give me a son to make up for some deficiency in my life. It has always been for me. Now, I'm asking for one for You. You are my sufficiency and my treasure, and if You give me a son, he will belong solely to You."

And God gave her a son. She would name him Samuel, which means "God has heard." Samuel grew up to be a great prophet, a priestly figure, and an almost-king of Israel (see 1 Sam 8). Although Samuel is great in the story of Scripture, he anoints another king, a coming king. Eventually he would be the prophet to anoint David to be the king of Israel.

Hannah, David, and Jesus

Hannah's story is included in 1 Samuel as more than an intriguing situation that led up to David's coronation. Her story sets a pattern for the story of David. Recall that Israel was searching for a king. Why did they want a king so badly? They wanted a king for the same reasons Hannah had wanted a son. They desired prosperity, stability, and security. Hannah sought these in a son; Israel sought them in a king. To Hannah, God says, "These things are not found in sons." To Israel He says, "These things are not found in kings." To both of them He says, "These things are only found in Me."

There is also a strong pattern that connects Hannah's story and Jesus' story. Hundreds of years later another woman would face an impossible birth like Hannah. This woman's name was Mary. Yet her pregnancy was even more unlikely. She was not barren; in fact, she had never slept with a man! And for Mary, having a child would mean losing everything she held onto for significance and security. To be pregnant out of wedlock in the first century meant the loss of reputation, most likely the loss of her intended spouse, and financial hardship. It would have been a type of death! (See, for instance, Joseph's reaction to Mary's untimely pregnancy in Matt 2:19.)

Like Hannah, however, Mary grasped the gospel. She understood that God was a more certain source of identity and security than reputation, than family, than money. She surrendered herself to God and found her identity and hope in Him. She expressed that hope, as Hannah did, in a song. Luke 1 records what we call "Mary's Magnificat," with wording nearly identical to that of Hannah's prayer: "My spirit has rejoiced in God my Savior. . . . He has toppled the mighty from their thrones and exalted the lowly" (Luke 1:47,52; cf. 1 Sam 2:1,4,8). Mary's song, like Hannah's, declares that security and significance are found in a God who would care about the broken and poor enough to give Himself to them.

Note all the parallels between Hannah's story and Mary's story.[6] Hannah gave birth to Samuel, who would be both priest and prophet, a man who would anoint the king of Israel. Mary gave birth to the One who would be Priest, Prophet, and King of all kings. Most scholars recognize that Hannah's Song in 1 Samuel 2 is the foundation for Mary's song that she sang after the angel announced that she would carry God's Son, the Messiah (Luke 1). The parallels (indicated by the symbol "//") are too strong to ignore:

Hannah (childless)	//	Mary (childless)
Divine Intervention for Hannah	//	Divine Intervention for Mary
Hannah's Praise	//	Mary's Praise
Praise for her Savior (1 Sam 2:1-10)	//	Praise for her Savior (Luke 1:46-55)

These connections are helpful. They remind us that God answers the prayers of those who fervently cry out to Him. They remind us that

---

[6] Scholars have long recognized the connections between their songs. See Ellis, *The Gospel of Luke*, 74–75; Green, *The Gospel of Luke*, 100–105.

God looks on the "lowly" state of ordinary people and loves them with extravagant love. We don't have to be rich or perfect or glamorous or religious or Democrat or Republican or anything else for God to love us. He loves us because He made us and as a result has gone above and beyond for humanity. He meets us right where we are.

But the parallels between Hannah and Mary take us further than what we have described above. The story of Scripture takes us straight to Jesus. Hannah prayed for a baby, and God gave Samuel to Hannah. The world prayed for a Savior, and God gave Jesus to Mary. Scripture turns to Jesus. Jesus, like Hannah, would pray for deliverance from a curse and shame. But whereas God answered Hannah, He would turn His back on Jesus. Why? So that Hannah's real shame could be taken away. So that our real shame would be abolished. So that we would have the joy of being restored to God.

Our real shame and brokenness come not from the fact that we can't have kids or that we aren't successful. Our real shame comes from the break in our relationship with our Creator. We don't need children. We don't need more money. We don't need better sex. We need to be reunited to God. This is what Jesus would accomplish for us. By being forsaken for our sakes, He would restore us to God.

The story of Hannah is not just an isolated incident about a woman, her aloof husband, and a miracle child. It's about lost people—us!—and how Jesus came to save us. This is the message of the whole Bible. From beginning to end, the grand narrative weaves a beautiful tapestry of a Creator seeking His people to reconcile them to Himself.

Hannah, David, Jesus, *and Us*

Hannah's life sets a pattern for the life of David. It even sets a pattern for the life of Jesus. What is most pressing is that Hannah's life parallels our story. Hannah looked to a son for security and significance; Israel looked to a king. Where will we look? What is the king we seek? What one thing must we have for life to be good? What one thing could we not imagine life without?

We all crown someone or something king over our lives. This is true of both religious and irreligious people. For the irreligious, something is needed *instead of* Jesus. Life is found, for instance, in money, fame, or family. For the religious, something is needed *in addition to* Jesus. The point of the Bible is that knowing Jesus is enough. He is life, stability, and security. This has at least four practical applications for us today.

Most of Our Hurt and Disappointment Comes from Seeking Another "King" besides God

When we are disappointed, hurt, or stressed, these feelings indicate that we have chosen another "king" besides God. These feelings are like smoke from a fire: you can follow the smoke back to the source of the fire. Follow these feelings back to their source, and we will find the altars that have been built to the things we are worshiping. This happens, for instance, with married couples who have placed too much weight on their marriage. They look to a spouse to fulfill them and to be their functional king. When that person lets them down, their world falls to pieces. Bitter, insecure, single people don't get better by getting married. They only become bitter, insecure, married people. Problems like loneliness and insecurity are not cured by the love of another human being; they are cured by the love of God.

God Is Better Than "Many Sons" or a King

The point of Hannah's story is not that if you trust God and ask for things long enough, He will give you what you ask for. Of course, this doesn't mean we never pray to God out of hurtful and difficult situations. We do. But we cannot strong-arm God into giving us what we want just by attempting to "have more faith." Hannah's attitude changed before she became pregnant, and she would have had joy even if she never had any children. Many among us will never have a child, despite pleading with God for one. Many will never get rich. Many will never get well again from their sicknesses. By all the world's standards, we may die "barren."

But if we have God, we have enough: the one who has God has everything. God is significance and stability. If a loving, all-powerful God is in someone's life, the approval of others becomes inconsequential. If a loving, all-powerful God is in someone's life, her future is in capable hands. And if a loving, all-powerful God is in someone's life, she can endure the harshest struggles because He is enough. God plus nothing still equals everything.

Barrenness Does Not Mean God-Forsakenness

Have we not all heard that voice inside telling us that the problems we are experiencing are God's repayment for our sinfulness? Have we not all felt abandoned by God? When we experience times of barrenness and brokenness, our natural reaction is to assume that God has forsaken us. It may be a natural reaction, but it certainly is not a biblical one. The gospel is that Jesus Christ was forsaken for us. Jesus' death on the cross took on our barrenness, our brokenness, and our hopelessness. He was forsaken so we would never have to be. When we approach the cross, we find that all that has been defeated, once and for all. We still experience barrenness and brokenness in this life; but because of Jesus, we can face them, knowing that God is for us. God has not abandoned us in our hour of darkness. He is present in that hour, working all things for good. If we have placed faith in the cross, we can be assured that we are not, and never can be, forsaken.

God Loves People the World Casts Away

Hannah's story teaches us that God cares for people that the world no longer cares for. Many of us may feel like the story of our lives has been a gigantic failure. We have not accomplished what we set out to accomplish. We are still childless. We are still addicted to alcohol. Our kings have failed us and have cast us aside. In times like these, we need the faith of Hannah. We need to be reminded that God cares for us and has offered Himself—the world's greatest possession—to us as our treasure. This is the unique message of the Bible: God cares for the outcast. He gives Himself to the broken. There is no greater consolation for those who feel that the world has cast them away.

Let us run to the cross and find there the love of God that pursues each of us. God has not forsaken us but desires to draw us back to a relationship with Him. No matter our situation, we can say with Hannah, "There is no rock like our God!"

Reflect and Discuss

1. What does this passage help you understand about God's love?
2. How does this passage of Scripture exalt Jesus?
3. What does it do to your heart when you realize that Jesus is the Savior we need?
4. How have you experienced the kind of hopelessness and rejection Hannah faced?
5. When you get to that place of hopelessness, what is your response? To which "savior" do you turn?
6. How does it free you to know that "barrenness does not mean God-forsakenness"?

7. Notice the definition of *faith*: *Faith* means rejoicing in God when our dreams are still unfulfilled and resting on God when life is still falling apart all around us. How would you apply that definition of *faith* to your life today?
8. How does Hannah's life anticipate the coming of Jesus?
9. How have you been frustrated or disappointed by other "saviors" in your life?
10. If you are still trusting in "saviors" other than Jesus, what are you thinking they provide that is more than what Jesus can provide?

All Worship the King

1 SAMUEL 2:1-11

Main Idea: Hannah's praise reveals the King who is worthy of worship.

I.   A Definition of *Worship*
II. True Worship Centers on the True God
III. True Worship Transforms

Introduction

As we have studied Hannah, it is worth taking a closer look at her worship, which we will accomplish in the exposition that follows. There is value in thinking about worship, and it is remarkable how closely worship and sporting events often parallel one another. People go crazy over sports. They (no, really, *we*) dress up, scream and shout, and do things we normally wouldn't do in everyday life. Think about going to a favorite team's football or basketball games, for instance. People enter into the gates of the sporting arena singing their teams' praises. They watch the warm-ups to get excited about the game. They give one another "peace" and high fives as they anticipate the event. They sing songs (the national anthem or the official team songs), watch special rituals (coin toss or tip-off), and then participate in the spectacle of the game.

If you think about it, for many, sporting events are similar to religious services. The sporting arenas are like houses of worship, sacred spaces, and holy places. At least that is how we can treat them. Everything feels like a worship service:

Sporting Events		Church Worship Services
Entrance through the gates	//	Procession to worship
High fives before the game	//	Passing the peace
Singing special songs	//	Singing worship music
Getting involved in the game	//	Worshiping and listening to preaching
Rituals of coin toss, kickoff, etc.	//	Baptism and Eucharist
Exit the stadium	//	Recessional

The reason sporting events carry so much power and influence for modern people (and indeed American Christians!) is because they give a place where we can express our need for worshiping something greater than ourselves. Do you doubt that? Well, just take note of how we do things in a sporting event that, at least one would think, we would do in a worship service (but often don't!): expressing emotion, praising, lamenting, and no doubt lots of prayers!

In light of the similarities we have drawn between worship events and sporting events, we wonder if a helpful insight has been exposed. We wonder if it is worth considering something important, and we frame it in the form of a question. Is it possible that sporting events draw out the *right kind of worship* to the *wrong god*?

It is easy to replace the right God with the wrong god and right worship with false worship. If we have gotten off track and fallen into false worship, we can get back on track as we learn from the Scriptures. From 1 Samuel 2, we discover the *right worship* to the *right God*. This text helps develop the theme of kingship in 1 Samuel and reveals the meaning and transformative power of worship to the King and its impact on life.

Hannah lived a long time ago—about 3,000 years ago. She shows us the way forward into true worship, which is what we're talking about in this chapter. True worship transforms our lives for the better. So let's look at Hannah's worship in 1 Samuel 2:1-11. What do we learn about worship from Hannah's experience in this text?

A Definition of *Worship*

First, let's raise a question that needs answering: What is worship? Here is a preliminary definition: Worship is our glad response to the goodness of God.

Almost everyone worships one way or another. The majority of human beings throughout history have a built-in tendency to worship. That is because God has placed in our hearts the desire to worship something greater than ourselves.

You might say, "What about atheists or purely secular people?" Even secular people (or atheists) today have a tendency to worship something. A recent article revealed that atheists in London have a weekly gathering on Sunday (called "Sunday Assembly") to get together and engage in a kind of worship. One of the founders says about the new "religion": "The more time you spend thinking about how awesome life is, guess what? The more awesome it is," he explained. "Just being alive;

to become conscious that you are alive, and celebrate that, is just as transcendental as anyone's God" (Hines, "Sunday Assembly Is the Hot New Atheist Church").

We all tend to worship something greater than ourselves. For these friends the object of worship (though no doubt they would object to such language!) is life itself and the sheer joy of life. And although we would agree that life is incredible and worth celebrating, we would encourage our friends to press more deeply into the meaning of life and find that life, humanity, and the Author of life belong together. Once we take the concept of Creator out of reality, then reality itself loses sense.

From Hannah's Song we see the heart of true worship. What can we learn from this ancient song?

True Worship Centers on the True God

Since we've been speaking about sports, imagine going to a football game. You go through the parking lot where everyone is tailgating in their team's colors. They are talking and laughing, eating and debating about the upcoming game. Hopes are high and excitement is real. You make your way through the parking lot with the masses of excited fans, hearing the team's song as you walk, people bursting out in song as they go. You are ready to see the game! And then you make your way through the gates of the stadium. Does everyone have his or her ticket? Yes, OK, we're all good! And now past the concession stands with eight-dollar hot dogs and five-dollar diet sodas. What a wonder! But now we must get our favorite player's jersey before we go through the tunnel into the stands. And then to the seats! You look out as you take your seat and see a great sight: tens of thousands of people crowding together, shouting and cheering for little ants running around the green field warming up. The cheerleaders (or yell-leaders) are there. Kickoff is about to ensue.

But what if, just as the game was about to begin, someone in your group declares that he or she is going to spend the next few hours doing other things, and you simply must come along. You ask if they have lost their mind because, after all, you have come to watch the game. But they respond that they will be looking at the concession stands and walking around the stadium to see the architecture and assessing the functionality of the electronics work at the entrance gates. They muse that they could go back into the parking lot to see how many cars there were or how many of those cars tailgated and how many did not. Then they urge you once again to accompany them. After all, together you could spend the next few hours counting each member of the audience one by one, or sketching the architectural design of the stadium. What would you say to that person? We don't know what you would say, but we know what we would say! "Do what you want, but *I've come to watch the game!*"

All the fanfare that is associated with a football spectacle is there to focus and highlight the main thing: the game itself. People don't go to a football game for the parking, the concessions, or the people. They go for the game.

Now let's take this thought to a worship service. It is entirely possible to be distracted away from the focus of worship. Lights, sounds, music, people, or clothes are not the focus of true worship. Rather, true worship focuses on the main thing, and the main attraction in worship is God Himself. When we look at Hannah's Song, we see the "main attraction" in worship. Others might go to worship for other reasons, but notice how many times Hannah focuses her worship on God. Just by the number of times she uses God's name in her praise, we count that she focuses her worship on God no fewer than 21 times in the span of these 11 verses.

Her singular focus on her God enables her to sing of His deliverance, her reversal from shame to honor, and the future hope of the coming Messiah! Only encounters with the living God in worship enable us to have a radical shift in perspective. Even if circumstances do not change, when we encounter the living God in worship, our perspectives on our circumstances do change! Hannah saw her God, and that changed everything.

People "go to church" for a number of reasons. Consider the following list:

1. To see people
2. To talk with people
3. To get the latest gossip
4. To make sure I am noticed
5. To feel better about myself
6. To get a better perspective on life
7. To hear the new music

Do any of these reasons sound familiar? If we are fully honest about what we do on a Saturday or Sunday, at least some of these in the list touch on real reasons we attend a service on the weekend. But Hannah's experience with God in worship reminds us of a powerful and terrifying truth: Our focus in worship is the living God and His Savior, Jesus Christ!

It is not merely about our needs or our hopes or our prayers. It is about encountering a living God who meets us and changes us in worship. This is the reason, for instance, that the writer of Hebrews encourages the church to hold fast to assembling together in worship: the living Christ has purified the church of her sins and meets with His bride as we anticipate His second coming (Heb 10:25). His encounter with His people is grand and powerful; as we are encouraged and transformed to stay the course, hold to the faith, and proclaim the gospel to a world that desperately needs the Savior:

> *Let us hold on to the confession of our hope without wavering, for He who promised is faithful. And let us be concerned about one another in order to promote love and good works, not staying away from our worship meetings, as some habitually do, but encouraging each other, and all the more as you see the day drawing near.* (Heb 10:23-25)

We have heard it all our lives, and likely you have too, that God wants us to "go to church." Maybe parents scolded us at some point or another for not "going to church." But we must remember this bold reality: God does not want us to come to church; we are the church! And as we gather together to worship the living Christ, we are encouraged and changed.

At the Summit Church in the Raleigh-Durham metroplex, we have to ask the same question readers ask as they make their way to worship each week: When we make the pilgrimage to worship on the weekend, why exactly do we do it?

Of course the admonition from Hebrews 10 is one reason. But on the other hand, no one is forcing us to do this. Why do we sing songs and hear God's Word preached, and pray and thank and plead with God? Why do we receive the ministry of the Spirit? Why do we look for God to do miracles when we enter into this sacred space?

We do this not to fulfill an obligation but to encounter the Holy One who has saved us and has changed us forever through the shed blood of the risen Christ! We gather together to worship for an audience of one. We worship our God and Him alone.

It is a good thing to reflect on the purpose and motivation of our participation in worship. Before the service begins, it may be helpful to ask yourself the following leading questions:

Why have I come today?
For whom am I here?
Whom do I want to see most of all?

As these questions open us up to our true selves, we can then turn our mind's attention and heart's devotion to the person who heals and saves, the object of our worship: the living Christ!

Hannah's Song in 1 Samuel 2:1-11 is the embodiment of praise. It is a radical song of worship to the true God. Her focus lay firmly on the living God, her "rock" and her "salvation." Her experience opens all of us to worship the King!

True Worship Transforms

Through Hannah's worship in 1 Samuel 2, we discover that her life was transformed. When we read of her experience from chapter 1, it is apparent that the text presents her as agitated, irritated, troubled in spirit, anxious, and in deep pain. Another way we can describe this is that she was at war with others, herself, and God:

She was **at war with others**, particularly her rival and her husband. She was provoked and abused by a woman (Peninnah) who ridiculed her infertility (1 Sam 1:6-7). This is perhaps one of the most sensitive issues in the biblical story: barrenness and infertility. It is a potent source of pain, and here the other woman mocks the deepest wound in her life. Have you had that experience? Have you ever experienced the shattering effect of another person scorning you for something you cannot control (especially what others see as physical deficiencies)? This is no small matter. But to make this issue worse, her husband is absolutely clueless. As we discussed in the previous chapter, Elkanah cannot comprehend why she is so upset! He thinks he is everything she needs in life! Easy for him to say. He already has children with Peninnah. Hannah, however, is all alone. For those who are married and are reading this commentary, is it not possible to hear Hannah's experience with her spouse ringing in your ears? Have we ever had the experience of our spouse not understanding or supporting us the way we think we ought to be supported? The loneliness and frustration, the pain and the agony of not being known and understood can be all too immense, leading us to be, like Hannah, "deeply hurt" (1:10).

But Hannah's conflict did not simply come from without. She experienced emotional and spiritual turmoil from within that the text describes as Hannah having a "broken heart" and experiencing "anguish and resentment" (1:15-16). She was at war with others, but she was also **at war with herself**. Hannah's story is not unusual in the biblical material. Oftentimes those who experience trouble all around them also reflect the storm within.

But finally, Hannah was **at war**, in a sense, **with God**. She wept bitterly and pleaded with Him (1:10) and poured out her heart to her God (1:15). She wondered what in the world God was doing with her! Why was He allowing her rival to do this to her? Why did God create her for barrenness rather than fertility? It was a bitter and jagged pill to swallow. She could go to no other court of appeal than the highest court imaginable: to the throne of God Himself!

That was Hannah's story in 1 Samuel 1. But look at her story in chapter 2: she is radically transformed! Look at her worship now: it is radically transformed. She is transformed in a number of ways we see in 2:1-11:

1. Her first word is praise to God (v. 1).
2. She thanks God for overcoming the enemy (vv. 3-5).
3. She sees her story in God's story (v. 8).
4. She knows God's character—His holiness and justice (vv. 2,10).
5. She sees God's coming salvation—a coming King (v. 10)!

When we read her song, we see that the life of Hannah moves from emptiness to fullness. She moves from pain to praise. Her heart moves from mourning to joy.

Worshiping the Lord transforms because in worship God meets with His people.

It is vital to note something extraordinarily important in the light of this. Worshiping the Lord transforms us whether we "feel" like it or not! Now, we may not feel like worshiping. Well-known pastor and author Eugene Peterson captures this point about feeling and worship in his fantastic book, *A Long Obedience in the Same Direction*. Peterson says,

> I have put a great emphasis on the fact that Christians worship because they want to, not because they are forced to. But I have never said we worship because we *feel* like it. Feelings are great liars. If Christians worshiped only when they felt like it, there would be precious little worship. Feelings are important in many areas but completely unreliable in matters of faith.

Paul Scherer is laconic: "The Bible wastes very little time on the way we feel."

We live in what one writer calls the "age of sensation." We think that if we don't *feel* something there can be no authenticity in *doing* it. But the wisdom of God says something different: that we can *act* ourselves into a new way of feeling much quicker than we can *feel* ourselves into a new way of acting. Worship is an *act* that develops feelings for God, not a *feeling* for God that is expressed in an act of worship. When we obey the command to praise God in our worship, our deep, essential need to be in a relationship with God is nurtured. (*A Long Obedience*, 54)

No doubt worship stirs up feelings for God, but worship is not about feelings for God alone. Transformation through worship comes as a result of our bowing our hearts and lives before our Maker, through the good and the bad, whether we feel like it or not. As we worship God in times of trouble and "press through," as an Anglican pastor friend has said, we experience the radical transformation that comes through communion with God.

The point is this: worship is the doorway to transformation.

In times of trouble, we want to commend the importance of talking with friends, spouse, family, and those closest to us. We want to commend the importance of exercise and leisure when times are difficult and the pain of life extends its icy fingers into our world. Still, while we commend these things, we would ask whether our first action in times of distress is, in fact, worship. Worship brings transformation.

First Samuel 2 is really the last word we hear of Hannah in the Bible. Hers is a story of transformation from pain to joy because of the radical experience with the God she worships. She will forever be known as that woman greatly transformed, that one whose life ends in worship. Can you say the same of your life?

Reflect and Discuss

1. What does this passage help you understand about God's love?
2. How does this passage of Scripture exalt Jesus?
3. "Right worship, wrong god!" Do you idolize sports or something else? Write down your thoughts.

4. In light of the list of reasons people attend worship services on a weekend, which of those reasons (or others not listed) resonates with you? Write down your thoughts.

5. How has worship transformed your life? Be specific and write down your thoughts.

6. Do you participate in worship (on a weekend or otherwise) "for the audience of One"? If not, what distractions get in the way?

7. Notice the definition of *worship*: Worship is our glad response to the goodness of God. How would you apply that definition of *worship* to your life today?

8. How does Hannah's praise anticipate the coming of Jesus?

9. How have you been frustrated or disappointed by worship in your life? Is it the style of music (contemporary vs. traditional)? Is it the overall type of service (liturgical vs. free church)? Is it the focus of the worship (self-help vs. focusing on Jesus)? Or is it something else (like preaching, etc.)? Write down your thoughts.

10. To what degree are those things you have written down in number 9 above really good reasons to distract us from worshiping Jesus?

Hearing God

1 SAMUEL 2:12–3:20

Main Idea: As Samuel heard God, he found his purpose and meaning as priest, prophet, and judge. It gave him courage to speak hard words to his spiritual father, Eli.

I. **Eli's House Was Judged for Not Hearing God.**
II. **God Still Speaks.**
III. **Ways God Speaks to His People**
    A. His voice: the Spirit of God
    B. His Word: the Scriptures
    C. His people: the church
    D. His world: the creation
    E. His Son: Jesus
IV. **Barriers to Hearing God's Voice**
    A. Inexperience
    B. Expectation
    C. Sin
    D. Unwillingness
V. **Hearing God Clarifies Meaning and Purpose.**
    A. Our purpose: to bring glory to our Creator
    B. Our purpose: finding the sweet spot

Introduction

Hannah's vibrant worship in 1 Samuel 2 contrasts with the willful sin of Eli's children and the dulled vision of the priest Eli in 1 Samuel 2:12–3:20. This section serves as a transition away from Eli's priestly family and toward the priestly and prophetic duties of Samuel. The narrative achieves this transition most immediately by presenting the judgment of Eli (2:12-36) juxtaposed against the beautiful worship song of Hannah (2:1-11). Hannah experienced the Lord and worshiped Him in faith, but 2:12 opens with, "Eli's sons were wicked men; they had no regard for the LORD." The remainder of the narrative clearly shows why Eli's household will fail and fall and why Yahweh raises up Samuel. Samuel will be a priest who will serve the Lord (unlike Eli's family).

Chapter 3 reveals the fact that Samuel will not only be a priest but a prophet as well. The chapter opens with, "In those days the word of the LORD was rare and prophetic visions were not widespread." This is the first instance in the book of Samuel that we have mention of prophetic terminology ("word of the LORD" and "prophetic visions"). The role and office of the prophet are given in Deuteronomy 13 and 18, but in the days of Hannah and Elkanah, prophetic activity was limited. Neither Eli nor his children would be prophets, but Hannah's devoted little boy would be the prophet and priest God's people would need.

The language, the "word of the LORD" and "visions," indicates prophetic activity in which prophets hear from God words of encouragement or rebuke and deliver these words to God's people. That such prophetic activity was "rare" reveals that God's word was not permeating the hearts of the community of the Lord. Without the word of God, the people of God perish. Moses' injunction to God's people just before his death reveals the seriousness of the word of God for His people. Moses has delivered the stipulations of the covenant with God as His people enter into the promised land. He urges God's people to follow the command of the Lord and to receive it gladly. Moses says plainly, "For they are not meaningless words to you but they are your life, and by them you will live long in the land you are crossing the Jordan to possess" (Deut 32:47). Without God's words and God's vision, God's people would perish.

In these days (1 Sam 3:1), the prophetic activity that brought the word of the Lord was "rare." Hearing the word of the Lord was like finding a pearl of great price that was hidden in the field. And apparently, God's priests were ineffective in teaching the people the word of the Lord. In verse 2, Eli, the great high priest at Shiloh, has about as much "vision" as the people. He cannot see and he cannot hear very well, as we noted in the introduction (p. 31).

The brief introduction here gives the setting for the focus of this passage of Scripture: hearing God. Imagine that you are in a coffee shop, a mall, or a concert with your family or friends. The noise around you is loud and distracting. But you are able to hear the person across from you or close to you. You are able to talk with them and carry on a full conversation. If you have children, you know what it is like to be able to pick out your child's call in a crowd. "Daddy!" from one of our children immediately causes us to turn to our kids, even if there are other kids and parents around. Why are we able to screen out other voices and hear those we want to hear? How are we able to do it?

In a word it is *focus*. We focus on what we want to hear, and so we are able to pick it out. We give our attention to the voice that is most important amid all other distractions. It is like those *Where's Waldo?* books. Do you remember those? Your job was to find Waldo in all the distractions. Sometimes it feels like hearing God is like finding Waldo—very hard to do, but once you find Him, you don't want to lose that focus.

From 1 Samuel 3 we discover that hearing God is not like finding Waldo because God wants to be heard, so He speaks clearly and truly to us. God really speaks to His children so hearing God is possible, beneficial, and necessary to meet His call for our lives. God says in Jeremiah 29:13, "You will seek Me and find Me when you search for Me with all your heart." However, as we see from this verse, hearing God does require a certain kind of openness and a tenacity from us. This is the kind of openness we see in the life of Samuel, which is one of the reasons God uses him as the prophet and priest for God's people.

What do we learn about hearing God from the experience of Samuel?

Eli's House Was Judged for Not Hearing God

Often we look for handwriting in the sky, a special message in the milk we pour into the coffee, signs, or thunderclaps. We look for the special sign that tells us God is really there and He wants to talk to us. We look for an image of Jesus to show up on our pancake in the morning or a picture of the virgin Mary to show up on our toast. It may be true that He does sometimes speak like that. But more often than not, God does not speak with handwriting in the sky. In reality God is wonderfully diverse in how He speaks.

A key way God speaks is through Scripture. The book of Samuel is about God speaking: the entire book is a message given to His people so they might know Him. In other words, God really does speak, and today He speaks from Scripture. Samuel heard God's voice because God really speaks. And this is the first point we ought to understand: there is a God who speaks today.

God longs for us to hear His voice. A beautiful picture is the little boy Samuel responding to God's voice, saying, "Speak, for Your servant is listening." Sometimes our ears are unable to hear Him. This was true of Eli. He could not hear God's voice. His eyes were dull, and his ears were stopped up. Perhaps God spoke to him over and over, with no response from the priest, to the point that Eli's ears were covered from the voice of God. It took him a number of times to recognize that it was Yahweh who was speaking to Samuel. And we have already seen in 1 Samuel 1 that Eli thought Hannah was drunk at the site of worship and did not perceive that she was earnestly praying. Eli could not see or hear God very well.

Modern people may be in the company of Eli, saying, "I just don't hear Him. I just don't see Him." That is understandable. Life is so loud with phones, television, iPods, iPads, music, work, and other noises that it can be difficult to discern the still, small voice of God. However, just because we may not hear God speaking right now does not mean (1) there is no God, and (2) God does not speak. Eli's deafness to the voice of God and blindness to the vision of God is not a reflection of the lack of existence or presence of God. Rather, his blindness and deafness indicate his spiritual state. Sometimes modern people are in the same boat.

God Still Speaks

We will explore below some reasons people today don't hear God's voice. But for now the important thing to grasp is that the experience of Samuel reminds us that God speaks. Samuel was a little boy with no experience with God. His mom gave him in service to the Lord. Still, despite his youth and inexperience, the text is unequivocal: God spoke to Samuel. Granted, Samuel didn't know who the voice was, but God continued to speak: four times God spoke to Samuel.

And in the last instance, God walks in and stands before Samuel and calls his name: "The LORD came, stood there, and called as before, 'Samuel, Samuel!' Samuel responded, 'Speak, for Your servant is listening'" (1 Sam 3:10). I've always found this imagery as extremely curious. How in the world does the living God come and stand before a little boy in the tabernacle? How can the God of the universe walk into Samuel's room? Is He not too big? The text presents to the reader a God who walks right up to a little boy and speaks to him; the great and majestic God of the universe walks into Samuel's room because He wants to speak to the boy. This text testifies that God really speaks, and we can really hear Him. The remainder of Samuel's life is a story of a man listening to God.

The God of the universe wants to walk into the rooms of ordinary people to speak to them because He loves to speak with His people. The book of Samuel is about God speaking to His people: about His love, His plan, and His people's sin. But the book of Samuel ultimately reveals God's plan to heal their sin in Jesus. If it is true that God speaks, then we must ask, How does God speak to us?

Ways God Speaks to His People

His Voice: The Spirit of God

God audibly spoke to Samuel, and He did so to others as well. When Jesus came, He told His disciples that He had a great many other things to teach them; but when He went away, the Spirit of God would come to teach them, guiding them into the truth (John 16:12-13). In the Gospel of John, truth has a name, and it is Jesus. So the Spirit of God reveals Jesus. But the Gospel of John also affirms that the Holy Spirit would continue to teach and bring to remembrance all that God has said through His Word (see John 14:26).

His Word: The Scriptures

Scripture is God's primary way of communicating to us. It helps us understand and confirm God's voice. The writer of Psalm 119 says it this way: "Your word is a lamp for my feet and a light on my path" (v. 105). John Calvin, that famous theologian from the seventeenth century, said that the Scriptures serve as "spectacles"; as we look through these spectacles, we see the world aright. Without the true vision provided by the Scriptures, then our sight of humanity, our world, and our work becomes distorted in sin. So God's Word illuminates our path and gives us the true story of the whole world, which culminates in the truth, Jesus Christ.

His People: The Church

God speaks through His people, as Colossians confirms:

> *Let the message about the Messiah dwell richly among you, teaching*
> *and admonishing one another in all wisdom, and singing psalms,*
> *hymns, and spiritual songs, with gratitude in your hearts to God.*
> *And whatever you do, in word or in deed, do everything in the name*
> *of the Lord Jesus, giving thanks to God the Father through Him.*
> (Col 3:16-17)

Consider for a moment that God gives His people the great privilege of speaking the word of God to one another—not in a way that we provide "new" information about God, the church, or the world but rather that we teach and encourage one another in life through Christ and His Scriptures.

His World: The Creation

It is important to remember as well that God speaks through His world. As Romans informs,

> What can be known about God is evident among them, because God has shown it to them. For His invisible attributes, that is, His eternal power and divine nature, have been clearly seen since the creation of the world, being understood through what He has made. (Rom 1:19)

God speaks through the created world, informing humanity that there is a God who made the world and it is not an accident.

His Son: Jesus

Although God speaks of Himself in creation, God has spoken definitively in His Son, Jesus the Messiah. Jesus is the "firstborn" of creation, and all God's work was accomplished through the Son (John 1). Because of this, our ability to hear what God is saying in His creation is made perfect in the One through whom all things were made (Col 1:15-20). Jesus is the definitive Word from the Lord.

As the writer of Hebrews says,

> Long ago God spoke to the fathers by the prophets at different times and in different ways. In these last days, He has spoken to us by His Son. God has appointed Him heir of all things and made the universe through Him. The Son is the radiance of God's glory and the exact expression of His nature, sustaining all things by His powerful word. After making purification for sins, He sat down at the right hand of the Majesty on high. So He became higher in rank than the angels, just as the name He inherited is superior to theirs. (Heb 1:1-4)

Even the life of Samuel testifies about the Son of God, Jesus Christ. I (Heath) remember clearly a spiritual hero writing in my Bible when I was a little boy (about 10 or 12 years old). He wrote, "Luke 2:52." The idea behind writing the verse in my Bible was that I would go back and read the verse, which I did. The verse is about Jesus, when He was a boy. It reads, "And Jesus increased in wisdom and stature, and in favor with God and with people" (Luke 2:52). It was only years later, when I was reading through 1 Samuel, that I saw similar verses that caught my imagination:

> *The boy Samuel grew in stature and in favor with the LORD and with men.* (2:26)

> *Samuel grew, and the LORD was with him, and He fulfilled everything Samuel prophesied. All Israel from Dan to Beer-sheba knew that Samuel was a confirmed prophet of the LORD. The LORD continued to appear in Shiloh, because there He revealed Himself to Samuel by His word.* (3:19-20)

The description of Jesus in Luke 2:52 is the same as that of Samuel in 1 Samuel 2:26. Samuel's divine favor and calling mirror those of Jesus, and vice versa. As Hannah recognized that Samuel was from the Lord, Mary recognized that Jesus was from the Lord. As Samuel grew, Jesus grew. As Samuel was priest and prophet (and almost king; see 1 Samuel 8), Jesus was the true priest, prophet, and king. In other words, Samuel's life sets a pattern that testifies to Jesus. So while Samuel is a great character in the story of the book of Samuel, his life looks toward One who will come: Jesus the Messiah.

God's Spirit, the Scriptures, creation, God's people, and even Samuel provide testimony that God speaks. If this is true, and if these are really several ways God speaks, then we must ask a significant question: Why is it so difficult to hear God's voice today?

Barriers to Hearing God's Voice

Inexperience

When one looks at 1 Samuel 3:7, it becomes apparent that Samuel was inexperienced in hearing God's voice. Samuel did not know it was God's voice until Eli, who was more mature, began to help him. Those who are older and more mature in the Lord need to help those who are younger in the faith. Inexperience with the Lord prevents people from recognizing that what is heard is actually the voice of God.

Expectation

A question we must ask is whether we expect to hear God's voice in the variety of ways described above. Do we read God's Word and carry out our daily business with the expectation that God will speak? It is apparent that God does speak, but do modern people live with the expectation of God's speaking *to them*? Once Samuel understood (through Eli) that it was God who was speaking, he turned up his expectation and tuned his antenna to the voice of God. As a boy, Samuel put into practice something he lived out for the rest of his days—an attitude of expectation: "Speak, for Your servant is listening" (3:10). Expectation positions us to hear God in the everyday of life. Expectation creates the ordinary moments of grace where God breaks in.

Sin

Unfortunately, Eli no longer could hear the voice of God or see the work of God. First Samuel 2:12-36 depicts the demise of Eli's household, primarily because of sin. The text records the fact that he can hear all the things his sons are boasting about that are wicked and vile (2:22). He can hear the voice of others talking about the sins of his boys (2:23). He can hear others, but due to his sin he can no longer hear God. Yahweh says (through a prophet), "You have honored your sons more than Me, by making yourselves fat with the best part of all of the offerings of My people Israel" (2:29). Apparently, Eli and his sons were receiving the sacrificial animals from God's people, but instead of giving the choice meat that belonged to God as a sacrifice on the altar, they were taking it for themselves as a meal. They literally "got fat" off of God's people and God's offering. As a result, God stripped Eli and his family of their priestly duties. As we saw in the introduction to this volume (pp. 27–28, 31–32), God then raised up a faithful prophet and priest to lead His people in the land, and this faithful one is Samuel (2:35-36). The reason for Eli's deafness to God's voice is sin, as the narrative of chapter 3 bears out.

But the story of Eli becomes the story of God's people in the book of Samuel. They, like he, tend to listen to the wrong voice because of their sin. God still speaks, but God's people cannot hear because of their brokenness and complicity and sin. What is worse, God's voice may be heard, but it sounds terrible and frightening rather than the voice of a loving father, a heavenly King who cares for His people. Consider the primal pair (Adam and Eve) in the garden of Eden. When they sinned, God's voice became a source of anxiety and fear rather than of hope and companionship. So too in Samuel. Sin either stops up our ears from God's voice or makes God's voice terrifying rather than comforting. Sin causes us to fear God's voice rather than love God's voice.

Unwillingness

The notion of "unwillingness" stands out as a strange but powerful idea. In the book of Samuel, one notes a contrast of people. There is Samuel, who willingly hears God's voice and obeys Him. But then there is Eli and his boys (Hophni and Phinehas), who are unwilling to hear God's voice and thereby disobey Him. A barrier to hearing God's voice is an unwillingness to be open to His voice and what He has to say. Unwillingness may derive from selfishness, the fear of change, or general rebellion. However, unwillingness to obey God's voice ends in disaster, as the book of Samuel teaches with startling lucidity.

So God speaks, and He wants to speak to people today. How does He do this? He will use Scripture, His Spirit, His people, His creation, and His Son to communicate with people. So first and foremost, modern people must move beyond the barriers in order to listen to these instruments of God's voice. God wants to speak to people, real people, today. But what in life prevents us from hearing His voice? We must learn to experience texts like Psalm 40:6:

> *You do not delight in sacrifice and offering;*
> *You open my ears to listen.*
> *You do not ask for a whole burnt offering or a sin offering.*

The phrase "You open my ears to listen" can be reasonably translated from the Hebrew "two ears You have dug out for me." The image is powerful. God takes a pickax to our heads to mine the deafness and hardness of sin, inexperience, unwillingness, and sloth out of our spiritual ears. As Eugene Peterson comments, "The primary organ for receiving God's revelation is not the eye that sees but the ear that hears—which means that all of our reading of Scripture must develop into a hearing of the word of God" (Peterson, *Eat This Book*, 92).

We need God to attune our ears in order that we might hear Him. As J. D. has said to the Summit Church over and over again, God reveals Himself to us, opens Himself to us, when we put our *yes* on the table with God without reservation or hesitation. God gives us an open ear as we lay our *yes* to God on the table. But why is it good to hear God? What are the benefits of hearing God? The book of Samuel clarifies and exemplifies the benefits of hearing God.

Hearing God Clarifies Meaning and Purpose

Samuel was prophet and priest and almost a king (1 Sam 8). No one holds all three titles in Israel except Jesus, who was Prophet, Priest, and King. Traditionally this is known as the trifold office of Jesus. Still, as Jesus follows and expands on the pattern of Samuel, it is clear that Samuel is a towering figure in the story in the books of Samuel. So this raises a good question for us: Are modern followers of Jesus to emulate Samuel?

We might be tempted to say yes. After all, he heard from God, preached the word of God, confronted evil, and followed God faithfully, even until his death. And it is true that Samuel illustrates the life of faith. But when we ask whether or how modern believers should emulate Samuel, we must respond negatively. Our goal should not be (at least in the first place) patterned on the life of Samuel.

Our goal should be to follow the One to whom Samuel's life points: Jesus the Messiah! Jesus is our life and model as Christians. The Scriptures testify of Him, and we must not miss our Savior as we read Scripture. Jesus is the clue that unlocks the whole of creation. Paul reminds the Colossian church that Jesus is the image of the invisible God and the firstborn over all creation (Col 1:15). He says that all things are made through Him and for Him and must return to Him.

Dietrich Bonhoeffer, the famous German pastor and theologian, captures the magnitude of Jesus:

> He is the centre and the strength of the Bible, of the Church, and of theology, but also of humanity, of reason, of justice and of culture. Everything must return to Him; it is only under His protection that it can live. (*Ethics*, 56)

Our reading of Scripture must return over and over again to the center of everything, Jesus the Messiah.

Bonhoeffer's words are helpful as we read the narrative about Samuel. As good as Samuel was, we must remember God spoke to Samuel because God had a purpose for Samuel that was specific to Samuel. But in Jesus we find our meaning and purpose in life. We find why Jesus has placed us in His world and what He calls for us to do in His world. In Jesus we discover life, and life to the fullest (John 10:10).

Why did God speak to Samuel? God spoke to Samuel so that Samuel would know God's purpose for his life. God spoke to Samuel to raise him up as a prophet. God speaks to you and me to give our lives purpose.

Our purpose will not look exactly like Samuel's. God told Samuel he was to speak His prophetic word to Israel and her kings—specifically to Saul and David. God told Samuel he would anoint Israel's true king, King David.

You and I don't have that purpose. God has something different and unique for you and me. But this drives us to ask a foundational question: What are God's purposes for our lives? We need to answer this question at two levels. God has already spoken on the first level, so it is not a mystery.

Our Purpose: To Bring Glory to Our Creator

At the most fundamental level, the purpose of every human ever created by God is that we would please, honor, and bring glory to the One who made us. Or as the apostle Paul says: "So, whether you eat or drink, or whatever you do, do all to the glory of God" (1 Cor 10:31 ESV). We exist to bring glory to the One who made us.

What does it mean to bring "glory" to God? It means to show God's weightiness, His worth, His value, His majesty, and His beauty in everything that we do. It means to honor the Lord more than we honor ourselves. It means to put the beauty of God on display in the little and big things in life.

It is tempting to hear that and make it into a kind of "billboard" Christianity. In this way of thinking, to be a faithful Christian means to eat "Testamints™," to model Christian T-shirts, to wear a cross around the neck, or to use churchy language in our tweets (#blessed). The thought is that these acts will demonstrate, like a billboard, that we love Jesus first and foremost.

Not to denigrate that stuff too much, but bringing glory to God is much deeper than those showy and often shallow expressions of Christianity.

Bringing glory to God in the whole of life means working out exactly what it means to live in such a way that honors God in everything—how we speak and work, what we wear and eat, how we care for our bodies and for those around us, and how we live in God's world. We consider His pleasure and joy before we consider ours. We give Him the weight in our lives. And working this out can be really difficult because it's deep and not shallow.

So how do we give God the glory in all that we do, practically speaking? Each person must work that out for himself or herself. However, there are some practices that will help us get on track when it comes to giving glory to God:

1. *Read the Scriptures to discover the way of life God loves.* Regular Scripture reading gives the shape and form of the Christian life, so we can encounter Jesus and listen to what He says about His world and our lives.

2. *Live and learn with fellow believers in a local church to discover what following Jesus is all about in the little and big things.* Common worship and life with fellow Christians is important because it provides the fertile soil for growing in Jesus and giving glory to God. When we listen to God's Word preached in a local church week in and week out, we discover what God has said about a pattern of life that is pleasing to Him. Small-group Bible studies and study groups are a good place to understand the specifics of following God. Regular prayer opens us up to hear what God is saying about our lives—what we need to take up in life and what we need to put down for God's honor and our well-being.

So what has the Lord already said when it comes to our purpose? He has already said to put Him first and give Him glory in all things. You and I will only know fulfillment when we begin to hear from God. We can talk to Him about any and every need we have. When you look at the experience of Samuel, you see a boy discovering what it means to live a fulfilled life as he hears God's voice and follows Him, even if it is hard.

Our Purpose: Finding the Sweet Spot

Hearing God, second, clarifies for us more specific questions about purpose in life. Specific calling and purpose in life are often termed "vocation." In her book *Kingdom Calling: Vocational Stewardship for the Common Good*, Amy Sherman speaks about practical ways we find our purpose. Finding one's purpose in life is that journey of discovery where we locate the places where God's priorities, our gifting (and passion), and the world's needs collide. The collision point is called the vocational "sweet spot." See the following diagram (Sherman, *Kingdom Calling*, 108):

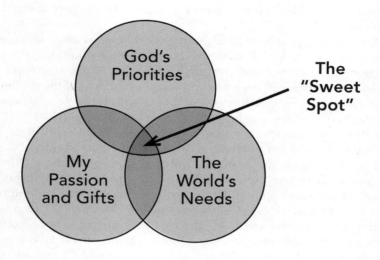

The collision point of divine priorities (discovered in Scripture), personal gifting (discovered in natural abilities and gifting), and the world's needs (discovered by attending to areas of brokenness and sin in local communities) reveals the sweet spot for our purpose. We must understand that our sweet spot may change. We develop new talents and gifts as we grow and mature, and the world's needs are always changing, at least to some degree.

The deepest need for people of the world is to know and love the God who made them. Because of this, it is vital that the world hears and receives the gospel of Jesus Christ, who reconciles all things back to God (Col 1:15-20). Broken people need to hear that they are far more sinful and broken than they could ever imagine, but they are more deeply loved by God than they could ever conceive. They need to hear that out of His love, God sent His one and only Son, so that through His sacrificial and atoning death on a cross, broken people might find forgiveness and hope. As broken and sinful people simply repent and believe in the Savior, they find themselves reconciled to God. This is the message of the gospel: not that we have loved God or could have earned our way to God but that God has loved us and sent His Son to be the atoning sacrifice that takes away the wall of separation and brings us home

(1 John 4:7-12). Hearing this good message is the deepest need of a broken world.

But it is not enough to proclaim the good news; we must also combat a broken world. We all know that broken people do terrible things: human trafficking, corruption, greed, and the like. At the root of all of it is sin and a separation from God. So we go to the root of the problem by proclaiming the gospel. But we also show a broken people who do terrible things that Jesus reigns in all things and over all things (Col 1:15-20). Jesus is King over everything, and so as Christians we discover the places of brokenness in the world and redirect them to the honor and glory of God.

For example, at the Summit Church in Raleigh-Durham, North Carolina, we have seen God clarify for many of us in the congregation the vocational sweet spot and take broken things in the community and redirect them for God's glory. We saw the challenge of parentless children in the county and state. The overwhelming reality of orphans exposes a deep brokenness in the area: some parents are not able to care for children. But God loves the orphan! In the Summit Church we recognized the deep need of the community, and we saw that some in the congregation had a passion and a gift for caring for these children. So they leveraged their lives for the sake of the gospel. They knew God cares for the orphan and widow through the church, they have a passion for the orphan, and so they establish a way for the church to be the instrument God uses to raise up folks to foster and adopt children without homes. This is a good example of how one can find the sweet spot. J. D. often speaks of how believers can "leverage" their gifts, talents, and passions for the gospel of Jesus Christ. As we do, we discover that God uses us to be the instruments He uses to impact the lost and broken world.

But finding our sweet spot, leveraging our lives, and discovering our purpose is not a microwave-quick moment. In her book, Sherman reminds us that finding the sweet spot of our purpose is a journey, and it does not happen overnight (*Kingdom Calling*, 107–8). Although there are lots of needs in the world, not every need has your name on it. We must discern what God has for each of us to do today. This is why prayer and hearing God are so essential for clarifying our specific sweet spot of purpose. As we think about going on the journey to find our purpose, we will discover that it is a journey of prayer, of hearing God at various levels:

- Personal, private prayer times where we focus in on what God is saying to us

- Corporate prayers where we gather to declare back to God His immeasurable beauty, and we bring to God the needs of the community
- Praying "at all times" as we are attentive to the Spirit as He guides us into truth and highlights the needs of the day and the gifts God has given us to meet those needs

As we walk the journey of prayer, we will find a road that takes us inward: toward God and His greatest desires for us and toward understanding our gifting and passion. And the journey inward will then propel us outward: toward the needs of the world. In and through multi-leveled prayer and hearing Him, God clarifies our gifts, our talents, and our desires so that we can be instruments in our Redeemer's hands.

As we will see in this commentary, when we lose our focus on hearing God, disastrous things follow. Eli lost God's voice and so lost his position as priest. Saul preferred hearing himself to hearing God. His disobedience to God's voice proved to be his undoing (1 Sam 15:22-23). Hearing God is vital to a vibrant and purpose-filled life. We must hear God because He is the great King who rules all of life, as we will see in the following chapters.

Reflect and Discuss

1. What does this passage help you understand about God?
2. How does this passage of Scripture exalt Jesus?
3. Do you believe God speaks today? Why or why not?
4. How do you most often hear God in the ways described above?
5. In what ways do you think God is prompting you to look to the other avenues of hearing Him from those described above?
6. Do you agree that giving God glory is our most basic purpose in life? If yes, then how are you giving Him glory now?
7. In the discussion on the sweet spot of purpose, do you need to hear God to find your sweet spot? How are you going to pursue hearing God this week?
8. Why can Eli no longer hear God? Are your spiritual ears hardened like Eli's? Why or why not?
9. What barriers to hearing God most relate to your experience with the Lord?
10. Why do you experience those barriers, and what do you need to ask God to change for you to move through them?

Yahweh Is King

Main Idea: The ark narrative reveals the unrivalled authority and power of Yahweh, the King.

I. The Ark Captured and Returned
II. Who Do You Say That I Am?
III. Repentance and Victory
IV. The Anatomy of Repentance
V. The Search for a Leader

Characterized as odd or "strange" (Doorly, *The Religion of Israel*, 60), this small story sounds almost too fantastic to believe—a tale to be told to little children or to adapt to a Hollywood movie. Just think about it: the journey of a mysterious golden box that holds the power of God! What a story! And Hollywood has capitalized on the story. Does anyone else remember Indiana Jones and *Raiders of the Lost Ark* (1981)? In that movie the ark is described as a source of unrivalled power that Hitler and the Nazis want to co-opt for themselves. Once discovered, the "wrath" and "power" of Israel's God would become a weapon for the Nazi war machine. Marcus Brody summarizes the ominous stakes for the one who holds the power of the religious artifact: "An army which carries the ark before it . . . is invincible." The remainder of the film shows just how powerful the relic is: at the finale, the power of God wipes out the Nazis (by . . . *ahem* . . . melting their faces off or shooting lightning through them!), while Indiana Jones and Marion Ravenwood are saved.

The Ark Captured and Returned

It is no surprise that this narrative, often called the "ark narrative," inspires wonder. The action of 1 Samuel 4–7 is indeed fantastic and proceeds as follows:

1. The people of God carry the ark before them into battle to defeat the enemy nation, the Philistines. They say: "Let's bring

the ark of the LORD's covenant from Shiloh. Then it will go with us and save us from the hand of our enemies" (4:3).

2. The Philistines capture the ark, defeat Israel in battle, and the chief priest's sons, Hophni and Phinehas, die (4:8-11).

3. The chief priest, Eli, hears of the capture of the ark, the defeat of Israel, and the death of his sons, and he keels over dead (4:18).

4. Eli's daughter-in-law goes into labor, has a baby, and gives him a horrible name to commemorate the total disaster:

She named the boy Ichabod, saying, "The glory has departed from Israel," referring to the capture of the ark of God and to the deaths of her father-in-law and her husband. "The glory has departed from Israel," she said, "because the ark of God has been captured." (4:21-22)

5. The Philistines take the ark and put it in the shrine of their god, Dagon.

6. God's power manifests in the shrine, lopping off the head and hands of the idol of Dagon before the ark (5:1-5).

7. While the ark is in their territory, God afflicts the Philistine people with tumors (5:6-12).

8. The Philistines send the ark back to Israel with a gift to Yahweh of five golden tumors and five golden mice as a restitution offering (6:1-18).

9. The ark enters the town of Beth-shemesh, and when 70 men look inside the ark (which is forbidden) they die (6:19-20).

10. The ark is taken to Kiriath-jearim, where it rests for 20 years (7:1-2).

11. Samuel rallies the people to worship Yahweh alone, and the Philistines try to surprise Israel while they worship Him at Mizpah, but God prevails and Israel defeats the Philistines (7:3-17).

So the content of the narrative has two major battles between the Philistines and Israel (chs. 4 and 7) and two major exhibitions of the power of God and the ark (chs. 5 and 6). Extraordinary!

Who Do You Say That I Am?

Through the progression of the narrative, a major theme emerges from the speech of the Philistines: Yahweh's unrivaled royal power will be known among all nations. This is the theme of the ark narrative. Notice how the Philistines come to recognize the awesome, unrivaled authority of Yahweh in this narrative.

At first they believe the ark of Yahweh is special and even a religious power. But they mistake the ark as one of the other "gods" of the nations. In 4:6-8 the Philistines speak about Yahweh:

> When the Philistines discovered that the ark of the LORD had entered
> the camp, they panicked. "The gods have entered their camp!" they
> said. "Woe to us, nothing like this has happened before. Woe to us,
> who will rescue us from the hand of these magnificent gods? These are
> the gods that slaughtered the Egyptians with all kinds of plagues in the
> wilderness.

Their response to the things of God is not unusual for most people. Modern people, like ancient people, tend to miss the true identity of the Lord. They have preconceived ideas about religion and use those notions as a grid by which to understand Israel's God. We must understand that the peoples of the ancient world in which Israel lived were polytheistic. Israel most likely recognized that other gods existed (we would call these false deities "demonic powers" or "forces" today). These were not true gods at all because they are not the true God, Yahweh. However, the nations (and, all too often, Israel as well) treated many gods with value and respect.

For instance, notice how the Philistines worshiped Dagon. Who is Dagon? He was the principal Philistine god, with the others being Ashtoreth (Dagon's wife or lover) and Baal-zebub. These three deities appear in other biblical texts and were worshiped by other people in Canaan and the ancient world.[7]

Each nation worshiped a principal deity as the high god over all other gods (often the high god was known as El or Enlil), but then a patron deity protected individual cities (e.g., Baal-zebub was the patron deity for the Philistine city of Ekron). They believed that all deities,

---

[7] For a good introduction to other nations in the Old Testament, as well as their religious views, we recommend interested readers consult Hoerth, Mattingly, and Yamauchi, eds., *Peoples of the Old Testament World*. For the Philistines, see idem, 231–50.

however, deserved honor. So the peoples would create temples and shrines in which various idols were housed.

So when an enemy nation was defeated, it meant their god defeated a rival god. To avoid offending the rival deity now defeated, the nation victorious in battle would bring the idol or relic or talisman of the defeated nation into their temple or shrine. In short, they would "add" the defeated deity to their pantheon of gods. For this reason we can understand why the Philistines captured what they thought was Israel's deity (the ark) and brought it into the temple of Dagon. They believed the Philistine god Dagon defeated Israel's deity (Yahweh). They simply viewed Yahweh as one of the many "gods" of the nations around them. But they did not understand who Yahweh truly is.

It would be easy to call these people "primitive" or "unenlightened." But let us not forget how common it is for us to miss the true identity and power of God. Consider how people in Jesus' day missed the reality of His identity. Jesus boldly asked His disciples, "Who do people say that the Son of Man is?" (Matt 16:13). The disciples informed Him of the popular views of the day: Jesus is John the Baptist come back, Elijah come back, Jeremiah come back, or one of the other prophets. The general view of the day, then, was that Jesus was a prophet—one like the prophets of old. And Jesus was a prophet: the true Prophet!

But Jesus turns the prophetic expectation on its head: "But you," He asked them, "who do you say that I am?" (Matt 16:15). Peter's confession reveals the true identity of Jesus. Peter proclaimed Jesus as the Messiah of Israel and the Son of the living God! Jesus is a prophet but more than a prophet. He is a priest but more than a priest. He is a king but more than just a king. He is *the* Prophet, Priest, and King. As the suffering King, Jesus bears our sin and forgives it. He pays the debt of sin, and our slate of sin is wiped clean by His blood, which He freely gives as payment. He gives us hope and life. He makes us fully human. This is who Jesus is. But the Gospels tell us more. Jesus the Messiah is also God in human flesh.

People missed Jesus' true identity in His day, and people still miss His identity today. Just think about the Easter or Christmas holidays as they roll into our lives. Is it not true that people all too often speak of Jesus as a "wise sage" or a "good example" or a "guru" figure? Or they speak of Him as a good person, someone of great inspiration and religious zeal. These portraits of Jesus may hold some truth, but to stop there is to miss the Savior completely.

C. S. Lewis captures our tendency to miss the true identity of Jesus.

I am trying here to prevent anyone saying the really foolish thing that people often say about Him: "I'm ready to accept Jesus as a great moral teacher, but I don't accept His claim to be God." That is the one thing we must not say. A man who was merely a man and said the sort of things Jesus said would not be a great moral teacher. He would either be a lunatic— on a level with the man who says he is a poached egg—or else he would be the Devil of hell. You must make your choice. Either this man was, and is, the Son of God: or else a madman or something worse. You can shut Him up for a fool, you can spit at Him and kill Him as a demon; or you can fall at His feet and call Him Lord and God. But let us not come with any patronising nonsense about His being a great human teacher. He has not left that open to us. He did not intend to. (*Mere Christianity*, 52)

These are strong, strong words, but so true. If Jesus was not the person He claimed, then no matter how one cuts it, Jesus is a madman at best or a deceptive phony at worst. If someone today went around calling himself or herself the son of God or the Messiah, or if he or she proclaimed the ability to heal diseases or forgive peoples' sins, we would probably have that man or woman locked up for lunacy, megalomania, or a messiah complex! But if he did what he did and claimed what he claimed and knew he was misleading people, then he would be a liar of epic proportions!

Jesus claimed to be divine, to heal disease, and to have risen from the grave. He claimed to offer forgiveness of sin, to provide peace and life, and to be the essence of what it means to be human. He claimed these things because He was God and what He said was true. Either He is who He says He is, and He is Lord, or He is lunatic or liar. We must learn to recognize Jesus for who He truly is.

Unfortunately, we are like the Philistines or the people of Jesus' day, missing the identity of the Lord again and again. The Philistines did not recognize the God of Israel for who He is. For them He was one of the "gods" but not the God of creation, the King of Israel, and the Father of our Lord Jesus Christ. He was a god but not the true God.

However, as the narrative progresses in 1 Samuel 5–6, the Philistines go on a journey of discovery. Although seemingly captured and subjected to their idol, Yahweh exerts His magnificence in the Philistine sanctuary, humbling the Philistines, humiliating their false deity, and exalting Himself in a moment. When their false god, Dagon, is humiliated by Yahweh (5:1-6), the people of the Philistine city of Ashdod exclaim: "The ark of Israel's God must not stay here with us, because His hand is strongly against us and our god Dagon" (5:7). They go on to ask: "What should we do with the ark of Israel's God?" (5:8). Notice how the Philistines' language about Yahweh changes as they come to realize His authority. At first He was one of the "gods" (4:7-8), but after Yahweh defeated the pagan Philistine deity, Dagon, the Philistines describe Him as the God of Israel.

As the story progresses, Yahweh afflicts the Philistines with plagues of tumors. They come to know Israel's God as the same One who afflicted the Egyptians with plagues. The people of Israel also come to recognize Yahweh's royal power both in their defeat and in their sin. In both ways human beings come face-to-face with Yahweh, the unrivaled power and Lord of all nations.

Repentance and Victory

Through His power God helped His people get the ark back; but in the journey to bring the ark back home, some Israelites (not priests) touched the ark (6:18-20). That was a big problem because only God's appointed priests were to touch God's ark and even then only in a specified manner (see Lev 16:2; Num 4:15). As a result God struck them dead. God's people mourned this terrible occurrence, and they carefully moved the ark to a place called Kiriath-jearim and left it there for about 20 years. God's people mourned the Philistine capture of the ark, the death of the Israelite people, and the fact the ark wasn't where it was supposed to be for two decades.

Israel experienced life when it went badly. As the narrative progresses, we see that their sin was not isolated to improperly handling the ark. Notice Samuel's words in 7:3:

> "If you are returning to the LORD with all your heart, get rid of the foreign gods and the Ashtoreths that are among you, dedicate yourselves to the LORD, and worship only Him. Then He will rescue you from the hand of the Philistines."

The verse is significant because it reveals that Israel's sin lay not only in handling lightly the things of God; it also lay in worshiping other gods.

In the Western world it seems silly to worship other deities, especially ones made out of metal, stone, or wood. But it is not silly at all.
Baal was a male storm deity. Ashtoreth was a female fertility deity. When
the two would copulate, it would produce crops from the ground. At
least this is what the ancient people thought. That may seem strange to
us until we understand this was an agrarian society that needed appropriate rain at the appropriate time for food, life, and security.

Today we depend on different gods, but they are no less gods.
For instance, we trust a retirement account or a monthly paycheck to
provide food and security for our lives. We think a job, relationship,
or position will provide the hope we need to survive. Jobs and money,
relationships, and retirement are not necessarily bad. They are good
gifts but terrible gods. The gods we worship today are still deified as
things that will provide us health and security. Samuel's words in verse 3
reminded the people that only Yahweh would provide the security and
life they needed and desired. All other gods are empty and useless and
so must be "put away."

In the midst of their mourning and sin, Samuel called Israel to a
fresh start. Who does not need a fresh start in life? We all do at some
point or another. And how do we gain a fresh start in life? Fresh starts
begin with repentance.

The Anatomy of Repentance

What is "repentance," and what does it mean in practical terms? What
is the anatomy of this theologically laden term? We see a beautiful picture of repentance in 1 Samuel 7:3-6. Repentance has the following
characteristics:

1. *Hearing what is wrong*: actually listening to the sin in our lives
2. *Recognizing what is wrong in our lives*: owning our sin and not
   deflecting or blaming it on others
3. *Realizing that God is right*: affirming God is in the right when He
   exposes sin
4. *Confessing where we got it wrong*: verbally acknowledging sin to
   God and confessing that it is wrong and displeasing to Him
5. *Turning to God and living for Him*: turning away from sin and
   toward the Lord

Repentance is a choice. God's people choose to put away idols and embrace Yahweh. Repentance is a decision we make to honor and value the Lord more than anything else. Repentance is our loving response to God, who loved us first.

Victory followed repentance (7:7-11). These verses are powerful because they show that as we turn to God, God is no longer our adversary but our emissary. Instead of coming against us, He goes out on our behalf. That is what happened with the people of God. They experienced the power of God against the Philistines.

We love the phrasing in verse 10. As God's people worshiped the Lord in repentance and faith, the Philistines went in to wipe them out. But as they worshiped, the text reads that "the LORD thundered loudly against the Philistines that day and threw them into such confusion that they fled before Israel." Some of us need to hear that the Lord "thunders" on our behalf. As we turn to God and start fresh with Him, He "thunders" out for us. He is a stone of help ("Ebenezer," v. 12).

The Search for a Leader

A subsequent focus of the narrative in 1 Samuel 7 is to show the importance of true and faithful leadership among God's people. The failure of Israel's leadership at the beginning of the narrative is counterbalanced by the fidelity of Samuel at the end of the narrative. The narrative abruptly shifts away from the character of young Samuel in chapter 4, leading the reader to see a subtle shift away from the appropriate, divinely chosen leader for God's people. Moreover, Eli and his house fall away in chapter 4, leaving a vacuum of leadership of sorts. Who would lead? God raises up His faithful leader in Samuel in chapter 7, who leads God's people to repentance and faith.

Yahweh is the king God's people need, and out of His goodness Yahweh will provide for Himself a leader to represent them to Him. Remember what Yahweh said of Samuel: "Then I will raise up a faithful priest for Myself. He will do whatever is in My heart and mind" (2:35). When God's people respond to Him faithfully, led by the true priest and prophet (in this narrative, Samuel), then good things follow. When they follow corrupt leaders and do not respond faithfully to their God, then horrible things follow! But the true hero of the story is neither the people nor Samuel but rather God Himself. In the ark narrative God assures for Himself that all peoples will know that He is King, powerful and worthy of worship.

Reflect and Discuss

1. What does this passage help you understand about God?
2. How does this passage of Scripture exalt Jesus?
3. Why did the Philistines capture the ark?
4. Why did the Philistines send the ark away?
5. What mistake did the Israelites make in handling the ark?
6. When do you find yourself mishandling sacred things? Why do you do this?
7. Repentance is key in 1 Samuel 7. What stands out to you when you work through the anatomy of repentance? Why does that stand out for you?
8. How do you miss the identity of Jesus or take Him for granted?
9. What are the key barriers that stand in the way of your living a life of repentance?
10. How does this narrative reveal the role of appropriate leadership for God's people?

Israel's Rebellion and the Rise of Saul

1 SAMUEL 8:1-18

Main Idea: Israel's rebellion in requesting a king "like all the other nations" is answered by God's grace in providing a king they need.

I.   A Rebellious Demand
II. What Was Wrong with the Demand?
III. What Was So Devastating about the Demand?
IV. What Did God, in His Grace, Do with Their Demand?

David's life is not just a random personality profile of a cool guy in the Old Testament. It is not just the tale of a fascinating man who killed a giant and fought great battles and slept with a woman who was not his wife. No, the Old Testament has a lot of stories, but they are all part of one grand story, and that is the coming of Jesus Christ. All these stories are designed to show readers that Jesus Christ is the ultimate answer to humanity's problems and that Jesus Christ is essentially what mankind is searching for.

David's life, specifically, is the story of Israel's search for a king. At this point in Israel's history, Israel has taken possession of the promised land. In 1 Samuel 8, they are demanding a king who will protect them, prosper them, and fulfill them.

There is nothing wrong with Israel's request for a king per se. In fact, God had already told Israel He would one day give them one (Deut 17:20). However, the reasons behind their request show a complete lack of faith in God. God was supposed to be their true King. He was supposed to be the one they depended on to meet their needs. But here they are saying, "Well, sure, it is all well and good to have God there like a safety net—something to fall back on in an emergency. We certainly do not want to tick Him off so that He sends us to hell. But in the here and now, we have real bills to pay, real enemies who want to hurt us, and real social issues to deal with. Frankly, we need something more than an invisible God whose whereabouts are unknown half the time. We need somebody we can depend on, someone we can hold accountable."

God rightly calls this a rejection of Him. It was not total rejection, as if they wanted nothing to do with God. It was rejection through demanding that God give some other source of happiness and security. Both are forms of rejection, and they still persist today: Irreligious people reject God by not wanting Him to be a part of their lives at all; religious people reject God by letting Him be a part of their lives but not really trusting Him or depending on Him.

A word picture may help explain the difference. When I was in high school, I (J. D.) took up rock climbing as a hobby. One day a friend suggested that instead of climbing up the rock face, we rappel down it. Even though I had never rappelled before, I got volunteered to go first. The belay rope was tied around me, and I stood with my back toward a 75-foot drop. The guide told me to "lean back."

I stood there for a few seconds working up my courage, and then I leaned back. Fully committed. What was surely no longer than a nanosecond seemed like an eternity as I waited for the rope to catch me. But it did, and there I stood, perpendicular to the rock face and parallel to the ground, suspended in the air by a rope.

My best friend was next. He had never rappelled before either. From 75 feet below, I could hear him being given the same instructions I was given. But when it came time to lean back, he did not budge. Instead, he took one of his legs and felt down below for a foothold. He found one, and then another and then another. He slowly worked his way down the rock face, one foothold at a time. Of course, that is not rappelling. That is rock climbing with rappelling equipment.

Both my friend and I had all the same equipment. Both of us were going the same general direction—down the face of the rock. Still, there was a huge difference in what we were doing. When you rappel, you are leaning your full weight on the rope, trusting it to keep you off the ground. When you are rock climbing, you are using your hands and feet to move up the mountain, and the rope is there as a safety net. My friend did not lean his weight back on the rope because he didn't trust it. He trusted his own arms and legs and wanted the rope there as a safety net if he slipped.

That is the picture of what is happening with Israel here. They want God as their safety net but are still primarily trusting in their own strength.

A Rebellious Demand

First Samuel 8 begins with Samuel. Remember him? He was the one who was miraculously born to Hannah. He grew up to be one of Israel's greatest prophets. He heard directly from God and told the people what God wanted. Unfortunately, his sons turn out to be dirtbags, and they do not follow God (8:3). All of this provides an opportunity for Israel to request something they have been itching after for some time.

> So all the elders of Israel gathered together and went to Samuel at Ramah. They said to him, "Look, you are old, and your sons do not follow your example. Therefore, appoint a king to judge us the same as all the other nations have."
>
> When they said, "Give us a king to judge us," Samuel considered their demand sinful, so he prayed to the LORD. (1 Sam 8:4-6)

Why is Samuel displeased? Is this just a personal insult? Is he just upset because they wanted a change of regime and had stopped liking him? Certainly, that is involved. But Samuel senses something deeper in this request than just disapproval of his children, and he is correct.

> But the LORD told him, "Listen to the people and everything they say to you. They have not rejected you; they have rejected Me as their king. They are doing the same thing to you that they have done to Me, since the day I brought them out of Egypt until this day, abandoning Me and worshiping other gods." (1 Sam 8:7-8)

Their request represents a complete lack of trust in God and satisfaction with Him. God was supposed to be their real King. They were supposed to depend on Him for everything. But from the beginning that had never been enough for them. They never trusted Him enough to say, "God, I am just going to do Your will; and I will let You worry about everything else."

No, they had constantly demanded golden calves and strong armies and guaranteed food and water sources and safe land conditions to feel secure.

They had never rejected God outright; they had always said, "God, yes, we want You . . . but we also need a guarantee of this, and that, and this, and that." There are two ways to reject God: one is to reject Him outright; the other is to say you follow Him but then not really to depend on Him. It is still rebellion to claim to follow God but to insist

on a number of other things being present in your life before you will
feel secure.

This is not just an ancient Israelite problem. This is our problem. Is
it not easier to "trust God" when everything that you feel like you need
for life is right in front of you? Your job is secure, your marriage is fulfilling, everyone you care about is healthy. But when one of those things is
missing, do you not have this feeling of insecurity or anxiety or unhappiness? Israel is not content to lean back and trust God. So they feel they
need something they can get their hands on and control.

What Was Wrong with the Demand?

Wouldn't it be easier to trust God and follow Him if you had some
kind of binding, legal guarantee of what He would do? Imagine some
sort of guaranteed overdraft protection on your bank account, so that
when you were out of money, it would automatically dip into God's,
and you could look online and see how much money God had at the
moment. Or maybe you would like a security system on your house
that automatically tied into God, so that when a burglar came in, a
couple of angels showed up to "whup up on" the bad guys. Or maybe
you would like a little God medical insurance card that came in the
mail and said, "May get sick temporarily but will be always be miraculously healed."

It would be so much easier to trust God if we could control Him.
But we cannot, and so we have a list of requirements that we demand
in addition to God. We will "follow" Him, but we have some stipulations
as well.

God calls that a rejection of Him because it is a rejection of trust in
Him. The author of Hebrews says that without faith it is impossible to
please God because those with faith must believe that He rewards those
who seek Him (Heb 11:6). To know God, you have to trust Him, to lean
on Him.

You see, when you do not trust someone, you feel like you have to
control them. The reason we require contracts enforceable by law with
people we do business with is because we do not inherently trust them
to keep up their end of the bargain. So we control them with contracts.

My kids do this with me (J. D.). I took one of my daughters out for
some daddy-daughter time recently, and on the way to the mall, she
tried to get me to promise her all sorts of stuff. "Daddy, do you promise
that we will get candy? Do you promise that we will go to the toy store?

Daddy, do you promise that if we eat lunch, we can get ice cream for dessert?"

What is going on? She does not trust me, so she wants guarantees that I will perform to her expectations. What is so sad about this is that my whole philosophy as a dad is to spoil her, to take good care of her, to be so gracious to her that every boy she dates in the future is a letdown.

This is where Israel is. They want a king they can see and touch and control because they do not fully trust God. And God rightly calls this rejection because everything about His character proves that they should be able to trust Him.

"Listen to them," God says, and give them a king (v. 9). God calls their request for a king disobedience, but then He acquiesces. This is a little confusing. If this request was so bad, why did God give it to them? Why not simply say no? This is why: God will sometimes answer your prayers to let you learn the hard way that what you were asking for was wrong.

Have you ever had that happen? Have you ever wanted something so badly that you worked for it, you obsessed over it, and you prayed about it—but then when you got it, it was not what you thought it would be? What you had hoped would be a blessing turned out to be more of a curse in your life.

This happens all the time for people who win the lottery. Most people still assume that life would be so easy, so good with millions of dollars. But what happens? Most people who win the lottery have none of the money left within just a few years. And throughout the process, they are harassed by so many people who want their money that countless relationships break down. What they had wanted as a blessing turned out to be an enormous curse.

Some people work feverishly to get a particular job or a particular promotion. But once they reach the apex, as they look back on their lives, they realize it was a curse because it destroyed their family. Having the "job you always wanted" does not lead to happiness because it so often comes with enormous stress or with relational dysfunction.

Many people think this way about marriage. A certain woman, for instance, may demand a husband. "Oh, God, I have to be married. Please, God, do not leave me single! I need to be married, and now!" Sometimes God says, "Fine. So you do not trust Me? Here is Mr. Perfect. Enjoy." But Mr. Perfect can never satisfy the role God is supposed to fill, so the marriage becomes a mess.

One of the worst judgment statements in the Bible is Romans 1:26: God turned them over to the desires of their heart. In other words, God's judgment on them was to answer all their prayers with a yes.

The reverse is also true. Some of God's greatest mercies to us come in the form of unanswered prayers. This should change how we think of unanswered prayers. Some people get so mad at God for not answering their prayers. But what if He is refusing to answer your prayer as a way of protecting you? It may not seem like protection. After all, what is the harm in being married? What is so bad about making an extra $20,000 a year? But the greatest blessing God could ever give is the ability to be happy in Him alone. Sometimes He has to teach us that lesson by withholding blessings we think would be beneficial.

This happens with ministers just like everyone else. Some pastors get really upset at God for not answering their prayers to make their churches big. But many of them may be experiencing God's *no* because they are incredibly arrogant. The worst thing for them would be for God to give them success and fan the fire of their ego. So God keeps their ministry small as a mercy to them, so that they would learn to trust Him and be fulfilled in Him.

To clarify, it is not inherently wrong to desire money or marriage or success. It is not wrong to ask God for them. There is nothing sinful about praying, "God, I really want to be married," or, "I really want to have children," or, "I really would like a raise."

The problem comes when a person craves those things and feels like they could not be happy or secure without them. That sort of passion is what the Bible calls *epithumia*—a desire that has taken on so much weight that it drives everything about a person. It is the "lust" for worldly goods in 1 John 2:16-17. *Epithumia* is a craving that controls (Rom 1:24). This is what Israel feels about a king. Their desire for a king is a craving they could not live without.

Israel was not supposed to avoid having a king at all costs. They were supposed to avoid being consumed by the idea. Whenever life is consumed with things—even good things—then it shows that God has been displaced. He has been outweighed by some lesser thing.

The result of this displacement is never pretty. It leads to unhappiness, anxiety, and depression. These things are like smoke from a fire, and if you follow the smoke down to its source, you will find the fires of idolatry.

So God gives Israel their king, telling Samuel, "You must solemnly warn them and tell them about the rights of the king who will rule over them" (v. 9). Samuel does exactly that, warning Israel of the devastating consequences of their idolatrous request (vv. 11-18).

What Was So Devastating about the Demand?

The dominant word in this description is *take*. The king will take your sons and daughters; he will take your crops and your lands; he will take the best years of your lives. And he will exploit them for himself.

The irony here is tremendous. The Israelites look to a king to guarantee prosperity and security. What they receive instead is a king who would take those things from them. They wanted a king whom they could control. Instead, that king ends up controlling them.

This is an Old Testament version of a New Testament principle: when you have other kings besides God, those kings do not save you; they tyrannize you.

Whatever you depend on for happiness and security, you become the slave of that thing. For example, if you have to be **married** to be happy, you become the slave of marriage. You feel miserable all the time if you are single. You live with depression because you are alone. You make bad relationship decisions and end up dating terrible people and doing foolish things.

This does not get better once you get married, either. If you depend on marriage to be happy, then once you get married, you become codependent. You constantly feel like your spouse lets you down. You are constantly tempted to leave your marriage and find fulfillment in a new marriage or an extramarital affair.

If you have to be **successful** to find fulfillment, you become the slave of success. You overwork; you get jealous of other successful people; you resent others their opportunities, promotions, and praise. You are devastated when people talk about you without giving you due credit and recognizing your value. We say that certain people are "driven by success," but a better way to say it might be that they are "enslaved by success." Success drives us until we destroy our families, our health, our very lives.

If you have to have some **physical escape** to release stress or feel relaxed, it can quickly enslave you. It starts out as an enjoyable escape that you can control, but it ends up as a tyrant that controls you. The type of escape varies—pornography, drugs, alcohol, overeating. But the pattern is the same. It begins as something you can go to on your own terms to escape the tedium of your day. But then you begin to crave it, and more of it, and worse types of it. And you cannot turn the drive off. The physical pleasure you once mastered quickly masters you, ruining relationships and souring every aspect of your life.

Every life has a king. A king in your life is whatever you must have in order to be happy and secure. And kings make all their subjects into servants. The apostle Paul says it this way: "But in the past, when you didn't know God, you were enslaved to things that by nature are not gods" (Gal 4:8); and "Don't you know that if you offer yourselves to someone as obedient slaves, you are slaves of that one you obey . . . ?" (Rom 6:16). Or as Bob Dylan says, "You're gonna have to serve somebody."

Now, there are always some free spirits who feel like they have gamed the whole system. "'You're gonna serve somebody,' huh? Well, not me. I don't need anything or anybody. I'm not enslaved to any of that stuff. I'm a free man." But these are the same people who are afraid to commit in their relationships. Precisely because they are "free," they will not allow anything to stand in the way of their absolute independence. Independence becomes their king, and they become its slave. They must have selfish independence to be happy.

Everybody serves something. There are no exceptions. You are either enslaved to something that brings life (God), or you are enslaved to something that brings death.

First Samuel 8 ends with God warning the people of Israel of all the bad consequences of receiving a king. They demand one anyway, and in the next few chapters, God gives them exactly what they ask for. God gives Israel a king named Saul, who was smart, a good leader, and physically buff. Saul promises change, gives the people hope they could believe in, and guarantees that Israel's status in the world would be restored.

But after a good start, Saul starts to do exactly what God said he would. He starts to use the people for his own advantage. He turns out to be a self-idolizing, self-willed tyrant.

What Did God, in His Grace, Do with Their Demand?

Christians who read the story of Saul cannot end by saying, "Poor Israelites, they should not have done that. Bad Saul, he should not have been so bad." No, Saul is being set up in contrast to God's true King,

Jesus. What Saul fails to deliver for the people of Israel, Jesus would fulfill in magnificent ways.

Note some of the parallels between Saul and Jesus. When Saul is anointed king, he is filled with the Spirit and he starts to prophesy (10:1-13). When Jesus is anointed, the Holy Spirit descends from heaven like a dove, and Jesus begins to speak with the voice of God (Matt 3:16-17; 4:17).

But note the contrasts. Saul would start well, but Jesus would end well, faithful unto death. Saul thought of his own interests, but Jesus thought primarily of ours. Saul made Israel his servants, but Jesus said, "The Son of Man did not come to be served, but to serve" (Matt 20:28). Saul's sinful, selfish choices would cause many in Israel to die. Jesus' loving choices would cause many in Israel to live. Israel had to die for Saul's sins, but Jesus would die for ours. Saul was harsh and unforgiving with those who disappointed him. When Jesus' subjects disappointed and rebelled against Him, He laid down His life for them.

Jesus, God in the flesh, was the King the people of Israel were seeking. He alone could satisfy and save. Every king says, "Please me, obey me, and I will guarantee you happiness." Money says, "Find me and you will be happy." Marriage says, "Find me and you will be happy." Family, success, fame, independence—all make these claims.

But every king also says, "If you disappoint me, I will make you miserable." Money says that: "If you fail to get me, and you become poor, you will be miserable." Marriage says, "If you fail to get me, and you grow old single, life will be terrible." As Tim Keller says, "Jesus is the only Lord who, if you receive him, will fulfill you completely, and, if you fail him, will forgive you eternally" (*The Reason for God*, 179).

We all have to choose a king. Each of us has already chosen one. We are either enslaved to something that brings life or enslaved to something that brings death. What will we choose from this point forward?

All earthly kings disappoint. But God is an altogether different King. He showed Israel time and time again that He had been faithful to them, even when they were not. They were unbelieving in the wilderness, but God gave them manna. They served idols, which led to other nations afflicting them; but when they called out to God in repentance, He immediately came to their aid and delivered them. Here is a King who not only supplies the needs of His own but also forgives and has mercy on those who fail Him. Why would anyone desire another king than Him?

We have the chance to make the choice that Israel did not make—the choice of faith. And we have more evidence to analyze than they did. We have a longer history of God's faithfulness to reflect on, more stories of His faithfulness in the midst of human faithlessness. Most importantly, we have the cross, the ultimate display of God's love and faithfulness to us. There is no king we could serve who gave more for us than God did.

Many people find the idea of the Christian God just fine—provided they can institute certain conditions. "As long as God does this, prevents me from that, provides me with this, then I will follow Him." But that is not faith at all. That is rebellion because conditional obedience is still disobedience. To follow this King, we must step out in faith, with absolutely no conditions and no exceptions.

How can we be sure God will take care of us? How can we lean back into the unknown with confidence that God will actually hold us up? We need only to look at the cross, where God poured Himself out for us. There, on Calvary, God proved that His compassion for us was beyond anything we could have imagined. There, once and for all, He proved that He is a King worth trusting with absolutely everything.

Reflect and Discuss

1. What does this passage help you understand about God?
2. How does this passage of Scripture exalt Jesus?
3. Why is Samuel displeased with the demand of God's people?
4. How do you make the same mistake of treating the Lord as your "safety net" while still wanting to live as you see fit?
5. What are some of the parallels between Saul and Jesus?
6. What are some of the differences between Saul and Jesus?
7. We have said that "everyone serves something." What do you serve, and why?
8. Why does Jesus not disappoint when other kings do disappoint?
9. Compare Deuteronomy 17:14-20 and 1 Samuel 8. What language is similar between these texts? Write down your thoughts.
10. Why is it important that God still dealt with the Israelites out of His grace and mercy?

God's Grace and Saul's Rise

1 SAMUEL 9–14

Main Idea: Although the people wanted a king like the other nations, God graciously provides a king who could serve effectively though imperfectly.

I.   **Saul's Rocky Rise**
II. **Victory and Failure**
III. **Saul's Last Words**

Saul's Rocky Rise

1 SAMUEL 9–10

The people wanted a king "like all the other nations" (8:19-22), so God granted their request. One of the things they stated in their demand is that they wanted a king to "go out before us, and fight our battles" (8:20). This is not a bad thing, as the king in the ancient world was the exemplar and representative for the people. So on the one hand, you cannot really blame them.

However, the real issue at hand here is that they are actually rejecting the Lord. Remember that God is the great King, the One who goes out and fights for the people.

> *Come, let us shout joyfully to the Lord,*
> *shout triumphantly to the rock of our salvation!*
> *Let us enter His presence with thanksgiving;*
> *let us shout triumphantly to Him in song.*
> *For the Lord is a great God,*
> *a great King above all gods.* (Ps 95:1-3)

In the exodus, God is remembered as the One who defeats enemy nations that threaten His people and plan.

> *The Lord is my strength and my song;*
> *He has become my salvation.*
> *This is my God, and I will praise Him,*
> *my father's God, and I will exalt Him.*

The Lord is a warrior;
Yahweh is His name. (Exod 15:2-3)

These texts remind us (as Israel should have remembered!) that God is the King and deliverer, the salvation we all need. But they reject Yahweh as King and want a king just like everyone else. This demand and God's acquiescence to it signal an ominous beginning to the coming of Saul.

Chapters 10–14 depict the rocky rise of Saul and the ebbing role of Samuel in the life of Israel. The perspective on Saul's reign was mixed from the start. Samuel, following God's direction, anointed Saul and identified him as king. On this there could be no doubt. However, Saul's name derives from the Hebrew word *sha'al* meaning "asked" and reminds us that Israel got the king they "asked" for—a king like all the other nations—but rejected the true King they needed: the Lord God.

Chapters 9–10 introduce us to the figure of Saul. He is a Benjaminite, which is not a good thing when we saw what happened in Israel within the tribe of Benjamin in Judges 18–19. The tribe of Benjamin has a history of corruption, inhospitality, rape, and murder. We could say that the tribe was awash with sin. So it is not a good sign that Saul comes from that tribe.

First Samuel 9 depicts the comical choosing of Saul as the king the people wanted. This story reads like a comedy rather than a dignified tale of heroism, class, and valor. Saul is a bit of an idiot, fumbling here, there, and everywhere trying to find his daddy's donkeys. He searches and searches with absolutely no luck. In fact, Saul gives up on the search until the servant suggests they consult a nearby "seer" to help them find the animals. *Seer* is another name for a prophet, and the prophet about which the servant spoke was Samuel (10:9).

It is worth stopping here to focus on a couple of points: in the narrative, Saul is (a) unable (or unwilling) to make positive change to transform his situation, and (b) he is hesitant about consulting the prophet of God. Saul has a passivity problem and a prophet problem. He is not able to act, and when he does, he is hesitant to have God (or God's representatives) involved. Both of these themes will be spelled out in greater detail, especially by chapter 15. But in 9:5-10 the one who has all the ideas and makes them come to fruition is not Saul but the servant. All Saul does is say yes to the servant's ideas. One wonders how strong a leader Saul will be if he cannot come up with any ideas of his own! And how strong a leader will Saul be if he is inherently suspicious of the Lord's prophet? These are ominous signals for the reader. You know you are in trouble when you are hesitant or unwilling to consult God before you act!

The two men find Samuel, and the text records that God had appeared to Samuel and told him that he was to anoint a man from Benjamin to be "prince" over Israel (9:16 ESV). The word used here is the Hebrew word *nagid* ("prince" or "leader"), not the Hebrew word *melek* ("king"). So why does God use the word *nagid* rather than *melek*? It may be a way to reinforce the idea that there is only one King in Israel, Yahweh, and the Israelite king will always and ever be only a prince. The Israelite king will rule as God's undershepherd in accordance with the authority of the Shepherd of Israel, Yahweh (see Ps 23).

Why does God decide to make Saul king? Only one reason is given: "I have seen the affliction of My people, for their cry has come to Me" (9:16). This language is strikingly similar to Exodus 2:23-24:

> *After a long time, the king of Egypt died. The Israelites groaned because of their difficult labor, and they cried out; and their cry for help ascended to God because of the difficult labor. So God heard their groaning, and He remembered His covenant with Abraham, Isaac, and Jacob. God saw the Israelites, and He took notice.*

The text of 1 Samuel 9 depicts God as responding to the cries of an afflicted people. Certainly they are afflicted by the Philistines (9:16a), but they are afflicted by their sin as well, as we have seen from their rebellious demand in 1 Samuel 8. God is portrayed here as raising up a leader who will deliver His people from their oppression and sin. Previously, God Himself had done that.

First Samuel 9:16 gives a brief glimpse into the heart of God. His heart is full of love and compassion for His people. As He was moved to act on their behalf in the past (the exodus), He is moved to act on their behalf now. This is the mercy and love of God. But He has agreed to give them a *nagid* like all the other nations. So, as He gives them Saul, what did He think Saul would do for His people?

He would deliver the people from the Philistines (v. 16). But Yahweh tells Samuel that Saul will do something else: "It is he who will restrain My people" (9:17, authors' translation). Scholars do not know exactly what to do with the word we have translated "restrain" here. The word comes from the verb *'atsar*, and it usually means something negative: "to shut up, imprison, restrain, close, or detain." So a positive reading of the verb "to rule" (as in the HCSB, NRSV) is highly unlikely (see Firth, *1 &*

2 Samuel, 119). We would rather translate the phrase as we have done above: "It is he who will restrain My people." The reality is that Saul's actions for the people are a mixed bag of good and bad. Saul will deliver the Philistines and fight the people's battles (just like they asked!), but in so doing, it may be that he will imprison and shut up his people from true worship and fidelity to Yahweh.

Nonetheless, Samuel anoints Saul as king. There are three steps to Saul's installation as king, which will mirror the steps to David's installation, as Firth rightly points out (*1 & 2 Samuel*, 120–21):

Action	Saul	David
Private anointing	1 Samuel 10:1-8	1 Samuel 16:1-13
Public acceptance	1 Samuel 10:17-27	2 Samuel 5:1-5
Military demonstration	1 Samuel 11	1 Samuel 17

In 1 Samuel 9–10, we see the private anointing and public acceptance. Samuel proclaims to Saul the "word of God" (9:27), which is that God has chosen Saul to be "prince over His heritage" (10:1, authors' translation). Again the word *nagid* "prince" is used instead of *melek* "king," driving home the notion that Yahweh is King and Saul will only be the undershepherd under the authority of the true Shepherd. Samuel informs Saul that he will experience certain "signs" that will verify his anointing and choosing for kingship. One of these "signs" is that Saul will prophesy (10:9-13). In the book of Samuel, the true king will be an instrument of God and speak the word of God, like a prophet. Saul looks like a prophet as king but ultimately will be shown to be a false prophet, leading God's people away from the Lord. But for now, the appearance of true prophecy appears with the life of Saul.

Saul returned home to his father, and his father asked what happened to him. Saul told his father that the donkeys had been found and that he had encountered Samuel. But interestingly, he did not tell his father anything about the anointing or appointing as ruler over Israel. Why? Saul is passive and hesitant when it comes to following through with the command of God.

This becomes all the more relevant in 1 Samuel 10:17-27, when Saul is formally proclaimed as king and publically accepted by the people. Samuel brings all the people together and proclaims,

The LORD, the God of Israel, says: "I brought Israel out of Egypt, and I rescued you from the power of the Egyptians and all the kingdoms that were oppressing you. But today you have rejected your God, who saves you from all your troubles and afflictions. You said to Him, "You must set a king over us." Now therefore present yourselves before the LORD by your tribes and clans. (10:18-19)

Samuel does not pull any punches! The reason the people are mustered to proclaim a king is because they have "rejected" their God! Nonetheless, God has granted their request. But where is the king? When Samuel called on Saul to present himself, he was nowhere to be found! In fact, in a hilarious scene, we find Saul has hidden himself in some baggage so as not to be noticed.

They cannot find him, so they "inquire" of the Lord again, to see whether the man could be found! The text is clearly playing on the name "Saul" here because the people *wayyish'alu* "ask" for *sha'ul* "Saul." The narrative shows that they are asking for something that cannot be found! Saul eventually throws the camel bags, carpets, and blankets off of himself and appears to the people. Although Saul has just been hiding in baggage, Samuel proclaims, "Do you see the one the LORD has chosen? There is no one like him among the entire population" (10:24). Indeed! One wonders if Samuel was biting his lip and suppressing a laugh when he said it.

Still, Samuel dutifully reads aloud all the rights and responsibilities of the king to Saul, presumably something that was stable and known, perhaps Deuteronomy 17:14-20. Saul was to exercise his rule under the authority of Yahweh and His word. Would he do this? The rest of the narrative in 1 Samuel 11–15 reveals that he would not. Still, that fact will be unpacked as the story progresses.

Victory and Failure

First Samuel 11 records a great victory. Just after he is installed as king, Saul fights the Ammonites and defeats them. The reason for the conflict is because, in fact, the king of the Ammonites (Nahash) shamed Saul and the Israelites. Saul wanted to make a peace treaty with them, but Nahash would only do that if every Israelite gouged out their right eye, thus bringing "shame" on Israel. That did not sit well with Saul (as you could imagine!) so he went to war with them. He mustered the Israelites into a fighting army and led them to victory.

The people are rightly pleased because of the victory, and they attribute the victory to Saul (v. 12). In one of the strongest statements in
his reign, Saul boldly proclaims, "The LORD has provided deliverance
in Israel" (v. 13). This is so promising, as Saul leads God's people to
attribute praise to the appropriate person—Yahweh, who gives deliverance. Where God's people want to praise Saul, Saul leads God's people
to praise the Lord!

This is as much a victory as is anything else in this story. It is a strong
reminder for God's people:

1. When good things happen in our lives, to whom do we give the
   credit?
2. When others praise you for your work, do you point them to
   God's grace?
3. When others want to make much of you, do you make much
   of God?

But Saul's victories and fidelity to the Lord are not uniform in 1 Samuel
9–14. It is good in 1 Samuel 11, but things go badly in 1 Samuel 13–14.
The problem Saul faces as recorded in those chapters is the Philistine
threat. The Philistines were people from the region of Greece and Crete
who had sailed southeast across the Mediterranean and settled in the
coastal plain in Israel. They held five major cities in the plain: Gaza,
Ashdod, Ashkelon, Gath, and Ekron. They had been a constant threat
in the period of the Judges, and they were still a threat in the times of
Saul and David.

The Philistines maintained a garrison at a little place called Geba,
and Jonathan, Saul's son, defeated it. The Philistines, in response, went
to war against Saul and his armies. The Scripture records that 30,000
Philistine chariots, 6,000 cavalry, and troops like the sand on the sea-
shore came up and encamped at a place called Michmash to engage
Israel in battle. The text describes how the people followed Saul at this
point: "And all the people trembled after him" (13:7, authors' translation). They wanted a king who would lead them out in battle. Instead,
they got a king they followed in fear, trembling. This is not a ringing
endorsement of Saul or the people.

As they encamped, apparently Samuel told Saul to wait to go into
battle for seven days until he was able to get to Gilgal and offer a sacrifice
(13:8-9). Samuel did not arrive on schedule. As a result, Saul offered the
sacrifices himself instead of waiting for Samuel. This may not seem like a

big deal, but it reveals that Saul is more concerned with his own agenda and timetable than with following the word of the Lord.

Samuel's response to Saul is unequivocal:

> *You have been foolish. You have not kept the command which the*
> *LORD your God gave you. It was at this time that the LORD would have*
> *permanently established your reign over Israel, but now your reign will*
> *not endure. The LORD has found a man loyal to Him, and the LORD*
> *has appointed him as ruler over His people, because you have not done*
> *what the LORD commanded.* (13:13-14)

Is God's verdict far too harsh? We may think so. But in fact, God's verdict was absolutely just. God's word is sure and certain, just and good. For us to think we know better than God so that we operate how we wish rather than how He wants is the definition of pride and disobedience.

This reveals a deep failure in the life of Saul. He puts on the airs of a real, authentic spiritual relationship with God, but he has none of its power. The psychologist M. Scott Peck describes how pure evil is found most prevalently around religious things. The reason is because such evil is most attracted to light and hides in it. It is the reality of Lucifer, the son of the morning: beautiful and filled with light and yet pure evil and a rebel against God. Where there is light, a lie is not far behind (Peck, *People of the Lie*).

This is true with Saul. He does things that look so good and holy and right:

Saul enacts worship.
Saul makes a sacrifice to God.
Saul prepares his people for battle.

It looks worthy of the Lord, filled with light and life. And yet it is a lie. Saul did nothing to bring honor and glory to the Creator. He did it for himself. Saul has the appearance of godliness but denies the Lord's power (cf. 2 Tim 3:5). He attempts to manipulate the things of God to his own ends. This is, by some definitions, an act of sorcery.

The failure of Saul is a failure to be truly devoted to the Lord. When we have the *appearance* of faith without *authentic* faith, then we can anticipate absolute judgment. Saul's kingdom is torn from his grasp. "The LORD has found a man loyal to Him." God says that Saul at heart was disloyal to his Maker. The victory he experienced was short-lived because his faith in the Lord was inauthentic and did not last.

You can always tell whether a tree is rooted in the ground by seeing if it grows and bears fruit. For instance, a live Christmas tree, after it has been in the house for about a week, starts to deteriorate—the needles fall off and it bears no cones. Likewise, Saul did not bear fruits of victory and true righteousness because he was not planted in the Lord.

The rest of the story of Saul in 1 Samuel 14 highlights Saul's son, Jonathan, more than it exalts the greatness of the king. Jonathan is one who thinks of the health and state of the warriors in Saul's army more than his own well-being. He even dares to go up against his father and a death sentence to care for his men. We discover later in 1 Samuel that Jonathan is devoted to David and to God's plan with David. All in all, Jonathan is a good man who loves God and loves his fellow Israelites. But he is the exception. Saul is the rule.

First Samuel 14:47-52 provides a summary of Saul's kingship. It speaks of his victories and his family. It shows that Saul fought hard against the Philistines, as God said that he would. However, the summary statement in verse 52 is telling:

> *And the battle was strong against the Philistines all the days of Saul.*
> *So when Saul saw any valiant man or any brave man, he would*
> *gather him to himself.* (14:52, authors' translation)

On the face of it, this verse just indicates that Saul was a good recruiter. If he saw a warrior or brave man, he enlisted that man into his army. But the biblical narrative is sparse in its details. Why does the narrator tell us that Saul enlists men to himself? Because the text reveals that Saul enlists people into *his* army rather than *God's* army. Again, Saul builds his name but "restrains" God's people from embracing God's name. We have seen that Saul uses the things of God when it is expedient—he has no real desire for his men to follow the Lord.

The conclusion to this narrative reveals ultimate goals for one's life: Are we about building *our* kingdom or *God's* kingdom? Saul was decidedly in favor of the former! This narrative sets the stage for Saul's final downfall and judgment in 1 Samuel 15.

Saul's life is tragic and in many ways mirrors Eli's. As Eli was passive, so too was Saul. As Eli was lackadaisical with the things of God, Saul was manipulative with the things of God. Both Eli and Saul treated God's holy sacrifices with some contempt. Both Eli and Saul had their leadership stripped from them. Eli and Saul were told that the true priest (Samuel) and the true king (David), respectively, would replace them.

Samuel's Final Words

Set between Saul's victory in 1 Samuel 10–11 and failure in 13–14 are Samuel's last words as the prophet in chapter 12. He still appears in the remainder of the narrative, but these mark his final statement concerning the people and the king. These words should be remembered for all believers because they remind us of the story of God—a God who loves and delivers, who is holy and pure, but a God who works miraculous redemption for an undeserving people.

Samuel closes his speech to the people by stating these words:

> *Don't be afraid. Even though you have committed all this evil, don't turn away from following the Lord. Instead, worship the Lord with all your heart. Don't turn away to follow worthless things that can't profit or deliver you; they are worthless. The Lord will not abandon His people, because of His great name and because He has determined to make you His own people.*
>
> *As for me, I vow that I will not sin against the Lord by ceasing to pray for you. I will teach you the good and right way. Above all, fear the Lord and worship Him faithfully with all your heart; consider the great things He has done for you. However, if you continue to do what is evil, both you and your king will be swept away.* (12:20-25)

What do we learn from Samuel's final words?

1. *Learn to live in God's story.* Samuel retells the story of God's work with Israel from the Exodus to the present day. He situates their story within God's story. It is always good to situate our lives within what God is doing in the world. Why? It reminds us that God is not something we fit into our lives; rather we fit our story into God's life and God's plan. It's *His* world, and we fit into what *He* is doing.

2. *Sin is real.* As if we have not seen it clearly enough in the life of Saul and the people, Samuel's words remind us that sin is real. It will not go away, and we must deal with it. But *we cannot deal with sin on our own. We need divine help!*

3. *Love God's redemption.* Divine help comes from the gospel. The God Samuel describes is not a violent and abusive God. He is a loving and redemptive God. He does not leave wicked people alone. Despite our sin, He goes to the distant country and draws us back to Himself. Samuel's words, then, point us to the

gospel. Jesus has gone to the far country and forgiven us of our sin; He has died on the cross so that we don't have to.

4. *Celebrate the gospel.* "Consider the great things He has done for you" (12:24). The gospel is not merely something to be understood and known—a cerebral recognition of random facts. No, the gospel is a *wonder* that must be lived, loved, and celebrated. Consider and reflect on the mighty and wonderful things God has done on our behalf!

5. *Follow closely.* Samuel reminds God's people to watch continually how closely they follow the Lord, how they walk with Him. He says, "Don't turn away from following the LORD." The temptation is to embrace worthless things we think will satisfy. They don't. The only satisfaction comes from following Jesus in the little and big things, from the deepest parts of who we are.

Reflect and Discuss

1. What does 1 Samuel 9–14 help you understand about God?
2. How does this passage of Scripture exalt Jesus?
3. Identify the victories of Saul. Who granted him these victories?
4. Saul was, in many ways, a false leader. He drew the people of God away from following their Lord. Have you ever committed this same sin? Are you doing so now?
5. What are some of the reasons you lead others away from the Lord and exalt your name instead of His name?
6. What makes Jonathan different from his father, Saul?
7. Saul used sacrifice as a way to achieve his purposes and carelessly manipulated the holy things of God. Have you ever manipulated the things of God for your own ends? How have you done that, and why?
8. How does Saul's life contrast with the life of Jesus?
9. Reread Samuel's last words in 1 Samuel 12. What stands out to you? Write your thoughts.
10. Samuel's words encourage God's people to celebrate the Lord, to consider the great things He has done. How do you celebrate the gospel?

Saul's Fall: Setting Up a Rival Kingdom

1 SAMUEL 15:1-28

Main Idea: Saul falls into sin and has his kingdom stripped from him because he failed to serve the Lord alone but instead set up a rival kingdom against the true King.

I. **The Command: Destroy the Amalekites**
   A. God is a holy, good, and loving Creator.
   B. "Holy war" in the Bible is not "holy war" at all.
   C. Divine warfare is limited and non repeatable.
   D. Divine warfare is commanded by a merciful God.
   E. Divine warfare is not genocide or ethnic cleansing but the elimination of false worship.
   F. Justice is meted out communally in divine warfare.
II. **The Battle: Saul's Halfhearted "Obedience"**
III. **The Cover-up: Saul's Stubborn Rebellion**
IV. **The Fallout: The Beginning of the End of Saul's Kingdom**
V. **The Anatomy of Disobedience**
   A. Disobedience is anything less than full, immediate obedience.
   B. Disobedience grows out of greedy desire.
   C. Disobedience further estranges us from God, leading to increasingly irrational behavior.
   D. Disobedience can only be overcome by the gospel.
   E. Disobedience exposed creates a choice: self-deception or repentance.

Introduction

King Saul started off well. He was good-looking and physically fit. He was a great military leader. He was a prophet. He was popular among the people. Most importantly, he was chosen by God to be king over Israel. But it would not last. First Samuel 15 shows the beginning of Saul's long and painful demise.

The Command: Destroy the Amalekites

Samuel told Saul, . . . "This is what the LORD of Hosts says: 'I witnessed what the Amalekites did to the Israelites when they opposed them along the way as they were coming out of Egypt. Now go and attack the Amalekites and completely destroy everything they have.'" (15:1-3)

The Amalekites were the perpetual enemies of Israel, and they were— to put it simply—some pretty bad people. The whole conflict between Israel and Amalek began when Israel was on their way out of Egypt and headed to the promised land. They were alone and defenseless in the wilderness, and the Amalekites raided them (Exod 17:8-16; Deut 25:17-19). God rescued the Israelites, but He never forgot the Amalekites' treachery.

The Amalekite opposition was not a one-time event, either. Throughout Israel's history the Amalekites were constantly provoking and pillaging Israel. They were renowned for their excessive violence and ruthlessness. So God finally declares, "Enough." He gives Saul the command to wipe them out completely: "Do not spare them. Kill men and women, children and infants, oxen and sheep, camels and donkeys" (1 Sam 15:3). The language here describes what people normally call "holy war."

This was not a war of conquest but a war of justice. The goal of the attack was not to make Saul rich but to execute justice on a rebellious group of people. Saul was explicitly told to take no prisoners and to leave the wealth alone.

This is a disturbing concept for modern minds. Why in the world would God order something as brutal as this? A self-defensive war may be justified, perhaps, but total warfare? Why destroy the animals? the women? *the children?* For modern ears this sounds disturbingly like Islamic *jihad.*

It is impossible here to give a full treatment to the question of Old Testament warfare. Entire volumes have been filled—and more will be—addressing questions about God's justice and war.[8] We encourage readers to consult these sources.

---

[8] See Thomas, Copan, and Evans, eds., *Holy War in the Bible;* Thomas, "The Old Testament, 'Holy War,' and Christian Morality"; Longman and Reid, *God Is a Warrior.*

Still, we cannot breeze through passages like these without at least considering the question: What is going on with the command for holy war? We will put forth six points for help as we think about preaching and teaching the text, though no doubt more needs to be said, and this simply does not answer everything (we do not pretend that it does!). However, these six points do provide guides to help us work through the concept of "holy war" in the Bible.

God Is a Holy, Good, and Loving Creator

This is neither the first nor the last picture of God in the Bible, as we saw from the introduction (pp. 22–27). The book of Samuel (including 1 Sam 15) fits into the larger story of Scripture. God created the world, and then humanity committed cosmic treason against their Creator. When we consider how we can begin to make sense of "holy wars" in the Bible, we must remember God's redemptive plan. This overarching narrative should form the backdrop to any such investigation. The Bible, from creation to new creation, reveals a God who is holy, just, and good. As one scholar has said,

> Old Testament "holy wars" can only be rightly understood
> within a story that reveals a God who is committed to
> eradicating sin and renewing his creation. This point seems so
> simple, and yet it remains so profound. "Holy wars" (whatever
> they may be) are not the *only* part of the story or even the *most
> important* part of the story. If we rip the troubling accounts of
> the Old Testament out of their broader creation–new creation
> context, then we may well distort their contents. (Thomas,
> "The Old Testament, 'Holy War,' and Christian Morality," 22)

"Holy War" in the Bible Is Not "Holy War" at All

The term *holy war* was coined by a German scholar (Friedrich Schwally) early in the twentieth century to describe the wars found in the Bible that are similar to what we see in 1 Samuel 15. In his work he compared the wars of the Bible and Islamic *jihad*. No wonder he uses the language of holy war, but he is wrong on the comparison. Biblical warfare is not primarily about people going out to fight in the name of God but rather God going to fight on behalf of His people. Most scholars today do not use "holy war" to describe what we find in 1 Samuel 15. Rather, they use

the language "divine warfare," and we will follow suit in the remainder
of this discussion.

Divine Warfare Is Limited and Non Repeatable

These wars were fought in a particular time in Israel and are neither
to be repeated by the Church nor to be justified for any peoples in the
present world. The Church cannot use texts like 1 Samuel 15 to ground
their obedience to Jesus in the world today and go out and "kill the
infidel." Such an application baldly rebels against the clear teaching of
Jesus.

Divine Warfare Is Commanded by a Merciful God

As we have seen, there comes a point where God says "Enough!" Sin
has consequences, and God does not allow creation-destroying sin to go
unchecked forever, as a quick read through the book of Revelation will
make clear! God will go out and defeat evil because He is merciful to
the plight of the suffering. Moreover, He does not act on a whim or out
of an outburst of wrath. Rather, He has extended grace on grace, with
each kindness refused. Finally, His justice toward sin will be revealed.

Divine Warfare Is Not Genocide or Ethnic Cleansing but the Elimination of False Worship

Divine war represents a focused attack on sinful and idolatrous *religion*
rather than simply an attack on *people* (Deut 7:3-6; 12:2-3; compare Exod
34:12-13). To get at the religious heart of an ancient people, one had to
engage more than their spiritual lives. The ancients refused to separate
the realm of the "secular" from that of the "sacred" as we do today. Ancient
peoples like Israel and Amalek saw their national identities bound up
with three factors: their particular place, their particular god, and their
particular people group. For example: the Moabites lived in the land
southeast of the Jordan River and worshiped Chemosh. They believed
Chemosh cared for the Moabites in that particular place. The Canaanites
revered the god Baal, who governed them in the land of Canaan. The
Israelites (obviously) worshiped Yahweh in the promised land. Divine
warfare fundamentally breaks the bonds within deity-people-land. When
the Amalekites were displaced and defeated, their gods were defeated
and revealed as powerless and false.

In order for Yahweh to show the gods of the nations to be false,
and in order to punish sin, a simple sermon would not do. Yahweh

demonstrated His authority over gods and sin so the world would know that He alone is God.

Justice Is Meted Out Communally in Divine Warfare

As Westerners, we tend to think about justice individually. Every person stands before the court of law alone. But other peoples, especially from majority world countries in the East—like those represented here—think about justice communally. Against us, they would claim that a person never truly "stands alone." Each person is always a part of a group, and the group lives and dies together. The ancient world saw things this way (see "Individual and Community" in the introduction, p. 15).

Both the individual and the communal concepts of justice contain an element of truth. We in the West probably need to be reminded of the communal aspects much more often. We are, in fact, inextricably united to our community. No one is ever just a lone individual. What we do affects others in our community, and what they do affects us.

It is not difficult to think of modern examples of this. When a child is born with fetal alcohol syndrome, it is not the fault of the child. That child did nothing different from the child born physically healthy. No, the child with fetal alcohol syndrome is suffering for the mistakes of her parents. The sins of our parents really do affect us, whether we find the idea objectionable or not.

This can work positively as well. Children are blessed by their parents' obedience to God. Look, for instance, at verse 6. God singles out a group of people, the Kenites, and commands Saul not to touch them. They were to be preserved because their ancestors helped Israel when they were in need. The descendants are blessed by the righteous acts of their parents.

So the Eastern and majority worldview of justice, not to mention the ancient Near Eastern view, is right as far as it goes. We can never be separated from our community.

It is also true, however, that justice has an individual element. Everyone will ultimately stand before God's throne individually, judged not for the sins of their fathers but for their own.

Eastern, ancient, and Western conceptions of justice reflect sides of complete justice. In a passage like this, when God delivers someone over to death because of the actions of another, one side of the equation is more prominent. We should not, however, skew the picture by assuming this is a normative pattern for exacting justice. This was a unique situation: no contemporary nation or individual hears from God as Saul does here. We can recognize that God was at work in a way that normally offends our sensibilities without prescribing that pattern for the world today.

Finally, we would like to reiterate that divine warfare is not an acceptable practice for the church today. The following words are instructive:

> In Jesus' teaching, which is a revitalization of the Old Testament law, the task of people of the Kingdom of God is to love their "enemies" (including enemy nations) and serve them with the good news of the Kingdom (Matthew 5:43-8, 28:18-20). The book of Ephesians powerfully teaches that because of God's victory in Christ, the Christian wages war neither for land nor for a place in the world. The whole world sits under the authority of Christ (Matthew 28:18), and so the world is the Lord's. Wherever a Christian lives in God's world, he or she engages in a spiritual battle against the cosmic rulers that futilely wage war against God's victory in Christ (Ephesians 5:1-9, 6:10-18). Christian "warfare" involves learning to rightly live in the triumph that God has provided in Christ and His Kingdom. This is not physical, militaristic action. This subversive instruction in Ephesians reveals that God's Kingdom is and will be established not through coercion and/or domination but through self-sacrificial love, in the manner of Christ. (Thomas, "The Old Testament, 'Holy War,' and Christian Morality," 25)

Nonetheless, divine war is in play in 1 Samuel 15, and so we need to unpack its meaning and significance. The main point to remember, though, as it relates to this passage, is that this was not a war of conquest. Saul was not to enrich himself and expand his empire. He was to be God's instrument of justice and was therefore forbidden from growing rich off of the spoils of war. In fact, growing rich off the wealth of conquered nations was the grievance for which the Amalekites were being punished.

The Battle: Saul's Halfhearted "Obedience"

Saul, then, goes to meet the Amalekites in battle and does what God commands—though not entirely.

> *Then Saul struck down the Amalekites from Havilah all the way to*
> *Shur, which is next to Egypt. He captured Agag king of Amalek alive,*
> *but he completely destroyed all the rest of the people with the sword.*
> *Saul and the troops spared Agag, and the best of the sheep, cattle, and*
> *choice animals, as well as the young rams and the best of everything*
> *else. They were not willing to destroy them, but they did destroy all the*
> *worthless and unwanted things.* (vv. 7-9)

Modern readers might find God's command to totally destroy the
Amalekites harsh, but even we would admit that the command was clear.
Yet here Saul refuses to utterly destroy what God explicitly told him to
utterly destroy.

The verb in verse 9, "spared," is singular in Hebrew (Owens,
Analytical Key). This is nearly impossible to present in English translations, in which the singular and plural forms of this verb are identical.
Thus "the people," although explicitly mentioned, are not the subject
of the sentence. The implication, then, is that although the people are
involved in this disobedience, the main actor in view is Saul.

God, of course, was not unaware of this deviation, so He informs
Samuel about Saul's disobedience, going so far as to say that He
"regrets" making Saul king (v. 11). This is a strange emotion to attribute
to God, and the original language does not immediately resolve the tension. The Hebrew word used here is *nacham*, which is often translated
"repent." What does it mean for God to regret a past decision, or—even
worse—to repent of something He has done?

There are theologians who, in attempting to take passages like this
seriously, posit that there are some limits on God's knowledge. Certainly
He knows more than we do, but Saul seems to prove that even God can
be caught off guard. This has been made popular through an entire
school of thought known as "open theism," which is based on the notion
that the future is as open to God as it is to humanity.

As interesting as this position is, it hardly does justice to this text.
When God uses language like "I regret," He is speaking in terms we
can understand. It means that He really feels the pain of our current
circumstances but not that He is unaware of the future. A quick glance
ahead to verse 29 should suffice to illustrate this: "The Glory of Israel
will not lie or have regret, for he is not a man, that he should have
regret" (ESV). In one sense, then, God has regrets but certainly not in
the same way humanity does. He feels sadness and regret for our sake
when our decisions are harmful, but He most certainly does not share

the pervasive human sentiment of wishing He could just go back and fix a past mistake.

This is the sort of thing that happens when you set about thinking deeply about God. He refuses to be reduced into neat categories that can be shelved in a person's mind. He is not a topic to be mastered. He is the Lord who commands obedience, whose ways are never contradictory but are ever mysterious.

The Cover-up: Saul's Stubborn Rebellion

God delivers the unsavory news to Samuel, who is rightfully angry. It moves him to cry out and pray all night long, and to go to Saul at the first chance he has—early the next morning. Samuel wants to get this confrontation over with.

When Samuel arrives, Saul is throwing his victory party, complete with dancing girls, beer kegs, and karaoke machines (or the ancient Israelite equivalent). Before he even arrives, word gets to Samuel that Saul has set up a monument in honor of his recent victory. Not only is Saul disregarding the clear command of God, but he is in the midst of recasting the entire battle to make it about him. Samuel is none too pleased.

> When Samuel came to him, Saul said, "May the LORD bless you. I have carried out the LORD's instructions."
> Samuel replied, "Then what is this sound of sheep and cattle I hear?" (vv. 13-14)

Do you see how ridiculous Saul's claim is, how absurd he seems? The evidences of disobedience are literally all around him, making noises and filling the air with the smell of livestock. Yet he carries himself with the air of approval. "That's right," he says proudly, "I am faithfully following the Lord."

We are not off of the hook here, either. Too many of us show up to worship services every weekend, thinking everything is just fine between us and God. We sing worship songs and tell everyone that we are right with God. Yet the evidence of disobedience is all around us: our spouse (or child or roommate or coworker) knows our hypocrisy. Do you realize how offensive that is to God—and how silly?

We all get caught in our sin—all of us. We are all hypocrites from time to time. But what we do next when the Holy Spirit confronts us is of life-or-death importance. At this point Saul still has an opening, a chance to choose a path toward repentance. But he hardens his heart, going further down a road that becomes harder and harder to return from.

> *Saul answered, "The troops brought them from the Amalekites and spared the best sheep and cattle in order to offer a sacrifice to the LORD your God, but the rest we destroyed." (v. 15)*

Look at what Saul has done here. Recall that in verse 9 the verb for "spared" was in the singular because Saul was the one that spearheaded this endeavor. Now he decides to shift blame to the people. Not only that, but like Adam and Eve in the garden of Eden, he ultimately tries to pin this back on God. The people spared the best sheep to sacrifice to God! That must justify this, right?

Samuel, however, will have none of it. He stops Saul in the middle of his excuses and says, "Although you once considered yourself unimportant, have you not become the leader of the tribes of Israel? The LORD anointed you king over Israel" (v. 17). Samuel brings Saul back to the beginning, pointing out that Saul was nothing when God decided to give him an entire kingdom. He says, in essence, "God made you everything, Saul! Was that not enough for you? After all that God has given you, you feel like you need more than that?"

Saul is after a name for himself—his own kingdom, his own stature. That is why he spares Agag and keeps him prisoner. Refusing to kill Agag is not an act of mercy. No, having an enemy king in your prison is an enormous status boost. In those days conquering kings would frequently parade out all the kings they had captured—emaciated, in chains—as a sign to the world: "I am the conquering king. I am the king of kings."

The Fallout: The Beginning of the End of Saul's Kingdom

Samuel is not finished scolding Saul. Samuel sees through Saul's revisionist history. Saul was not strong-armed into sparing some of the spoils; he pounced on them at the first opportunity he had. And when Saul responds that he did most of what God had asked, Samuel fires back: God is not nearly as thrilled with this token offering, Saul, as you might hope.

> *Then Samuel said: "Does the LORD take pleasure in burnt offerings and sacrifices as much as in obeying the LORD? Look: to obey is better than sacrifice, to pay attention is better than the fat of rams.*

"For rebellion is like the sin of divination, and defiance is like wickedness and idolatry. Because you have rejected the word of the LORD, He has rejected you as king." (vv. 22-23)

The same could be said for many people sitting in our churches today. God is not fired up about people singing some songs, giving some of their money. What thrills God is a heart that obeys Him. What thrills God is a surrendered heart.

The alternative to full surrender is rebellion. Even 98-percent obedience is rebellion, and Samuel says that we might as well be worshiping Satan. That is a bold statement. Imagine that you went to someone's house for dinner, and just as you were leaving, they said, "So glad you came tonight, but before you go, I want to invite you upstairs with me. I've got a pentagram and some candles spread out on the floor, and I thought we could have sex with some temple prostitutes, sacrifice a few goats, and generally just offer ourselves to Satan. Don't worry, we'll go to church on Sunday, like normal." How would you react to that? With revulsion, of course. And that is precisely how God reacts to our half-hearted "obedience."

Many people in our churches are giving 90-percent obedience, just like Saul, and are completely at peace with it. Some are cheating on their taxes or cheating on their school exams. Boyfriends and girlfriends are sleeping with one another under the excuse of being truly "in love." Some people are holding on to bitterness, refusing to forgive someone they know they should forgive. Many have heard a call to ministry or missions but are actively refusing to answer. And all these seemingly small acts of disobedience are just as disgusting to God as blatant worship of the Devil.

This is difficult to believe, but there is a common denominator between any act of disobedience and Satan himself. Satan's sin, after all, was telling God, "I want to do my own thing." He demanded autonomy to circumvent those of God's laws that he found offensive. When we follow in his footsteps by displaying the same attitude, we are declaring that he is our true lord.

Our conception of sin is so often warped, as if the important aspect is what you do. Sin, however, is not wicked because of what a person does but because of whose authority a person rejects. As Samuel says to Saul, "Because you have rejected the word of the LORD, He has rejected you as king" (v. 23).

Saul knows that something is amiss:

Saul answered Samuel, "I have sinned. I have transgressed the LORD's command and your words. Because I was afraid of the people, I obeyed them. Now therefore, please forgive my sin and return with me so I can worship the LORD." (vv. 24-25)

On the surface this looks like repentance. We should pat Saul on the back and raise him up as a model for this . . . right? Unfortunately, what looks like repentance is actually a fraud. This is evident in two ways. First, for the rest of Saul's life, he will repeat this same rebellious attitude. Repentance entails a change, but Saul never evinces one. Second, the phrase in verse 25 indicates that Saul is still thinking of the whole situation incorrectly. Saul wants to "worship the Lord," and he is not thinking of singing some God songs together or washing someone else's feet. Saul wants to have a national thanksgiving sacrifice on behalf of the victory. He wants a big ceremony.

The problem with this is that Samuel is the only one who can offer an official worship ceremony. If Samuel refuses, this will be a major loss of face for Saul. Sadly, this is what Saul is so worried about. His main concern is still how he looks in the eyes of the people. He is still concerned about his status.

Again, far too many people in our pews think along the same lines. Too many of us are more worried about being caught in our sin than about the flagrance of the offense before God. We would be embarrassed if our sin was exposed, but we completely ignore the fact that the person most offended, most involved—God Himself—sees and knows our sin completely.

Samuel replied to Saul, "I will not return with you. Because you rejected the word of the LORD, the LORD has rejected you from being king over Israel." When Samuel turned to go, Saul grabbed the hem of his robe, and it tore. Samuel said to him, "The LORD has torn the kingship of Israel away from you today and has given it to your neighbor who is better than you." . . .

Samuel said, "Bring me Agag king of Amalek." Agag came to him trembling, for he thought, "Certainly the bitterness of death has come."

Samuel declared: As your sword has made women childless, so your mother will be childless among women. Then he hacked Agag to pieces before the LORD at Gilgal. (vv. 26-28,32-33)

You must admit: the Bible has some vivid screenwriting. Imagine Samuel turning to leave, when Saul grabs his robe. *Rip!* Samuel takes one look at his torn shirt and says, "God has torn the kingdom away from you, fool, and given it to a better neighbor of yours" (see vv. 27-28). That neighbor will turn out to be King David. David would not be a perfect king, but he knew how to repent; and he knew how to let repentance be about God's kingdom, not his own.

But the cinematic spectacle does not end there. Samuel drags Agag before everyone, which does not seem to bother Agag in the least (v. 32 ESV, NIV). The scene is dripping with irony. Agag comes forward happily, thinking, "OK, I've killed people. You've killed people. I'm sure we can work out a deal. I know people with money, and no one has to walk away unhappy." But Samuel picks up his sword and puts a bloody end to a bloody king. This is one of those gory passages people are often surprised to find in the pages of Scripture.

The Anatomy of Disobedience

Saul's disobedience offers us a crash course. This passage reveals five truths about the anatomy of disobedience.

Disobedience Is Anything Less Than Full, Immediate Obedience

According to Samuel, witchcraft-level rebellion is seen in any partial, conditional, or delayed obedience. If Satanists are those who worship the Devil, practical Satanists are those who do not live fully under the authority of God. We must ask ourselves: Are there areas of our lives in which we are not obeying God fully?

Those of us who are religious are often tempted to cover over rebellion with rituals, to substitute ceremony for surrender. We disobey in one area and try to "make it up" to God with some offering in another area. So we refuse the call to missions, but we resolve to tithe heavily in our local church. Or we refuse to break off the relationship with an unbeliever but resolve to share Christ with them instead. Or we refuse to give our money to God's mission, but we resolve to "tithe of our time."

Religion tries to pay God off. But religious people labor under the delusion that they have the right to retain control of their lives. Religion wants to obey God but on its own terms—terms that mean partial, delayed, or conditional obedience. But all of those are just various forms of disobedience.

Disobedience Grows out of Greedy Desire

The heart of Saul's disobedience is that he wants to be a famous king with world-class power. That is why he spares Agag, why he keeps the spoils, why he builds a monument to himself, and why, when Samuel confronts him, his only concern is how he will look in front of the people.

Everyone has a king, something he craves and must have to feel happy and secure. Personal recognition is Saul's king. It fuels his rebellion.

Sin always grows out of some deep soul dissatisfaction, something we feel like we must have for a happy and secure life. The man who must have respect compromises his morals for the sake of his peers. The woman who must have romance will pursue it at the cost of every other relationship in her life, dissolving marriages and breaking promises to find new lovers and better thrills. The man who must have pleasure will pursue it in drugs or alcohol or pornography, even when it is damaging to his health. The woman who must have creature comforts will do everything she can to move into a larger house and will do everything possible to avoid living in that downtown area that God has laid on her heart.

In all these our real problem, like Saul's, is that our soul is not content in its possession of God. Our idolatrous, greedy desire for other things fuels our disobedience. Until we depose these false kings and deal with our idolatry, we will never really be able to quit sinning and truly surrender to God.

Disobedience Further Estranges Us from God, Leading to Increasingly Irrational Behavior

This moment is a defining one in Saul's life. From this point on he will plummet into an epic tailspin. Instead of repenting, Saul will harden himself further. In response the Spirit of God departs from him. The absence of God and His approval leaves Saul with an enormous void in his life, and jealousy virtually consumes him. The slightest criticism will send him into a violent rage. He will spend years of his life tracking David around in the wilderness, trying to kill a man who continually goes out of his way to honor him.

Saul's touchy spirit serves as a warning to us. Are we not like that at times? Does criticism shake us, if not completely unsettle us? Does jealousy consume our thoughts? Does being compared unfavorably with others send us into despair? We may not be as far from Saul's mania as we imagine. Selfish desire grows out of a feeling of separation from God; and the longer we persist in maintaining that separation, the more erratic and destructive our behavior will become.

Disobedience Can Only Be Overcome by the Gospel

Samuel reminds Saul that God made him a king when he had previously been a nobody. This is a beautiful Old Testament picture of the gospel. Saul should have responded in gratitude because of God's amazing grace. He should have allowed the value of God's gift to him to break the captivating power of sin over his life. But he hardened himself against God's grace instead.

God has said something similar to us: "When you were a sinner, I came to earth and hung on a cross for you." The God of the universe sacrificed Himself for us and loves us immeasurably. There is now no condemnation for those who are in Christ, who promises goodness and mercy to us all the days of our lives. When we understand this, it liberates us from the driving need to be great. Knowing the value of God's gift breaks us from the captivating power of sin over our lives.

The great news of the gospel is that Christ fulfilled obedience perfectly for us but then was given rejection and punishment at the end of His life. He did it in our place, suffering the penalty for Satan worshipers. He died the witch's death so we could have the saint's acceptance.

"To obey is better than sacrifice." The author of Hebrews alludes to 1 Samuel 15:22, applying it to Jesus: He obeyed fully and then sacrificed Himself on top of that (Heb 10:5-10). His obedience earns our acceptance before God—the one person whose opinion matters more than any other—if we will receive it. And when we do, the power of disobedience in our lives is broken, setting us free from anxieties, dissatisfaction, insecurity, and fear.

Disobedience Exposed Creates a Choice: Self-Deception or Repentance

Saul succumbs to the temptation of following the wrong narrative. He constructs a narrative that excuses his sin—blaming others for his disobedience, attempting to make up for his mistakes with other sacrifices, and generally asserting that he is still a pretty good individual. The revisionist history flows out of Saul's mouth so freely that it seems he believes the deceitful story he has crafted to dupe others. He is falling prey to his own web of lies.

When confronted with our sin, we all find ourselves in situations similar to Saul's. Like Saul we may rationalize our disobedience and follow a nonbiblical narrative. We can try to blame others for our disobedience, make up for our mistakes by giving extra money to the church, or point out that at least we are not as bad as that guy. But this is a path without an exit. Once we begin to rationalize, we begin to spin the web of our own demise, deceiving ourselves until, like Samuel's robe, our lives are torn in two.

God does not want our rationalizations; He wants our repentance. He does not want our sacrifices; He wants our submission. The choice has passed for Saul but not for us. The choice between self-deception and repentance, between death and life, stands before each of us, even today.

Reflect and Discuss

1. What does this passage help you understand about God?
2. How does this passage of Scripture exalt Jesus?
3. Do you identify with Saul's disobedience? Why or why not?
4. What aspects of the anatomy of disobedience described above resonate with you the most? Why?
5. In what ways do we cover up our disobedience?
6. Read 1 Samuel 15:22-23. What is God's judgment against Saul?
7. Out of this same text, what does God really want from Saul? What does He want from us?
8. What does it do to your heart to know that our disobedience can only be overcome by the good news of Jesus?
9. Too often we think we can obey enough to gain God's love. What does it do to your heart to know that God already loves us so much that He gave us Jesus?
10. What do you need to put away or give up as you say yes to Jesus?

An Ordinary King

1 SAMUEL 16:1-13

Main Idea: Out of His grace God raises up and anoints an ordinary, unexpected king to serve in His kingdom. This king pictures the true King, Jesus.

I.   Proclaiming the End of Saul's Kingdom
II. The Lord Looks on the Heart
III. David, the "Runt" King
IV. Lessons to Learn from the "Runt" King
    A. David was ordinary.
    B. Because David was ordinary, God could be extraordinary through David.
    C. God made David extraordinary in the pasture.
    D. Jesus would be the truly ordinary-extraordinary.

Introduction

The book of 1 Samuel is the story of Israel's search for a king. Ultimately, only God could be their true King, but He had allowed them to have an earthly king to mirror His reign. The first king of Israel was a gifted character by the name of Saul. Unfortunately for Israel, however, Saul turned out to be more interested in his own glory than in leading his people in a godly way. So even after Saul ascended the throne, the search continued.

Chapter 16 leaves Saul behind for a moment to focus on what God searches for in His king and how He goes about choosing that king. The man of the hour is a boy by the name of David, and he is not exactly the king anyone would expect. He will go on to be a great man of God, but his first entrance onto the scene is hardly impressive. In every way he is—to put it bluntly—ordinary.

The story picks up with Samuel in deep distress because of the sin of Saul. Samuel had anointed him, and he seemed like such a promising prospect. But he turned out to be nothing like what Samuel had hoped for. Samuel had a vision of a king that he had gotten from his mother, Hannah (1 Sam 2:1-10). He looked for a king who would be faithful to

God and faithful to his people, who would trust God and teach the people to do the same, who would use his power to bless and serve others, promoting justice and lifting up the needy. That kind of king would not have to command the allegiance of the people but would win it from them. They would be willing to die for him because they would see that he was willing to die for them.

Saul was not that king. He was faithful only to himself, which has gotten Samuel rather depressed. The one he had hoped in has been exposed as a fraud. Think of the disappointment he must have felt in trusting in someone so deeply, only to be left with false promises and unfulfilled dreams. We have all felt moments of betrayal like this, some more poignantly than others. And as we pick up 1 Samuel 16, Samuel is in the throes of that despondency.

Proclaiming the End of Saul's Kingdom

In 1 Samuel 16:1-5 God abruptly sends Samuel on a mission to find the next king of Israel, which is not exactly the remedy for depression Samuel would have concocted himself. He is more than a little reluctant to go out anointing a new king, knowing how passionate the current king is about his own kingdom and name and honor. God's plan sounds like a recipe for disaster.

So God gives Samuel some more detail, essentially providing an alibi for his trip to Bethlehem. Samuel needs to officiate a ritual sacrifice in the city anyway, so God decides to use the official occasion for another, more subversive agenda. The sacrifice would have been a huge affair, with the entire city coming out to a large public arena. Samuel's primary job in all this is to ensure that Jesse and his sons attend.

As he enters the city, however, tensions are already rather high. Word has apparently gotten out about the "hacked Agag to pieces" incident of 15:33. Samuel's arrival has the city leaders shaking in their sandals. They want to know, "Are you here to bring a reckoning?" Apparently, if he wanted to confront the city by himself, they were ready to lie down and take it. Whatever else is true of Samuel, this passage shows us that he had a commanding presence.

Samuel orders a consecration for the sacrifice in which all members of the community offer themselves to God. This is the perfect moment for Samuel to inspect the sons of Jesse, who will come marching by him in succession. Word must have spread through the crowd that Samuel's visit was more than a mere sacrifice, and the atmosphere must have been intense by the time Jesse's family came forward.

The Lord Looks on the Heart

When they arrived, Samuel saw Eliab and said, "Certainly the LORD's anointed one is here before Him."
*   But the LORD said to Samuel, "Do not look at his appearance or his stature, because I have rejected him. Man does not see what the LORD sees, for man sees what is visible, but the LORD sees the heart."*
(16:6-7)

Eliab is the oldest of Jesse's sons, so he naturally comes forward first, looking as kingly as possible. Samuel takes one look at him and thinks he has found his man—good looking, tall, strong. This must be kingly material.

God, however, is unimpressed. Eliab's appearance, height, and physique do not even register as relevant qualities. God never looks down from heaven and says, "Wow, that's a nice physique," or, "Sweet haircut," or even, "Nice résumé." His standards are different from what most of us value because He looks on the heart.

In one sense this is good news. Most of us have tried to measure up to the world's criteria, but few people ever feel as if they have succeeded. The stress of trying to have the perfect body, a successful career, a conflict-free family—all these have eluded us. It comes as refreshing, freeing news that God is not particularly concerned with our earthly successes.

In another sense, though, this is a bit problematic. Who among us has the kind of heart God would want? Our outward appearance may not be top-notch, but if we are honest with ourselves, our heart condition is usually worse! We spend hours caring for our bodies (decaying as they are), or on our résumés (trivial as they are in eternity), but many of us never think about the quality of our hearts. If that is the case, then we are more concerned with the approval of others than the approval of God.

"The LORD sees the heart." This may be challenging news for some of us, but it is surprising to see Samuel struggle to grasp this concept. Samuel is God's man, the prophet who should be attuned to the way God sees the world. And with Saul he had just made the mistake of allowing impressive credentials to blind him to a wicked heart. Is he really about to make the same mistake again, choosing Eliab because he looks like a king? Apparently so. This is such a counterintuitive lesson that even Samuel needs a consistent reminder. And so do we.

We are not given specific reasons why Eliab, Abinadab, Shammah, or the rest are rejected (vv. 8-11). Outwardly they may seem qualified, but God weighs their hearts and finds them lacking. One by one Jesse trots his sons out, and one by on Samuel shoots them down. It is an Old Testament version of Cinderella, as the brothers fruitlessly try to cram themselves into the glass slipper that is Israel's kingship. But so far, no Cinderella. All seven come and go, and everyone looks around awkwardly. Samuel asks what must be a strange question: "Jesse, did you, perchance, forget about any of your kids?"

David: The "Runt" King

Samuel asked him, "Are these all the sons you have?"

"There is still the youngest," he answered, "but right now he's tending the sheep."

Samuel told Jesse, "Send for him. We won't sit down to eat until he gets here." So Jesse sent for him. He had beautiful eyes and a healthy, handsome appearance.

Then the LORD said, "Anoint him, for he is the one." So Samuel took the horn of oil, anointed him in the presence of his brothers, and the Spirit of the LORD took control of David from that day forward. Then Samuel set out and went to Ramah. (16:11-13)

Jesse finally speaks up: "Oh right, there is the youngest one. I didn't think to have him come all the way down here." Several factors here imply that David is not the sort of man who seems fit to be a king. The first is his position as a shepherd. Keeping the sheep was not a coveted position in Israel. Slaves and social rejects were shepherds. Though demanding, it was a job that required no real skill set. No wonder the older brothers pawn this duty off on their baby brother.

The second aspect working against David is the way his father describes him. He is the youngest son, an English translation of the Hebrew word *haqqaton. Haqqaton* can mean, literally, "the youngest," but it also carries the connotation of "the tiniest" or "the smallest." Essentially David is the runt. His own father fails to invite him to the event because the prospect of David's being a king is laughable.

We are given more of a clue into Jesse's omission with the physical description of David. In contrast to his brother Eliab, who is imposing and strong, David is described as boyish and weak. Western readers may be tempted to read about David's beautiful eyes and handsome appearance as if these were complimentary attributes. They are not. The author points them out to show that David looks more like a cute kid than a possible warrior. The text intends to show us that David is outwardly unimpressive, even to those who knew him best; yet this is the one God chooses.

Lessons to Learn from the "Runt King"

David Was Ordinary

It is easy to rush past the realization that David was an ordinary person, especially if we are acquainted with some of the extraordinary events of his life. How can *the* David, who wrote most of the Psalms, who knocked off Goliath, be an ordinary man? Is he not the standard after which all future kings will be measured? Is he not the pinnacle of extraordinary?

David's life was certainly not ordinary but not because of any greatness in himself. The great aspects of David's life are all the result of the Spirit of God. Even some of the more magnificent scenes from his life paint him as an ordinary man: he challenges Goliath to a fight but only because his father sends him to the battle with sack lunches for his older brothers; he writes dozens of psalms but only because he has time on his hands while sitting in a pasture or hiding in caves.

David became extraordinary, but we must not miss that every extraordinary event in his life happened in spite of his own ordinariness. David had access to the power of an extraordinary God because he did not think he was extraordinary in himself. This is in strong contrast to Saul, who was fully convinced of his own greatness, a folly that led God's Spirit away from him and brought him crashing back down to earth.

Contemporary North American society would have us all be Sauls instead of Davids. And for the most part, the church repeats these lies in Christianized forms. Thus we teach people that they are special, unique, like a snowflake. In one sense, of course, this is true: we each have unique DNA, fingerprints, and defining experiences. But in another, more profound sense, none of us is all that special. Yes, we are fearfully and wonderfully made in God's image, but we do the Bible a great disservice when we try to show how these truths lead to self-esteem boosting and puffing up our egos. Even the prophet Elijah, the greatest prophet in the Old Testament, was—according to James—"a man with a nature like ours" (5:17). David did not achieve greatness because he nurtured narcissism.

Or we encourage people to get involved because "God needs them," as if God were shorthanded and in need of some talented leaders. But the God who created the universe out of nothing is not wringing His hands for lack of personnel. This may not make us feel particularly special, but the gospel does not aim to make us feel that way. God is special and we are not. Our entire faith consists in making much of Him because of His majestic uniqueness.

David was ordinary. We are ordinary. Accepting this is a big first step in being used by God because Christianity is a large collection of nobodies worshiping a great big Somebody.

Because David Was Ordinary, God Could Be Extraordinary through David

God does not revel in the ordinary for its own sake. In David's life, as in ours, He is interested in doing some extraordinary things. And that only happens as the Spirit of God is allowed to work. Samuel threatened that God would revoke His Spirit from Saul, and this passage ends with that same Spirit rushing upon David. This Spirit would make the extraordinary possible.

This is the case throughout Scripture. It is only by the Spirit of God that Joseph, a foreign criminal in Egypt, can become the second-most-powerful man in the world (Gen 41:38-41). Only by the Spirit of God could Gideon take 300 men and defeat an army of 100,000 without a single casualty (Judg 7:19-25). And the same Spirit enabled the early church to defy the Roman Empire, testifying boldly about Jesus even when it cost them their lives (Acts 7:55).

Zechariah would sum up all the great and powerful people in the Bible by saying, "'Not by strength or by might, but by My Spirit,' says the LORD of Hosts" (Zech 4:6). Only as we cease trying to be Saul can God be truly extraordinary through us. Too many of us have tried to become David by pursuing the path of Saul. But God will not share His glory. So He takes the ordinary, the plain, and the outcast and pours His power into them. Only one person in our lives can be seen as great—it is either God or us.

This is a strong blow to many of us who have been fed a steady diet of praise. Our parents, teachers, and peers have convinced us that we are distinguished, extraordinary, and just plain awesome. And perhaps we are more talented than some others around us. But the danger of relying on our talents and skills is that we run the risk of following Saul, not David. When it comes to making a lasting impact in God's kingdom, no one has what it takes, no matter how talented.

This is why David, even after he becomes a king, can pen a song like Psalm 23. He sees himself as a sheep, and sheep are dumb. They focus on the patch of grass immediately in front of them and know nothing else. Essentially every predator alive can easily dispatch a sheep. If a sheep thrives, it is always because of the care of the shepherd, not the skill of the sheep. David knew this intimately—that the Lord was his shepherd—and he embraced his "sheeply" role.

God Made David Extraordinary in the Pasture

Being anointed is a momentous occasion, and David must have been elated. Samuel, the most important prophet in Israel, comes on a covert mission to anoint David, reports that God Himself has chosen David, and as the oil pours down his head, the Spirit of God rushes on him. This is not an experience anyone present would soon forget.

But as often happens in situations like this, this mountaintop experience was followed by monotony and drudgery. Samuel returns to Ramah, and David goes back to tending sheep. No elite training program for future kings. No interviews with the *Israel Gazette*. No fittings for kingly robes and crowns. Just more of the same.

His father puts him back on sheep duty, which is where we find David even years later. His dad is apparently unwilling to have his chief sheep-keeper taken away from his duties, so despite the magnificent anointing, the next few scenes of David's life always start out in the pasture. Even when David's life starts to display a little more action, the trend is not in the upward direction. David will soon go from the pasture to the cave, hiding out and on the run for years from the increasingly jealous and insane Saul.

Can you imagine David's thoughts? "I have been anointed king! I know my destiny! But look at everything that is happening. Has there been a mistake?" We do not know if David entertained these thoughts, but we do know that God was not merely sloppy with His timing. God was using the pasture to prepare the king.

Years spent watching sheep would have been monotonous and obscure. There is a reason we are not given a catalog of David's daily events during this time: they would have been the same every single day. Walk the sheep from here to there. Lead them to water. Retrieve a wandering lamb. Sit. Wait. Repeat. Repeat. Repeat. But the pasture was also where David honed some of the most vital skills in his life. It was where he sharpened his slingshot accuracy. It was where he grew in courage, fending off lions and bears from his helpless flock. It was where he learned humility, cleaning sheep excrement off his robes and sandals day after day.

No wonder Psalm 78:72 says that David "shepherded them with a pure heart and guided them with his skillful hands." A pure heart and a shepherding attitude come from the pasture, not the palace.

This is still what God does with us today. Mothers who feel undervalued, changing diapers for unappreciative infants, experience their own pasture and can do so with joy if they realize that in whatever they do, it is for the Lord (cf. Col 3:23). Businesspeople often work dead-end jobs, unnoticed even by their own supervisors, but if they work with faithfulness where they are, God often does magnificent things. Students, many of whom are eager to get out into the world and "make a difference," pore over their books, learning material they may never use. But God is at work in them, forging their character, patience, and integrity. We ought not to despise the pasture or resent our suffering: these are God's laboratories for molding our hearts to look how He wants.

Jesus Would Be the Truly Ordinary-Extraordinary

We need constant reminders that David's story is not about us. I have heard enough sermons that say, "Look at David! He wasn't much, but he became king! So don't judge a book by its cover because sometimes good things come in small packages." A little rah-rah, a little motivational talk, and we can all go out and act the part of David in our lives.

But these stories are not primarily about us. We may see some of ourselves in David, but his story is not meant to resonate with our lives. It is meant to remind us of someone greater. David prefigures Christ, who would be the truly ordinary-extraordinary.

Consider that David is anointed by the Spirit of the Lord, only to spend the next 15 years in obscurity and suffering. Jesus was a carpenter with a regular, blue-collar job. He was not a rising ruler. He was not even a rabbi. Apart from a short story in Luke, we know nothing of His life from the time of His birth until He is 30 years old. When Jesus bursts on the scene, He is anointed, and the Holy Spirit rushes upon Him. But instead of marching on Jerusalem, Jesus' next stop is the wilderness, for 40 days of wandering and temptation.

Jesus' time on earth would be largely spent in obscurity, and those moments that were not obscure were filled with suffering. But the Father would use this life of suffering to save the world.

David's anointing is not an anecdote telling us to hang on until God puts us on the throne of victory. Jesus is already there. The gospel reminds us that He has won the victory, and if we want victory, it only comes by sharing in His victory, not anticipating our own. The most ordinary king of all, an obscure man from Galilee, has been raised to the most extraordinary position of all. If we know Him, our lives will never be truly ordinary again.

Reflect and Discuss

1. How does this passage help you understand God?
2. How does this passage of Scripture exalt Jesus?
3. Do you really believe God looks at the heart? Why or why not?
4. When we look at how the world views us, in what ways does it encourage you to know that God values the deepest part of who we are—our hearts?
5. How does it encourage you to know that God raises up the "ordinary" folk for His purposes?
6. In what ways do you think God wants to work the "extraordinary" using the ordinary in your life? Write your thoughts.
7. In what ways is God using your days in the "pasture" to shape you?
8. In sports, it is often said that athletes should "let the game come to them." In what ways did David "let the game come to him"?
9. What barriers did David have to move beyond in order to be the man God called him to be?
10. What barriers do you have to move beyond in order to be the woman or man God called you to be?

Courage

1 SAMUEL 17:1-54

Main Idea: Real courage comes from the One in whom we trust: David trusted in Yahweh and experienced victory over his giant to show us that Jesus is the victor and we experience victory as we trust in Him.

I.   **Enter Goliath, the Champion**
II. **Enter David, the Runt**
III. **The Runt Slays the Champion**
IV. **Jesus Is David and You Are Not**
V.   **Two Lessons from David and Goliath**
    A. Because Jesus took out the real giant in our lives, we can bravely face all the lesser giants.
    B. Through the story of David and Goliath, God also gives His people a pattern for how they will overcome the giants they face.

Introduction

Courage has never been a gift of ours. That may surprise a lot of people because we put on such a strong show of bravado. But that is mostly a veneer. Underneath it all, we often fear what our peers think, what the congregation thinks, what random strangers think. We struggle to be courageous in sharing the faith or in preaching the Word faithfully. And there have been moments in life where we have caved to the pressures around us and given way to these fears. Those have always been deeply embarrassing moments.

We suspect, however, that we are not alone. Perhaps some of you reading this book can be transparent enough to admit to yourself that you are not courageous. You have mastered the art of looking tough on the outside, but on the inside you are plagued by fears—fear that your marriage will fall apart, that your children will not turn out right, or that you will lose your job. Perhaps you lack the courage to be open about your own mistakes, admitting an addiction or owning up to your fault in a broken relationship. Perhaps you lack the courage to confront someone with a truth you know they need to hear.

So where does real courage come from? In this most famous of Bible stories, we get a glimpse into the answer. But there may be more to David and Goliath than most of us remember from Sunday school.

Enter Goliath, the Champion

First Samuel 17 is not our first encounter with the Philistines. As the reader will recall, the Philistines were a group of people living in the promised land of Canaan. God had given Israel orders to drive all of them out so they could have the land themselves. That was generations ago, and Israel still had not succeeded in driving the Philistines out.

One reason Israel had yet to drive the Philistines out is that, from the perspective of the Israelites, the Philistines were strong. They were technologically advanced. They were one of the first civilizations to work with bronze and iron, and they used those metals to make their weapons—hence the repeated mention of all of Goliath's bronze weaponry. Because of their military might, they controlled Gezer, Megiddo, and Hazor, three major cities along the most popular trade route in the world, called the "way by the sea" or the *via maris*. We might compare that to controlling all the commerce in New York, Washington, DC, and Miami.

But from a different perspective—a more appropriate view—the Israelites' failure to drive the Philistines out was ultimately a result of their disobedience. Had they truly believed God and fought the Philistines as God intended, *He* would have driven them out. None of the Philistine prowess cowed God in the least. His promise—to drive out all the inhabitants of Canaan so Israel might live in the land in peace (Exod 33:1-2)—was still valid, but Israel never fully believed it. That promise is the backbone of this story.

I (J. D.) have been to the Valley of Socoh mentioned in verse 1. It is a large valley with two mountains facing the center. The valley itself is about a mile wide, and if both armies had camped out as described here, they would have been largely visible to each other. So when Goliath swaggered out to challenge the Israelites, it was quite a scene.

A brief note about Goliath's height here is probably in order. If Goliath were "six cubits and a span," that makes him about nine and a half feet tall. Some scholars think this was a scribal error and that it should instead read "four cubits and a span." Instead of nine feet tall, that would put Goliath's height at about six feet nine inches.

We may never know for sure which is the original, but it is important to be aware of the discrepancy for two reasons. First, this is one of the parts of the Bible that skeptics like to point to in order to discredit its validity. So when a professor points this out and says, "Look, Goliath wasn't that big. Your Sunday school teacher was all wrong!" you can just yawn and respond, "I was already aware of this, thank you."

Second, even if Goliath is "only" six feet nine inches, that is pretty large—especially to David, who, as we pointed out earlier, was described as the runt of his family. Hebrews were not terribly tall as an ethnic group anyway, so to be a short Hebrew probably put him around five feet three inches. In just about any hand-to-hand combat, an eighteen-inch height advantage is substantial.

Verse 16 points out that Goliath came out and taunted the Israelites day after day for 40 days. As the Israelites ate their breakfast, he thundered at them: "Send me a man so we can fight each other!" As they gathered to discuss possible battle tactics: "Send me a man so we can fight each other!" As they sat around their campfires at night, smoking their pipes: "Send me a man so we can fight each other!" And Goliath struck such fear into the entire army that no one even entertained his challenge.

Enter David, the Runt

Meanwhile, back at the ranch, Jesse sends David out to visit his brothers on the battlefield. His father does not seem to be terribly impressed with the anointing ceremony that had recently occurred in front of his eyes because David is still tending sheep while his big brothers are off at war. To Jesse, David is still just a teenager suited for food deliveries or watching the livestock. But David is an obedient son, so he packs his bags and heads to the front line.

David walks onto the scene to find a lot of posturing but not much fighting. The Israelites would line up as if they were about to fight and would shout menacingly to the Philistine army. But the fight would never materialize once the Philistines responded with their own war cry: "We've got Goliath." That would send the Israelites scampering back to their tents to change their loincloths and spend the rest of the day shivering in fear.

Apparently news of the standoff had not reached the Jesse ranch because David asks the local Israelite soldiers two questions: First, what is the reward for the man who takes this guy out? And second, who is that big oaf, anyway, mouthing off about our God?

The second question is the more important of the two and is David's real motivation. But the first question gives us another clue as to the fear Goliath instilled. The reward for taking down Goliath is a serious haul: (1) riches from the king, (2) marriage to the king's daughter—which would make the victor royalty, and (3) no taxes for that person's family for life. You might think for that price tag at least one crazy soldier would take the risk. But even this high of an incentive has failed to budge anyone. What good is being rich and royal and tax free if you aren't alive to enjoy it?

In verse 28 Eliab is hardly out to win "Brother of the Year." Still bitter about not being chosen king, he lashes out at David and impugns his motives. His question about David's sheep is less intended to elicit information about the flock than it is to remind David of his rightful role—the young, insignificant servant.

It is a tragic irony that some of the most discouraging opposition Christians face comes from the people who should be on God's side. Confronting an enemy like Goliath is frightening enough as it is, but often added to that are the supposed believers who do everything in their power to prevent sincere young Christians from stepping out in bold faith. The cowardly people of God are always the biggest obstacle to the mission of God.

Goliath is not really the problem here. A leather strap and a little rock can fix him. The real menacing giant in this story is the unbelief that dominates the hearts of God's people. The obstacle is not found in God; it is not found in God's opponents; it is found in God's own people. I suspect God was more insulted by Israel's disbelief than He was by Goliath's blatant, blasphemous defiance. We should expect Goliath to respond the way he does, but the people of God should know better.

The same opposition is at work in our churches today. What should be a bastion for godly ambition becomes a place of cowardly timidity and unbelief. Churches are full of Eliabs who scoff at every grand vision to reach their community and their world. How different would our cities be if, instead of responding with Eliab's cynical spirit, we assumed with David that God was poised to work powerfully?

Unlike his brothers, unlike the entire Israelite army, David assumes God will bring the victory. He never questions the outcome of the battle but simply wants to know who the blasphemer is and what the spoils will be when he goes down. "Of course whoever fights Goliath will win," David seems to be saying. "Didn't God promise us victory over the Philistines? Did you all forget that promise? Why has no one believed it?"

The Runt Slays the Champion

Word gets back to King Saul that someone might be up for the challenge of taking on Goliath (v. 31). But as soon as David arrives, Saul takes up the same tone with him his brothers had: You don't stand a chance (v. 33). David, however, is unfazed. He had done his real training in the pasture, and compared to a lion or a bear, Goliath was not terribly impressive.

Saul is largely absent from this entire narrative, but he shows up long enough to discourage David and to offer him some poorly fitting armor. Remember, Saul was head and shoulders above the average man, while David was short. It is no wonder David opted out of using the oversized gear. Had Saul possessed the technology of his opponents, he might have had spare armor lying around. But Saul's armor served as the best shot for David to be protected, at least from Saul's (earthly) perspective.

The story becomes strikingly similar to most twenty-first-century action movies, complete with trash talking and vivid graphic imagery, in verses 40-54. This is gripping stuff and qualifies as one of the first DVDs I plan to grab off the shelf when I get to heaven. But other than being a fascinating battle story, what exactly is the main lesson to learn in David's triumph over Goliath? Contemporary audiences love to use this as an analogy about the underdog: No matter the odds, you can do it! Just believe in yourself! Christians are as prone as anyone to fall prey to this sort of interpretation, baptizing it with spiritual language: If you trust God, He will give you victory over all the "giants" in your life—cancer, a lousy job, a broken relationship. Just claim your victory, and God will give it to you!

Sadly this misses the point. God does not want us to read this story and come away with a cocky assurance that, given the right confidence, we can achieve whatever we set our mind to. Yes, David was able to overcome insurmountable odds. The interpretive problem comes not from recognizing the long odd but in identifying ourselves with David. This may strike you as bad news, but in this story you are not David. You and I are the cowering, helpless nation of Israel.

Jesus Is David and You Are Not

The entire scene of David's conflict with Goliath is cast in the light of representative warfare. When David takes on Goliath, it is not merely one man against another; this is Israel and Philistia, squaring off. What's more, the battle between Israel and Philistia represents the struggle between their gods, as both David and Goliath mention in their taunting monologues. Thus when David wins, the rout is on: the Philistines (and their god) are on the run, while Israel (and the one true God) pursues.

This helps indicate David's confidence. When he arrives on the scene, he is immediately enraged with the situation, not because he is being disparaged but because his God is. He goes to the battle line with confidence, not because he finds himself particularly worthy but because he sees the battle for what it is, a struggle between the God of Israel and the gods of the world. And when he wins, the entire nation of Israel shares in his representative victory, even though they had done nothing to earn it themselves.

We stand in a situation similar to Israel, in need of a representative to save us from the menacing giant of sin. Humanity's most serious and most fundamental problem—the problem behind all our problems—is our alienation from God. And just like Israel versus the giant, there is nothing any of us can do about that. In fact, there is nothing any of us, of our own accord, even desire to do about this. We are the hoards of Israelites hiding in our tents, not dealing with the threat of sin, guilt, and death. God's judgment looms over us, as terrifying as the giant Goliath, and we are powerless to stop it. What we need, like Israel, is a representative to challenge this giant of judgment on our behalf.

The devastating Indian Ocean tsunami of 2004 provides another powerful image of our helpless state before the giant of sin and judgment. I (J. D.) spoke with a friend who had been asleep on the beach the morning that tragedy happened. He and a dozen others woke up when the 7.0 magnitude earthquake shook their island, but they were unaware of the crushing wave that would follow. They walked out of their tents to see the ocean water rapidly receding half a mile away from the shore.

My friend decided to get on his motorcycle and go home to check on his parents. His friends, however, curious about what was happening, walked out onto the sand where previously there had been ocean. A few minutes later, a 70-foot wave crashed into the shore, killing every single one of them—except my friend, who by that time was on higher ground.

Can you imagine standing on that shore, watching a growing wall of water, as tall as a seven-story building and as wide as your eye can see, barreling toward you at 60 miles an hour? There is nowhere to turn. Death is all but certain. But then imagine that just before the wave swept you away, the ground between you and the wave opened up and the earth swallowed up every bit of the water coming toward you.

That wall of water, that Goliath, is the righteous wrath of God. And the pit that swallows up that water, the hero able to conquer Goliath, is none other than Jesus. Jesus was our unexpected representative, the One who fought the giant on our behalf while we stood on the sidelines and did nothing to help Him. Jesus was opposed by all His brothers, abandoned by all His friends, precisely at the moment of His greatest battle. Jesus was the only One who, like David, really believed the promises of God. And Jesus was the only One to run onto the battlefield with perfect confidence in God, winning a victory on our behalf, despite our disobedience and failure.

Two Lessons from David and Goliath

Until we see Christ's victory in David's story, we miss the central thrust of this passage. Yet once we recognize that we are much more like Israel than David, we see two practical lessons for us today.

Because Jesus Took Out the Real Giant in Our Lives, We Can Bravely Face All the Lesser Giants

The real menacing giant in our lives is not our present situation, however tragic. The real giant in our lives is the one that has already been defeated at Golgotha—the giant of sin, death, and separation from God. Because Jesus absorbed the wrath of God in our place, we can have confidence in the face of every other challenge.

In Christ we have no need to be afraid of death. So when cancer threatens to destroy me, there is nothing ultimately to fear. Even if cancer kills me, Jesus has taken away the sting of death. As Paul says, "For me, living is Christ and dying is gain" (Phil 1:21). Christ has freed us from the captivity to the fear of death, so the prospect of the grave simply does not have the same binding power it once did.

In Christ we have no need to be afraid of the future flying out of control. So when I lose my job, I have something more secure than a job. The real fear behind unemployment is not the job, anyway, but the fear of being taken care of. And Christ's sacrifice on our behalf assures us that we will never lack that tender care and compassion. Thus we can answer with David that even in the darkest valley we fear no evil because God Himself is with us (Ps 23:4).

In Christ we have no need to be afraid of pain in our relationships. So when a spouse dies—or worse, walks out—we can feel the weight of grief without drifting into outright despair. We can engage in close and vulnerable relationships without the fear of getting hurt because the prospect of betrayal would not be the end of the world. Jesus Himself took the "end of the world" into His body for us so that no relational pain would ever threaten to undo us.

In Christ we have no need to be afraid of the disapproval of others. We have the absolute approval of the only One whose opinion matters. The God who created the universe with a word, who rules eternity, with all power in His hand—if that God is for you, if He treasures you and approves of you, who can rightfully be said to stand against you (Rom 8:31)? If we have His smile, we can endure the fiercest frown.

Real courage does not arise from the assurance that we will never encounter trouble. Courage is not the absence of strife or the absence of fear in the midst of strife. Instead, courage comes from having a priceless and secure treasure that strife and fear cannot threaten. That treasure is Jesus Christ Himself.

Through the Story of David and Goliath, God Also Gives His People a Pattern for How They Will Overcome the Giants They Face

David's story, like all narratives in the Old Testament, primarily points us to the work of Christ (cf. Luke 24:25-27). But as the apostle Paul says, these stories happened *to them* as an example *for us* (1 Cor 10:11). So like the people of Israel, when we see Jesus, the true David, conquer death, the true Goliath, we should respond as they did—by triumphantly following Christ in His victory.

There are giants in our lives, huge obstacles, areas in which the kingdom of God is prohibited from going forward in the lives of those whom He loves. For the teenager, that may be her school, where it is laughable to live with faith in Jesus Christ. For the businessman, that may be his workplace, where integrity is consistently sacrificed in the name of growing profit. For the full-time mother, that may be her own home, where her children's future salvation looms like a giant she cannot overcome.

The kingdom of God is a kingdom of advance. But as in David's day, so in ours, obstacles from both inside and outside God's people threaten to hamper what God wants to do in the world. The size of Goliath was no problem to David, nor is the size of whatever giant stands before the church today. The more significant obstacle is the smallness of our confidence in God.

God expects the taunts of those who do not believe in Him, and we should not be overly anxious about those in our culture who deride followers of Christ for their faith. This may insult God, but what grieves Him more than their taunts is the church's failure to take God at His word. We must take our eyes off the size of the giant, stop listening to unbelieving "believers," and think instead about the size of the love and power of God. Until we do, we remain fearfully in the tents of Israel—hiding from risk but also from the work of God.

Reflect and Discuss

1. How does this passage help you understand God?
2. How does this passage of Scripture exalt Jesus?
3. This is a famous passage of Scripture. Prior to hearing this chapter on David and Goliath, what have you understood to be the major lesson of the story? Why do you think you thought that?
4. What does it do to your heart to know that Jesus is the champion we need?
5. How does it encourage and inspire you to know that Jesus has faced the giants of sin, death, and hell so we do not have to?
6. In what ways do you need to express gratitude to our champion, Jesus?
7. In what ways does this story highlight the character of David versus the character of Saul?
8. If David is a man after God's own heart, then what do David's actions reveal about his heart and his love for Yahweh?
9. What obstacles prevent you from following Jesus now?
10. Do you believe you can overcome the giants in life through Jesus? Why or why not?

David in Saul's House

1 SAMUEL 18–20

Main Idea: The distinction between Saul and his family reveals the difference between those who embrace God and His Messiah and those who reject Him.

I. Jealousy and Murder
II. Killing Jealousy through the Gospel

Introduction

After David's victory over Goliath, the tension between Saul and the young runt rises to an epic level. Not for David, of course, but for Saul. Saul sees the kingdom slipping from his grasp, and he knows it is just a matter of time before his reign will end and the reign of David will begin. Samuel has already anointed David as the future king (16:12-13). The Hebrew word *messiah* means "anointed one," so David is the "messiah" of Judah at this time.

In 1 Samuel 14:52, we saw that Saul co-opted young, brave warriors into his royal army. He also swayed the hearts of these brave men away from the Lord. When we pick up in chapter 18, we see that Saul will not let David go back to his own home. Rather, he brings David right into his royal family. The Hebrew is strong: Saul took David for himself and would not let him go back to his father's house (18:2). Saul attempted to sway the young David. He even gives his daughter Michal to marry the young David. More to that move in a moment.

But at this stage we can say that Saul comes to hate the coming messiah, the one who has been anointed to replace him. By contrast his own family members love, honor, and commit to the coming messiah. Their distinctive commitment to David is a picture for those who will embrace God's plan as opposed to those who reject it. This picture establishes a pattern we see later with Jesus.

Jealousy and Murder

It is no wonder Saul attempted to bring David into his royal retinue, since he was a young and promising warrior. David would be a great political and military ally. His presence in the royal house would certainly boost morale! However, the text gives other motivations at work in Saul as well. He experiences the burning pangs of jealousy in his heart and life.

The women of Israel start singing David's praises—literally! They sing songs about him, and they dance over him. They compose a song about his greatness: "Saul has killed his thousands, but David his tens of thousands" (18:7). In terms of the honor-shame dynamic at work in the book, it is clear they give slight honor to Saul, but they give greater honor to David! To say the least, Saul notices the slight. Observe what the text clearly states of Saul:

> *Saul was furious and resented this song. "They credited tens of thousands to David," he complained, "but they only credited me with thousands. What more can he have but the kingdom?" So Saul watched David jealously from that day forward.* (vv. 8-9)

He even goes so far as trying to pin David to the wall because of his rage. David played the harp for Saul, but Saul was so eaten up with jealousy that he threw his spear at the young boy trying to murder him (vv. 10-11).

Jealousy is a terrible emotion. Jealousy is the scab you keep picking only to have the wound fester. Jealousy is a hunger you simply cannot satisfy; the more you eat, the emptier you feel, and it forces you to feed it once again. Jealousy is a pain that will not abate; it persists and pounds us until we are pushed to the point of no return. Jealousy is a terrible and harsh master.

Saul felt the awful talons of jealousy dig into his heart to prevent him from loving David and loving God's plan through David. We mentioned that Saul gave his daughter, Michal, to David as his wife (vv. 17-30). On the surface that seems like a great thing: David will formally be in the royal house! But appearances can be deceiving.

As Saul has previously given the appearance of godliness but denied its power (chs. 13 and 15), he now gives the appearance of affection but actually felt hatred toward the young David. Beneath the surface of Saul's life lay a horrific, noxious brew of jealousy and hatred. Notice what the text says about Michal's potential marriage to David: "I'll give her to him," Saul thought. "She'll be a trap for him, and the hand of the Philistines will be against him" (18:21). Wow! What a loving father! He attempts to kill David through marriage. We know that in-law relationships can be tough, but have you had your in-law actively plan for your murder even before you were married? That is rough!

In fact, it shows Saul's overwhelming and disturbing jealousy. When we see Saul's hatred toward David, it expresses itself in chapter 18 in three plans to murder David:

1. Saul throws a spear at David (vv. 10-11).
2. Saul attempts to give his elder daughter Merab to David so David will have to fight the Philistines and die as a result (v. 17).
3. Saul gives his daughter Michal to David so he would die (vv. 21,25).

David escaped the first plot. David escaped the second by not marrying Merab. The third murder plot deserves further mention. David rebuffed Saul's offer of Michal, saying he needed to give something in return for the marriage of Michal. This is typically known as a *mohar*, or "bride price." So Saul sets the price: 100 Philistine foreskins (v. 25). Now that is a costly marriage! Saul's intention was that David would fail at gaining the bride price, dying in the attempt. He essentially plotted a murder for David.

But, true to form, David went out and acquired 200 Philistine foreskins instead! This is terrible bloody business! It seems absolutely horrific. Although the text describes the event, it does not prescribe the event for you and for me. The action works and communicates in an honor-shame culture: David honored Saul above and beyond what Saul deserved. That is the point we are to take from David's actions.

Saul, however, is not done with his murderous ways. In chapter 19 Saul speaks to his family and servants and orders them to kill David. Fourth time's the charm? From that point onward, David is in Saul's house, but David is the target for Saul's plots on his life. Saul is jealous and out of control, a man who has lost his sanity and his grip on life.

The reason? He "realized that the LORD was with David and that his daughter Michal loved him, and he became even more afraid of David. As a result, Saul was David's enemy from then on" (1 Sam 18:28-29). Michal was committed to, and loved, the coming messiah of Israel. It is telling that the stories of Michal and Jonathan open and close 1 Samuel 18 and 20. They serve as a kind of frame that contrasts with Saul's hatred, loathing, and fear of David.

After the last attempt on his life, the young David fled from Saul's household to Ramah and stayed with Samuel. He recounted to Samuel all that Saul had done. While he was there, Jonathan vowed to protect him against his father's ravings. Jonathan had entered into a covenant with

David over and against his father (18:3-4), and now in 20:16-17 Jonathan renews that covenant with David based on the new wave of attacks from Saul. Jonathan will not betray David but will remain true to him. He swears loyalty to David, tellingly, and the Lord is his witness (20:12-15). Jonathan defied his father's plans to murder David and instead helps him because of his commitment to the anointed one of God.

Saul's own family rebels against his plans to kill David. This should tell us something important: Saul does not have the support of the Lord, his family, or his people. This manifests itself in a few ways:

1. The people sing and rejoice over David and love him (18:6-8,16,30).
2. Michal and Jonathan both commit to David in covenant— Michal through marriage (18:27-28) and Jonathan through a covenant of friendship and commitment (18:3; 20:16).
3. The Lord is committed to David but sends an "evil spirit" to Saul (18:10-14; 19:9).

That God sent an "evil spirit" to Saul deserves mention. Why does God do this? It is important, as we said in the introduction, to see what the narrative *shows* and *says* (see pp. 7–8). The first mention of the evil spirit coming upon Saul is in the context of this summary statement: "Saul was afraid of David, because the Lord was with David but had left Saul" (18:12). God has said in Samuel's prophetic announcement that the kingdom is ripped from Saul and given to David, a king after God's heart (13:14; 15:22-29). The text now shows this reality of God's rejection of Saul by means of the evil spirit He sends on Saul. Each of these instances reveals that God has left Saul and was "with" David. This reality leads to radical fear, jealousy, and hatred of God's anointed man after His own heart.

Killing Jealousy through the Gospel

We can learn lessons from Saul's jealous heart.

Jealousy Appears on the Horizon of Our Lives When We Are Not Content with What God Has Proclaimed Over Us

Saul's kingdom was over; David's kingdom was on the rise. Jonathan knew this and committed to David. So did Michal. They got in on what God was doing. This meant Jonathan would never be king. But instead of resenting David over God's anointing, Jonathan embraced God's plan.

He killed jealousy by committing to God's plan for Israel. Jonathan was more interested in the Lord's kingdom over and above his own kingdom! Saul was not. He was more interested in his plan and holding onto his power than embracing the Lord's plan and divine power. Whenever anyone chooses self over the Savior, bad things happen!

Jealousy Reveals Our Deepest Loves

Saul's greatest love was himself, not Yahweh, the God of Israel. If we are jealous, we put more weight on ourselves and our wants, needs, and desires than the weight of God's desires for us. For example, if a pastor reads this commentary, we must ask: If revival broke out in the place where you minister, would you rejoice? But what if God broke loose in another church, in another denomination, and exponential salvation/baptism/growth occurred in all the other churches but not your church. Would you be jealous? Would you resent the anointing of God and the salvation of the lost in other churches, or would you embrace God's work and rejoice in God's plan? You see, jealousy reveals our deepest loves. If we love self rather than God and His plan, we are in deep trouble.

Jealousy Is Closely Related to Fear

Notice that Saul is constantly "afraid" of David. The text mention's Saul's fear of David at numerous places (18:12,15,29). Jealousy and fear go hand in hand. Saul was afraid of David and what he meant: others loved David, David would be king, David would be great, and God anointed him. But this meant Saul was set in the background rather than the foreground, and he feared losing power. As a result, he was jealous and resentful of this young man.

Life does not have to be filled with fear and jealousy! What kills fear and jealousy in life? Nothing other than perfect love found in Jesus Christ, found in the gospel. At the Summit Church, we have committed to embrace these key realities of the gospel:

1. In Christ, there is nothing we can do to make God love us more; there is nothing that we have done to make God love us less.
2. Christ is all we need for everlasting joy.
3. As Christ has been to us, so we will be to others.
4. As we pray, we will measure Christ's compassion by the power of the cross and resurrection.

This is an adaptation of the "Gospel Prayer" put forth and taught by J. D. over the course of many years (Greear, *Gospel*, esp. 45–190). Only the power of the gospel kills fear and jealousy in life. We see that Jonathan knew the power of the gospel. Jonathan knew he was deeply loved by God and cared for, regardless of whether he was king. Jonathan knew the Lord was his everlasting joy. As God had been gracious to him and his family, he was gracious to David. Jonathan measured compassion by God's overwhelming kindness.

If we experience debilitating jealousy, then we must learn to embrace the gospel. You can be confident in who you are because in Christ you are freed to be fully yourself, not someone else. Jonathan knew he would not be king, but he still embraced who God had made him to be. The gospel frees us. We learn that our identity is not bound up in our profession or what others say about us. Our identity is found in what Christ has called us through His gospel: deeply loved, forgiven from sin by His blood on the cross, valued, and set on His purposes. Only the power of the gospel will kill jealousy in life.

So, if you are allowing the seeds of jealousy to sprout into a terrible jungle of sin, one way you can kill jealousy is to pray to Jesus His powerful gospel, and allow Jesus to remind you of His love, His identity, His purpose for you, and His plan. A good start would be to pray the gospel prayer mentioned above.

Reflect and Discuss

1. How does this passage help you understand God?
2. How does this passage of Scripture exalt Jesus?
3. What does God's sending the evil spirit to Saul signify?
4. Who are the characters that love and support David in this chapter?
5. Where do you experience your deepest experience of jealousy? Why do you feel jealous? Is it based out of fear, threat, or something else? Write down your thoughts and discuss them with someone you trust.
6. How does it make you feel when others get recognition and you do not? Do you feel unloved, unrecognized, and undervalued? Why or why not?
7. Are you content with what God has proclaimed over your life through the gospel: deeply loved in Jesus, forgiven, and valued? Why or why not? Write down your thoughts.
8. What part of the gospel prayer stands out to you the most and warms your heart the most? Why? Write down your thoughts.

9. Jealousy is a powerful and debilitating emotion that can stay with us a long time. What obstacles prevent you from rejecting jealousy? Write down your thoughts and discuss them with someone you love and trust.
10. Take a moment to thank Jesus for the grace He has given in the cross and resurrection. Celebrate the good news that we are deeply loved, forgiven, and valued by Christ.

Saul versus David

1 SAMUEL 21–23

Main Idea: The interactions between David and Saul reveal God's favor and commitment to David the messiah, and they reveal characteristics of the coming Messiah.

I. **Food for the Messiah and His Disciples**
II. **Unholy War**
III. **Blessing and Salvation from the Messiah**

Introduction

After Jonathan saves David from Saul's wrath, David goes to the town of Nob (a priestly city) and stays with Ahimelech, the priest. The interaction at Nob is in many ways beautiful because it shows God's blessing of His messiah, David, the one who had been anointed as the next king. But it also gives a context for the coming Messiah, Jesus. Contrasted with the divine blessing and favor of David, we see the horrendous actions of Saul.

Food for the Messiah and His Disciples

Nothing is more satisfying than a good loaf of bread. When I (Heath) lived in England, we fell in love with the freshly baked bread that was offered day in and day out at the markets and bakeries. When I walked to my office at the University of Gloucestershire, I keenly remember the smell of the fresh bread coming out of the shops. It is a really good memory.

Bread is, in the ancient world, the staple food. You cannot get by without it. The bread might not have looked like bread we have in Western countries, but nonetheless, bread was essential for the ancient Israelites. David wanted bread when he came to Nob, for he was hungry (1 Sam 21).

Ahimelech does not have any freshly baked bread available to give David but instead gives him the holy bread called the "bread of the Presence" from the table in the tabernacle. The bread Ahimelech gives David is described in Exodus 25:23-30 and Leviticus 24:5-9, and it rests on a holy table in the tabernacle. The bread was there not to feed Yahweh (He wasn't hungry!) but to signify something special.

Jewish tradition holds that the bread was baked in a U pattern so that there were two ends facing each other. The reason it was called the bread of the "Presence" is that the bread signified that at the tabernacle God's presence met with the people face-to-face. In Leviticus 24:6 we see that there are 12 loaves on the table, no doubt signifying the 12 tribes of Israel. But the passage in Leviticus also stipulates that only the priests are to eat the bread: "It belongs to Aaron and his sons, who are to eat it in a holy place, for it is the holiest portion for him from the fire offerings to the LORD; this is a permanent rule" (Lev 24:9).

So how is holy bread that has been reserved only for priests an appropriate meal for David? Technically it is not. It is an inappropriate meal. But in the context of 1 Samuel, this story reinforces the divine favor, anointing, and blessing of David. David experiences provision and fullness at Nob. God is committed to His messiah. And those who bless David will receive ultimate provision from God (though, as we will see, those who bless David will not receive immediate provision).

A lesson about generosity. A word no doubt needs to be said about showing kindness and giving to those in need. Although technically inappropriate, Ahimelech's generosity toward David and his compatriots broke the letter of the law (Lev 24:9) but captured the spirit of the law. What is the spirit of the law? It is to love the Lord your God with all that you are (Deut 6:5) and love your neighbor as yourself (Lev 19:18). Giving to a hungry person in need of food is worth breaking the letter of the law if you capture its spirit. Or as Leon Morris says, "Human need must not be subjected to barren legalism" (*The Gospel According to Luke*, 122). Ahimelech did right by giving David and his compatriots food to eat.

A warm heart of generosity and a love for those in need is an indicator that the gospel of Jesus Christ has captured us. A loveless and cold obedience to God does not reveal a warm heart to Jesus. We like the way the apostle John puts it:

> If anyone says, "I love God," yet hates his brother, he is a liar. For the person who does not love his brother he has seen cannot love the God he has not seen. And we have this command from Him: The one who loves God must also love his brother. (1 John 4:20-21)

A lesson about Jesus. But the passage about David's experience at Nob is more than just a lesson on generosity! We must understand that the passage sets a pattern for the coming Messiah, Jesus, as well. In Luke 6, Pharisees criticize Jesus and His disciples for eating grain in the field on the Sabbath day. Jesus rebukes the Pharisees, and His illustration is the story of David at Nob in 1 Samuel 21. He says to the Pharisees,

> *"Haven't you read what David and those who were with him did when he was hungry—how he entered the house of God, and took and ate the sacred bread, which is not lawful for any but the priests to eat? He even gave some to those who were with him." Then He told them, "The Son of Man is Lord of the Sabbath."* (Luke 6:3-5)

As David could eat holy bread because God had anointed him for a purpose, God anointed Jesus for a purpose as well, and He could eat grain in the field. Leon Morris captures the thought of Jesus' words: "It is the Son of David who is Lord. If David could override the law without blame, how much more could the much greater Son of David do so?" (*The Gospel According to Luke,* 123). David's encounter with the holy bread at Nob prepares us to see the greater Messiah, the Lord of the Sabbath, Jesus.

Why does this matter for you and for me? Because we can see that Jesus provides all that we need. He is the Lord of provision and the Lord of care. He gives food to the hungry and presence to the lonely. In Him we meet God face-to-face. Jesus is the bread of the Presence.

Unholy War

The narrative has been building the tension between Saul and David to contrast the place of the kings in God's plan. Saul rejected God and so God rejected Saul. But David committed himself to the Lord, and we can see that the Lord committed to David. The difference between Saul and David can be seen in terrible relief in chapter 22, where Saul retaliates against Ahimelech and the priests at Nob because of their kindness to David.

Saul is in Gibeah with a group of his followers and warriors, and he angrily stews over David's successes and the love and favor he receives. He laments his own son's fidelity to David (22:8). He thinks he is all alone and vulnerable. And, in fact, he is because he has stationed himself against the Lord's anointed, the Lord's plan, and the Lord's purposes. Essentially, Saul is looking for any intelligence that will give him David.

Up stands a man named Doeg. This man is an Edomite, from the region just south and east of the region of Judah. Edomites have a contentious relationship with the people of Israel. They betrayed Israel on the trek to the promised land. They would betray the nation of Judah when the Babylonians came through and conquered the people of God in 586 BC (see Obadiah). So they have a bad reputation in the Bible, and deservedly so. The fact that Doeg is an Edomite actually casts a negative light on him as a character. It is this man who informs Saul that David was in Nob with his men. He knows this because he was there (21:7). Saul immediately receives this intelligence and summons Ahimelech and the priests of Nob to Saul's place in Gibeah.

When Ahimelech and the priests arrive, Saul questions them about their loyalties. Fearlessly, Ahimelech commits himself to David and swears allegiance to David (22:14-15). Ahimelech makes a choice to follow God's ways and God's plan with the messiah though it may cost him much.

And it did. Saul immediately ordered Ahimelech and the priests to be put to death. None of Saul's servants would lift a finger against these priests, for who on earth would murder a priest? Saul would! When he saw that none of his army would kill the priests at his command, he ordered Doeg the Edomite to commit mass murder (22:18). The text records that Doeg killed 85 priests for Saul. Moreover, under Saul's command, Doeg destroyed the city of Nob, and he murdered everything that moved: "both men and women, children and infants, oxen, donkeys, and sheep" (22:19).

Saul ordered unholy war. This is an act of genocide from a horrific leader. In many ways he has positioned himself as the anti-messiah. Instead of providing life and blessing to his people, as God's messiah would do, he brings death and destruction. Saul's inside qualities came out that day. The entirety of Israel would know that Saul was a terror. This narrative reminds us that the Scriptures don't present the best world or the ideal world but rather the real world. Because of jealousy, fear, anger, and deep-seated sin, Saul committed murder. In this case there is no statement of an "evil spirit" from the Lord overtaking Saul. No. This is all him.

We may think we are above Saul, more moral than him, but in reality the text serves as a mirror for our false morality. The text of Scripture only presents one true hero: the Lord and His Messiah. Pretty soon we will understand that God's Messiah is not found in David but will come in the true David—Jesus.

Blessing and Salvation from the Messiah

In contrast to Saul, David is the messiah who provides blessing and safety. One priest escapes the slaughter at Nob—Abiathar. Where does he run? He runs to David the messiah, the only hope he has. David says to Abiathar, "Stay with me. Don't be afraid, for the one who wants to take my life wants to take your life. You will be safe with me" (22:23). David is a life giver while Saul is a life taker.

This verse reveals that blessing, protection, and salvation come from God's messiah, David. Those who place their hope in him and what God is going to do through him will find the salvation they need. Saul is the antimessiah, at cross purposes with God and God's true savior.

We must remember that there are plenty of false saviors in the world today. Saul was a broken savior. Following him led to death and destruction. Broken saviors promise the world but leave us empty and hollow. As we have served churches in North Carolina, Texas, Oklahoma, Asia, and the United Kingdom, we have seen that people tend to embrace the following broken saviors:

1. *Self:* Especially Western society is awash with selfishness. This seeps into the church with what Eugene Peterson describes as the "replacement trinity," my wants, my needs, and my desires (Peterson, *Eat This Book*, 31–33). My wants, needs, and desires are important but not nearly as important as being captured by the love of the God who created us. Knowing Him sets selfishness to the side so we can serve Him. Self is a broken savior.

2. *Money:* In the West, to be sure, but all around the world money is understood to be a savior. We go to college and get an education. That is good, but the motivation behind it is so that we can get money to take care of our lives. In fact, we have a terrible problem with treating money like a savior. It is broken. Money is a good *gift* from God, but it is *not* God. Our retirement accounts, bank accounts, and benefits packages do not save—only God can save. So when we measure our worth by the size of our bank accounts, we will be trusting in a broken savior.

3. *Power:* Power is like a liquor that slips down our throats and makes us drunk. Power and authority are granted by God at creation—He made humans to serve under His rule in a way that imitates His rule of justice and order. But humans have the strange tendency to twist power to their own ends rather

than exercise power with justice. Just look at Saul: as king he uses his royal power to horrifically execute an entire city. This is power gone wrong. And when power slips through our fingers (as it does with Saul), we go crazy! Why? Because we have made power a god. Power is a *gift* from God, but it is *not* God. Power only works if we have submitted ourselves to the Lord and His care.

4. *Sexuality:* God made human beings as inherently sexual. It is good for man and woman to unite in marriage and have sex. It is right. But sexuality has become a broken savior that we hold tightly. We have made sexuality a right, not a gift, and as a result our practice of human sexuality has run amok, away from God's good design. Sex is wonderful. But sex outside of God's design leaves us broken and tattered. And for those of us who have experienced the wounds an unrestrained sexuality can have on our lives, we have come to know that this broken savior leaves us empty and cold. Sexuality is a wonderful gift but a terrible god.

5. *Relationships:* God made humans for relationship. He made us so that we would relate to God and our neighbor. However, we can treat relationships as the thing that will make everything OK. The problem is that relationships can never fill the hole that is in our soul. We were made for relationships, yes, but relationships with others (romantic or otherwise) will *never* replace the primary relationship with the God who made us! Relationships, on their own and put in the place of God, will be broken saviors.

Of course there are other broken saviors in life. And readers of this volume will no doubt think of others we have missed! However, the point is to show that broken saviors are all too present with us. But these second-rate saviors are like Saul: they cannot, and will not, save us.

We must understand that the only way we will experience blessing and salvation is to run to the Messiah, Jesus. Abiathar ran to David when he was in trouble. His action is instructive for us. We must learn to run to Jesus, the true Savior. In Jesus, we have the salvation and protection that only a true Savior can provide. So the encouragement is from the text.

David's words to Abiathar could be Jesus' words to us: "Stay with me. Don't be afraid, for the one who wants to take my life wants to take your life. You will be safe with me" (22:23). But no one can take Jesus' life. He has already given it up in death on the cross and gotten it back through the power of the resurrection. And He who has defeated death will protect you and me in life and in death. Jesus is the true Savior because blessing and salvation come through Him.

Reflect and Discuss

1. How does this passage help you understand God?
2. How does this passage of Scripture exalt Jesus?
3. How is Jesus like the bread of the Presence?
4. How does David's action with the bread of the Presence relate to Jesus being Lord of the Sabbath?
5. Compare God's command against the Amalekites in 1 Samuel 15 and Saul's command against the priests at Nob in chapter 22. What are the similarities and differences? Write down your thoughts and discuss them with someone you trust.
6. How are Saul and David contrasted with one another in 1 Samuel 21–23? Write down your thoughts and discuss them with someone you trust.
7. In what ways does Saul represent the antimessiah? Write down your thoughts.
8. We have discussed in this chapter broken saviors. Of the ones we listed, which broken savior stood out to you? Why?
9. What broken savior was not listed but represents one you embrace? What obstacles prevent you from rejecting the broken saviors in our lives? Write your thoughts and discuss them with someone you trust.
10. Hear the words of David as if Jesus were speaking them to you: "Stay with me. Don't be afraid, for the one who wants to take my life wants to take your life. You will be safe with me" (22:23). What do these words do to your heart? Do they engender love and gratitude to Jesus? In prayer express to Jesus your thoughts.

Patience

1 SAMUEL 24

Main Idea: David's experience with Saul reveals how believers can exhibit the rare virtue of patience.

Introduction

The story of 1 and 2 Samuel follows Israel's search for a real king. While most contemporary audiences have little experience with literal kingship, our daily lives prove that we, like Israel, are searching for a king as well.

This notion strikes most modern people as far-fetched. "I'm not very political, and even if I were, I wouldn't go looking for a king to solve my political issues." But this misunderstands the true heart of kingship. Israel's search for a king and ours have in common a quest for someone or something to guarantee happiness and security. A "king" is what a person hangs on to at the core of his life. For Israel that was a literal royal figure. For us that may be a political party, but it is just as likely to be romance, success, a drug, or an ideology. Even those of us who are not particularly religious have something we look to for happiness and security. The story of David, as we have seen, points us to Jesus, the only King who can actually deliver on those demands.

And yet, as the apostle Paul reminds, stories like David's also show us how to trust and walk with God—or, unfortunately, how not to trust and walk with God.

> *Now these things became examples for us, so that we will not desire evil things as they did.* (1 Cor 10:6)

150

> *Now these things happened to them as examples, and they were*
> *written as a warning to us, on whom the ends of the ages have come.*
> (1 Cor 10:11)

The passage before us shows David as he deals with an issue that all of us have dealt with at some point: How do we respond when a situation is not going as we expected it *would* and as we think it *should?* What do you do when the path you are on takes you a direction you never thought it would go?

I (J. D.) have had this experience more times than I care to recount. I suspect you have as well. Perhaps your career has not reached the heights you thought it would. Perhaps you are single when—by this age—you were certain you would be married. Perhaps you are in ministry like me, but your ministry has just stalled out and failed to grow. Or maybe you just feel lost, unhappy, unfulfilled. You look to heaven and say, "God, remember me? What's going on?"

Everyone who knows me knows that I am notoriously terrible with directions. Give me five minutes in a new city and I will get lost in new and creative ways. So my GPS is an absolute necessity. What I love best about this device is the British lady who interrupts me every time I take a wrong turn (frequent). She is always so cordial and polite, simply piping up at the opportune time, "Recalculating." Without fail she tells me how to get back on the right path.

Most of us wish God would be that direct (and polite!) with us in our lives. We would love someone to evaluate where we are and where we are headed—and, if need be, to recalculate our trajectory for us. While we wait and wish for that to happen, an enormous temptation for us is to take matters into our own hands, to get ahead of God, to sacrifice our integrity in the name of expediency.

When we sense the tension between where we are and where we think we need to be, will we follow a path we know we should avoid? Or will we, like David, exhibit the rare virtue of patience?

When Life's Circumstances Aren't God's Will

When we meet David in 1 Samuel 24, his life is not going well. His life to this point has followed a series of hills and valleys. He is anointed to be king, a high point by any standard. But he is immediately sent back to the sheep pasture where he is apparently forgotten—from hill to valley. He then has his big moment on the national stage when he takes down

Goliath, marries the king's daughter, and gets a job on Capitol Hill. Big times for little David!

But David's job in Saul's court turns out to be a mixed bag when King Saul turns out to be an incredibly jealous egomaniac. Saul uses the state-controlled media to trash David's reputation, takes David's wife away from him and gives her to someone else, and begins throwing spears in David's direction, hoping to impale him. Definitely valley material.

Despite repeatedly failing in his attempts to murder David, Saul is unrelenting. So when he hears that David and his merry men are in the wilderness called En-gedi, he goes after David yet again (vv. 1-4). But Saul is in for another surprise.

Add this to the many reasons I am glad my story is not in the Bible: awkward bathroom stories. Into the cave walks Saul, naturally enough, to find a private place to do his private business. Little does he know that his bathroom stall is also David's secret hideout. The awkwardness for David's men, however, wears off quickly once they realize their opportunity. Saul could hardly be in a more vulnerable position. Thus David's friends see this as a God-ordained moment for him to take revenge: "David, coincidences like this do not just happen. If ever circumstances pointed to God's will, here it is. God promised this, and here is your chance. Take it!"

There is an important lesson for us here. It is tragically easy to confuse both our desires and our circumstances with the will of God. As an example, this kind of confused justification arises all the time in two key areas—romance and finances.

I cannot remember the number of times I have heard circumstances enlisted to justify a terrible romantic decision. Potential affairs always seem so reasonable and so perfectly timed: "It must be OK to leave my husband because the spark I have with this new guy at work is just too perfect. Pastor, this must be God's will." Or a single person will defend their new dating partner, someone they know is not where they need to be spiritually: "But they make me so happy, and they just happened to be at the same place I was on Friday. Isn't that something?" In the end the circumstances are usually just a thin veneer for a person's underlying desire. Because I want this, because this feels so enjoyable, then I will find a way to make it seem right.

Consider also how people make decisions about spending their money—or, more accurately, spending money they do not have. A flat-screen television happens to go on sale the same day a credit card application arrives in the mail. Well, then, God must be behind this! A couple gets approved for a mortgage loan that far exceeds their income. It feels right at the time, but just a few years on, they are in debt up to their eyeballs and cannot even entertain the idea of giving to the church. Materialism and consumerism are the clear culprits, but when the circumstances line up just well enough, we fool ourselves into thinking that God's providence must be at work.

We must come to grips with this quite plainly: neither our desires nor our circumstances are good guides to the will of God. This is not to say they can never be used by God, but both are so deceptive that we would do better to evaluate our desires and circumstances by a more fixed measure—the Word of God. Only when the Scriptures take primacy can we rightly interpret our desires and circumstances.

So David finds himself in a conflicting position. His desires and his circumstances are pushing him to murder Saul, yet simultaneously God's Spirit is prompting David to choose another way. Which way will he turn?

> Then David got up and secretly cut off the corner of Saul's robe.
> Afterward, David's conscience bothered him because he had cut off the corner of Saul's robe. He said to his men, "I swear before the LORD: I would never do such a thing to my lord, the LORD's anointed. I will never lift my hand against him, since he is the LORD's anointed." With these words David persuaded his men, and he did not let them rise up against Saul. Then Saul left the cave and went on his way. (24:4b-7)

We should not be too quick to skip over that little phrase "got up" in verse 4. In Hebrew that word (*wayaqam*, "and he arose") indicates that David made a clear decision. The author is not simply telling us that David had to stand up to get to Saul but that the moment had come for David to choose. So he steels himself and picks up his knife, preparing—so it seems to his comrades—to assassinate the king of Israel. Yet David realizes that even though the circumstances seemed unique, killing a defenseless man was still an act of murder. So David relents and instead swiftly takes a souvenir—a piece of Saul's clothes.

David's men are dumbfounded by the entire situation. Not only does David refrain from killing Saul, but he seems to feel profound guilt about simply touching his robe. In their minds self-preservation and revenge took precedence over honor for the king. But David responds by pointing out that this is God's appointed king. Even if Saul is murderously wrong, it is not for David to take matters into his own hands. Nor would he let his men "rise up" and kill Saul (v. 7).

Killing Saul would have solved just about every one of David's problems. And David's men were right in pointing out that God had promised him the throne. Saul deserves death for his crimes. Yet David stands firm because he sees that it is impossible to achieve the purpose of God by breaking the commands of God.

Some might worry that an attitude like this would lead to conservatism or quietism, implicitly condoning Saul's reckless behavior. And those in positions of power are notorious for using supposed divine appointment as justification for abuse. Who are *you* to challenge *me?* A king, so it seems, especially a king appointed by the one true God, can get away with just about anything.

But note David's next move. David's response to injustice in verses 8-15 is more complicated than choosing between violent revolution and quiet acceptance. He refuses to kill Saul for his assaults, but he certainly does not "grin and bear it." He protests loudly that Saul is acting unjustly, and he takes measures to protect himself. (Note that he waits until Saul has put some distance between them before David confronts him.) The little piece of cloth David recently acquired also acts as an insurance policy (or so he hopes) against future attacks. And the entire tenor of his speech is both a plea for the violence to end and an indictment against Saul's wrong actions. David is hardly lying down.

Yet David refuses to succumb to the contemporary "wisdom" that the ends justify the means. Doing wickedness, he points out, makes one wicked no matter how justified a person feels while doing it.

David's Choice (and Ours): Taking Wrong Action or Patiently Waiting

Few of us will be presented with a situation as remarkable as David's, at least in the specific details of being the object of repeated murder attempts. Yet the same choices lie before any believer when confronted with injustice or disappointment. When the path we follow takes a direction we do not expect, will we take matters into our own hands, or will we trust God enough to wait?

The wrongful action of taking matters into our own hands takes several forms. As in this story it may be sheer revenge, taking vengeance into our own hands. Someone wrongs us, and we act to settle the score.

So when a man's wife treats him poorly, he cheats on her with little regret. Or when an employee is belittled by her boss, she responds by ruining his reputation or undercutting his authority. The common feature here is not the *extent* of the vengeance but the *heart* behind it: "You have hurt me, so when given the opportunity, I will respond in kind." The practical problem with such a response—in addition to the theological problem—is that we consistently overestimate the extent of the wrong done against us. We simply cannot be trusted to mete out justice justly, as the endlessly escalating cycles of revenge throughout history demonstrate.

Taking matters into our own hands may take the more subtle form of a stolen pleasure. Because life has not turned out as we expected, we find escape in something illicit. We drown out our present disappointments with distractions, imagining that a short-term thrill will cover our dissatisfaction. But whether the stolen pleasure is overt and societally frowned on (like using hard drugs or visiting prostitutes), or the stolen pleasure is more covert and accepted (like escaping into endless hours of television or overeating or fantasizing about the perfect spouse we wish we had), the result is the same. We drink poison, thinking it will satisfy our thirst for water.

Perhaps the most common way we take matters into our own hands is through bald compromise. We feel we deserve more money than we have so we hedge on our taxes or fudge our time sheets. "Stealing from a faceless corporation isn't really stealing anyway, is it?" We feel we deserve romantic satisfaction so we lower our dating standards. "Being with the 'wrong' guy is better than being alone anyway, right?" We feel we deserve approval and respect for our work so we exaggerate our accomplishments and minimize our failures. "Sure, this may be a little deceptive, but it's not outright lying, so that's something, isn't it?" Behind it all is the urge to bend on what we know to be right, to sacrifice integrity on the altar of an immediate perceived happiness. The tragedy is that the happiness always fails to deliver, usually to our surprise, and in the meantime we have done immense damage to our soul.

So we can take wrong action and wrestle our situations into our own hands. The prospects always seem promising, but the results never satisfy. On the other hand, we can choose to trust God and wait.

Our American culture despises waiting, and I (J. D.) admit that I share in that cultural sentiment. The idea implies helplessness and insignificance. It may help, however, to consider two meanings of the word *wait*. The first is simple inaction; the second is attentive readiness. What God wants from us is the latter, not the former. David's "waiting" does not lead him to inaction but to a passionate and fervent action. He protects himself by running. He confronts Saul and passionately pleads his case for justice. But he refuses to shortcut God's promises for him by crossing a line into compromise and sin. He does everything he can and waits on God to act.

We can see the two types of waiting in most current restaurant settings. The staff at Waffle House and a five-star restaurant may both be called "waiters," but they think of their role quite differently. At Waffle House the friendly lady assigned to your table will retrieve some ketchup for you, but it is largely up to you to initiate that transaction. She waits until you ask and then fulfills the request. (It's not her fault, of course. The same woman assigned to your table is also responsible for cooking an omelet, cleaning the bathroom, and waiting on 17 other tables at the same time.)

At many five-star restaurants, however, a single waiter will be devoted to a single table. At the slightest hint of a need, the waiter magically shows up. Just imagine that you want some Splenda, and he appears before the request even crosses your lips. He waits on you with a single-minded (and somewhat intimidating) attentiveness, not reactively or passively.

When we wait on God, it should be more like the five-star waiter than anything else. Our attention is single-minded, and our posture is attentive. As the psalmist said,

> *Like a servant's eyes on his master's hand, like a servant girl's eyes on her mistress's hand, so our eyes are on the* Lord *our God until He shows us favor.* (Ps 123:2)

We wait not by sitting still but by pursuing God's purposes in God's ways with God's timing. It may seem like the real enemy before us is Saul, seeking to destroy us. But from God's perspective the inability to wait is much more pernicious.

The Resources for Waiting: David's Psalm from the Cave

Counseling patience is one thing; finding the resources to actually be patient in a tumultuous time is another. Fortunately, we have another passage that shows us precisely where David found that strength. The superscript to Psalm 57 gives the circumstances of writing: "For the choir director: 'Do Not Destroy.' A Davidic *Miktam.* When he fled before Saul into the cave."

> *Be gracious to me, God, be gracious to me,*
> *for I take refuge in You.*
> *I will seek refuge in the shadow of Your wings*
> *until danger passes.*
> *I call to God Most High,*
> *to God who fulfills His purpose for me.*
> *He reaches down from heaven and saves me,*
> *challenging the one who tramples me. Selah*
> *God sends His faithful love and truth.*
> *I am surrounded by lions;*
> *I lie down with those who devour men.*
> *Their teeth are spears and arrows;*
> *their tongues are sharp swords.*
> *God, be exalted above the heavens;*
> *let Your glory be over the whole earth. . . .*
> *My heart is confident, God, my heart is confident.*
> *I will sing; I will sing praises.* (Ps 57:1-5,7)

First Samuel gives us a glimpse into the discussion between David and his men in the cave, but it give us little about David's internal struggle. But here in Psalm 57, we get a glimpse into David's heart. This psalm was written during the same span of time as our story here. For all we know, David may have been tidying up the last stanza just as Saul wandered in.

This psalm gives us four words that characterize the patient heart.

Sovereignty

In verse 2, David points out that God "fulfills His purpose for me." Contrary to his counselors' advice, it is not necessary to break God's commands to get where God wants David to go. David may not be sure precisely how God will do this, but he knows God's plan is certain. The sovereignty of God over a confusing situation gives David the strength to wait on Him.

Faithful Love

This phrase in verse 3 is an absolutely critical partner to sovereignty. Were David to see only the sovereignty of God, it is doubtful he would have felt that as a comfort. Sovereignty without assurance of love feels like blind fate. It leads to the resigned attitude that is common, for instance, among Muslims, who are convinced of God's sovereignty but not of His good purposes for their lives. When invoking the will of God (*"Inshah Allah"*), it always comes with a shrug. "If this is God's will," they are saying, "then we just have to deal with it." They do not doubt that God is at work in all things, but they lack the promise that God's work in all things includes their good.

The gospel gives us an assurance of steadfast love that nothing else can. Because of Jesus' sacrifice for us on the cross, we never have to wonder how God feels about us. When circumstances conspire to make us feel abandoned or condemned—whether that be a bankruptcy or a job loss or a divorce or a rabid king trying to kill us—we have only to look at the cross to see a God who took true abandonment and condemnation in our place. All that is left for us is goodness and mercy. We may not be given a reason for every bad turn in our lives, but if we are assured that God has a steadfast loving purpose for us, we can endure misfortune with not only patience but hope.

Selflessness

This is the surprising shift when, in verse 5, David says, "God, be exalted above the heavens; let Your glory be over the whole earth." Saul is hot on David's heels, so much so that David feels like lions are hunting him, and yet he lifts his eyes to pray for something bigger than mere relief—God's exaltation. Whether his prayer leads to rescue or more pain, David is less concerned with himself than with his God.

This is one of the primary differences between David and Saul. Saul thinks this entire ordeal is about his name, his reputation, his kingdom. So when David seemingly infringes on that, he cannot see anything else and lashes out. But David knows this is not about him or his kingdom. He is willing for his reputation to suffer and his body to ache because he sees something beyond himself.

Satisfaction

In verse 7, David uses the word "confident" to refer to his own faithfulness, not God's. The two are intricately connected: David can be faithful toward God because he knows God is faithful toward him. The backbone of obedience is confidence in the faithful love of God. Assurance of that love leads to satisfaction; a lack of assurance leads to revenge, stolen pleasures, and compromise.

As Martin Luther once said, all sin begins with unbelief. Believe in God's goodness, and you can rest content in the midst of a seeming lack of goodness. Disbelieve in that goodness, and you will invariably take steps outside of God's will to obtain it. The tragedy is that all our efforts to obtain the good life apart from God are endlessly futile and pathetic. We are like a man being taken to a steak dinner who, distrustful of the coming feast, is busily stuffing his pockets with cheap beef jerky.

Conclusion

When we are tempted to take matters into our own hands, tempted to sin because of our impatience, we are failing in one of those four areas. We do not believe God is really sovereign; we are not convinced of His steadfast love; we still, like Saul, think our lives are all about ourselves; or we are not truly satisfied with God's approval of us.

When we feel the tug to circumvent God's way, we should ask ourselves, "Why is God's love and approval not enough for me?" All our impatience ultimately goes back to a failure to believe the gospel. We either do not understand how God feels about us, or we fail to value His approval highly enough. And this unbelief often has us teetering on the precipice of disaster, entertaining a quick fix to a situation we dislike. Resist the urge to take that step. Trust in the all-satisfying God and wait on His goodness.

The resources for waiting are found in the steadfast love of Christ. David refrains from killing Saul when Saul deserves it, but Christ refrained from pouring condemnation on us when we deserved it. David rejects a sinful shortcut to the throne, but Christ rejected Satan's shortcut to the throne of the world in the temptation. Christ could have taken the rule of the world by sidestepping the cross but only at the cost of our lives. He chose to go the long route to the throne so that by His death we might live.

Reflect and Discuss

1. How does this passage help you understand God?
2. How does this passage of Scripture exalt Jesus?
3. Are you a patient person? Why or why not?

4. What needs to change in your heart for you to develop the virtue of patience? Confess that to the Lord right now.
5. Have you ever experienced a time when life did not go as you thought it should go? How did you handle it?
6. Why specifically did you handle that situation in that way? Write down your thoughts.
7. In what ways is God speaking to you about patience in life when life does not go the way you think it should go?
8. Identify the main stressors that generate in you a heart of impatience. Write them down. Can you hand those over to the Lord? He is big enough to handle them!
9. Is your satisfaction in God alone? Why or why not?
10. When in life have you taken the wrong action because of impatience? How can you learn from that experience?

Lessons on Trust

1 SAMUEL 25–26

Main Idea: Nabal's insults, David's response, and Abigail's intervention teach lessons on what it means to trust the Lord.

I. Violence for God? Or Who Is David's Defender?
II. Learning to Trust
III. Who Is Our Defender?

Introduction

During their tense encounter in the cave (1 Sam 24), David and Saul showed themselves to be polar opposites: Saul was concerned with his reputation, his name, and *his* kingdom, while David was able to rest in the sovereignty and steadfast love of his God. David stands as a model for all of us of godly patience in the midst of strong temptation. God's approval is all we need for lasting satisfaction, and David seems to be a man who understands that to his core.

When the reader arrives at 1 Samuel 25, we find David confronting another adversary; this time it is Nabal (whose name means "fool").

Violence for God? Or Who Is David's Defender?

Theologian and commentator David Firth reveals how this passage is a pivot for what goes on between 1 Samuel 24 and 26. David spares Saul's life in chapters 24 and 26. In the first instance David is ready to do violence against Saul, shaming him by cutting off a section of his robe (24:5). In the second instance David has the chance to kill Saul, but David's comments are telling:

> *"Don't destroy him, for who can lift a hand against the LORD's anointed and be blameless?" David added, "As the LORD lives, the LORD will certainly strike him down: either his day will come and he will die, or he will go into battle and perish."* (26:9-10)

By 1 Samuel 26, David knows without a doubt that God is his defender and source of strength. Yahweh will protect David and mete out justice against Saul. Violence is not the answer to his troubles with Saul. Rather, he should trust in God's providential care.

Where did David learn this lesson? He learned it when he was confronted with another Saul, a wealthy and powerful adversary. This other Saul's name was Nabal. The text gives us hints that Nabal is an idiot, greedy, and mean. His wife, Abigail, taught David to trust God above all else because the Lord sets right the wrongs—you can trust in His providential care. Listen how the Scriptures contrast the man and his wife: "The woman was intelligent and beautiful, but the man, a Calebite, was harsh and evil in his dealings" (25:3). Nabal was a fool and stood in the place of Saul as an adversary to David (although clearly the two should not be conflated—Nabal is not Saul, after all!).

Learning to Trust

Chapter 25 shows us a development in David's faithfulness with God, a moment when he learns that he can ultimately trust in the Lord rather than in his own strength. The story develops in verses 4-9.

David and Nabal were, in a general sense, business partners. David had been in Nabal's vicinity for some time and had protected Nabal's shepherds several times over the course of the year. Shepherding can be a risky venture, so it is always helpful to have a roaming band of soldiers like David's to keep bandits at bay. Apparently, David held up his end of this partnership well: Nabal's men even describe him as having been like "a wall around us, both day and night" (v. 16). David's presence had been nothing but positive for Nabal.

It was customary in those times for shepherds to dole out gifts during the time of sheep shearing to all those people who had assisted them throughout the year. So David sends a request for a small gift along these lines. It should be a simple and courteous transaction. But Nabal is, as verse 3 bluntly says it, "harsh and evil in his dealings." So an average token of appreciation becomes for him a major problem.

Not only does Nabal deny David's request, which is rude enough, but in verses 10-12 he sends back a stinging insult: "David? David who? Never heard of him. Sounds like some runaway slave trying to scam me out of my hard-earned cash." This was not merely cautious stinginess, either. (After all, as a rich man, Nabal probably entertained a lot of suspect requests. One might excuse a bit of suspicion from his end.)

But everyone knew about David—Nabal included. So this was just an unwarranted slap in the face. Nabal shames David. And as we have seen, in an honor-shame culture, such a shaming cannot go unnoticed. A modern equivalent might be waiting on a table at a restaurant and serving someone who not only refused to tip you but also said that you look like the sort of person who flunked out of school and would only waste the money on booze anyway.

Naturally, David finds Nabal's affront offensive. So in verse 13 he musters his men: "All of you, put on your swords!" Nobody crosses David and gets away with it! David takes 400 warriors and begins a furious march toward Nabal, determined to wipe out every single man he can find (v. 22).

A military showdown seems imminent until Nabal's wife steps in. Unlike Nabal, who is harsh and badly behaved, his wife Abigail is "intelligent and beautiful" (v. 3). When word gets to her that David is on the move, she puts together an enormous gift basket and hurries out to meet David, hoping to prevent David from his intended rampage. She gets to David just in time.

Nabal was probably not a popular name for Hebrew children because, as Abigail points out (v. 25), his name means "fool," and her husband is true to his name! No one intentionally names their kid "fool."

Abigail's argument here can be summed up rather simply: "David, you can trust your God to fight your battles for you. Taking matters into your own hands will only leave you with regret." Abigail truly proves herself to be intelligent, not only arguing with David logically but evoking a specific memory of David's as well. It is no accident that she reaches for the metaphor of the "sling" to describe God's avenging David's enemies in verse 29. With one little sling David had shown to the entire nation of Israel that the battle belongs to God. And as easily as David took down Goliath, Abigail reasons, would not God surely do what is just with regard to Nabal the fool?

Fortunately for Nabal's men the argument strikes home. David recognizes the folly of violence and stops himself from vengeance, sparing the lives of many. Unsurprisingly, however, the story ends much less favorably for Nabal. Abigail's words prove to be prophetic, and within two weeks Nabal is dead. God swiftly slung David's enemy out without David's lifting a finger.

When David hears of Nabal's death, his comments reveal he has learned to trust. He says,

> *"Praise the LORD who championed my cause against Nabal's insults*
> *and restrained His servant from doing evil. The LORD brought Nabal's*
> *evil deeds back on his own head."* (v. 39)

Whenever someone lifts a finger to strike down Saul or his family from this point on, David reacts with terrible resolve: only God is his defender (see 1 Sam 26:10-11; 2 Sam 1:14-15; 4:12). He also marries Abigail, who is the instrument God used to teach David to trust the Lord alone.

Who Is Our Defender?

What we must not miss in this account is David's need for correction and his need to learn God's ways. David may be able to stand as the paragon of nonviolent resistance in chapter 24, but by chapter 25 he is a vigilante soldier, ready to mete out justice on his own terms, in his own time. The man who talks his men out of performing an unjust mob hit in chapter 24 needs someone else to give him the same speech in chapter 25.

Everyone has lapses of faithfulness, which is why we need community. David is a famous figure, a household name, a known hero. In contrast Abigail is a relative nobody. This is her cameo in Scripture, and every mention of her from this point on simply mentions that she is Nabal's widow and David's (new) wife. Yet David needs Abigail. Without her he is no better than Saul or Nabal.

Too often when seeking the will of God in our lives, we ignore two majors gifts God has given us—the Word of God and the wise counsel of other believers. Countless sins and major episodes of foolishness have been preceded by Christian believers "praying about a situation" and then acting on their feelings. But God has given the church as the instrument God uses to answer prayers. We should pray for guidance—frequently and earnestly—but we must recognize our prayers find God's response through the wise words and actions of Christian brothers and sisters.

Believers who make terrible decisions almost always do so in isolation from good counsel. Like David, even the strongest of us is liable to forget what we know to be true and lunge forward toward our own solutions. We come to a crossroads in our marriage, our job, or our finances, and instead of seeking the Lord in prayer, seeking the Lord in Scripture, and seeking counsel from those who know the Word of God, we plow ahead all by ourselves. It should come as no surprise that cutting ourselves off from the body of Christ only leads to ruin and destruction.

In much of our study of 1 Samuel, we have needed to remind ourselves that we are not David, because David displays a faithfulness that reminds us of Christ. But here we should see ourselves in David, a man forgetful of God's grace and in need of a community to correct him. May God be merciful to us and give us all ears to hear the Abigails in our lives.

So, whom do we trust as our defender? Is it the Lord or is it us? Let us remind ourselves of the words of the following (Davidic!) psalm as we encounter other Sauls in our lives—adversaries, enemies, and those who wish to shame us:

> *For the choir director. Of the servant of the LORD, David, who spoke the words of this song to the LORD on the day the LORD rescued him from the hand of all his enemies and from the hand of Saul. He said:*

> *I love You, LORD, my strength.*
> *The LORD is my rock,*
> *my fortress, and my deliverer,*
> *my God, my mountain where I seek refuge,*
> *my shield and the horn of my salvation,*
> *my stronghold.*
> *I called to the LORD, who is worthy of praise,*
> *and I was saved from my enemies.* (Ps 18:1-3)

Reflect and Discuss

1. How does this passage help you understand God?
2. How does this passage of Scripture exalt Jesus?
3. Do you tend to take actions to defend yourself by your own hands, or do you generally trust in God? Explain your answer.
4. Do you believe in the deepest part of your being that the Lord is your defender? Why or why not?
5. What does it feel like when people shame you (or have shamed you in the past)? Be specific and write down your thoughts.
6. Do you believe God will be your "shield"? What would have to change in your life for you to really believe it? Write down your thoughts.

7. Where do you turn to first when you need counsel about dealing with difficulties? How does the teaching about learning and loving Christian community impact you?

8. How do you or your church need to change to embrace the teaching on the centrality of Christian community in answering prayer? Be specific and write down your thoughts.

9. Reread 1 Samuel 25. Is Nabal justified in shaming David? Why or why not?

10. Reread Psalm 18:1-3. What does it do for your heart to know that God stands to defend us? What does it do for your heart to know that God has already defended us in Jesus? "Therefore, no condemnation now exists for those in Christ Jesus" (Rom 8:1).

The Tragedy of Dying without God

1 SAMUEL 27–2 SAMUEL 1

Main Idea: Saul's death marks the failure of the Saulide dynasty and the horror of dying without the Lord. His death contrasts with the rise of the Davidic house.

I. **The Beginning of the End**
II. **The End Foretold**
III. **The End of Saul and His House**
IV. **Lessons from Saul, a Religious (and Lost) Man**
    A. Saul kept up religious practices without ever knowing God.
    B. Saul never learned how to repent.
    C. Saul died the sinner's death.

Introduction

Is it possible to be extremely active in God's church and not really know God at all? For some people this kind of question makes no sense at all. It may not even seem worth asking. How could a person not know God if they are active in God's church? But consider: Is it possible to be married to someone for 40 years and not really love them? Absolutely. Or does walking through a maternity ward automatically make you pregnant? Of course not. Simply being in the vicinity when God is at work is no guarantee of intimacy with Him.

In fact, as the Bible demonstrates repeatedly, it is often the religiously active who find it most difficult to know the true God. Some of the most self-deceived people in our society are those who are active in our churches. The passage we have in front of us gives us graphic detail of that self-deception and the tragic end of such a life.

The text from 1 Samuel 27–2 Samuel 1 is called the "Accession Narrative" because it shows the downfall of Saul but the accession of David to the throne (Firth, *1 & 2 Samuel*, 283). Strange things go on in this narrative. David moves down with the Philistines and lives with them. He becomes a servant of the Philistine king, Achish, who ruled over the city of Gath. Achish gave the city of Ziklag to David as a gift. And David regularly went on raids to the Judean cities. He killed a bunch of people and basically lived as a mercenary under the protection of Achish. Even Achish thinks David is sketchy and says of him, "Since he has made himself detestable to his people Israel, he will be my servant forever" (1 Sam 27:12).

To be honest, it is a strange opening to the accession of David to the throne. The question begins to fester in the mind of the reader: "Is this really the king that God wants? I don't know what to do with David's actions!" And we aren't meant to know what to do with David's life at this stage. Does God sanction David's raids and killing? The answer is no. He allows it but does not sanction it. After all, as Firth recognizes, the name of God and the speech of God are not mentioned at all in 1 Samuel 27—an interesting and significant omission (*1 & 2 Samuel*, 287). David never consults with God or the community. This action is all David. As a result, although the entire narrative from 1 Samuel 27–2 Samuel 1 solidifies Saul's demise and David's rise, the text sets a big question mark over David's reign. The remainder of the Accession Narrative reveals that only God can sort it all out. Furthermore, although we know Saul will not be the true king, we get hints that David will not be the true king, either! Only Jesus will serve as the King God has chosen to bring blessing to all.

But for our purposes, we want to focus on Saul. We have learned much from Saul—generally negative things! Saul's story is for our instruction, as will be David's story. These chapters reveal the end of Saul and why the end has come.

The Beginning of the End

Saul had started well. As 1 Samuel 28:3-6 notes, he had eradicated the nation of "mediums and the necromancers" (ESV), those religious experts who practiced magic and communicated with the dead. Contemporary audiences may be prone to view such practices with skepticism, especially considering our own context of sham fortune-tellers and vague newspaper horoscopes. But for those outside of the West, the presence and danger of witchcraft remains immediately relevant. Behind such practices lies a dark reality, a demonic power that we rarely recognize but that Scripture addresses at length. Saul was to be commended for successfully opposing such a demonic force.

Yet when faced with the threat of the Philistine army, Saul's good start begins to unravel. We see in verse 5 a repetitive theme of Saul's life—fear. Fear seems to motivate everything in Saul's life from his military decisions (or indecision) to his raving rampages against the young David. Fear transformed a man who stood head and shoulders above everyone in Israel into a cowering shell, a weakling incapable of following God when his own skin was at stake.

Saul is hardly alone. Fear is one of the defining characteristics of anyone living apart from God, and it seems particularly rampant among religious people. We are afraid of our future, of financial ruin, of possible health problems, of others' opinions of us, of our impending death. When life is going poorly, we fear that it will always be that way. When it is going well, we fear a turn for the worse. But the presence of persistent fear is a sign, as John says, that the love of God is far from us (cf. 1 John 4:18).

In addition to the imposing military force bearing down on him, Saul encounters another obstacle that heightens his fear—the silence of God (v. 6). Saul was actively seeking God for some guidance on how to approach his foes. The prophets, however, were silent. His dreams ran dry. Even the Urim, the Old Testament equivalent of a divine roll of the dice, was coming up inconclusive. God was supernaturally withholding an answer from Saul. But Saul simply would not wait.

It is difficult to imagine a more inappropriate course of action than the one Saul pursues in 1 Samuel 28:7-10. Met with silence from God, Saul decides to break a (good) law that he himself had instituted. Apparently his zealous opposition to the demonic was not terribly deep-seated: pragmatism drove out any remnant of integrity.

In just a few verses, the actors in this scene will find themselves overcome with horror. But as readers, we should not need to see what comes of this séance to have that response. The medium rightly has a sense that something is off about this encounter. So to put her at ease, Saul assures her—invoking God's name twice—that God's judgment is nothing to worry about (v. 10). Can you imagine the impudence? One wonders where exactly Saul thinks he is garnering such authority. Most likely he is not even thinking about that himself: his fear, and not his reason, is at the helm, driving him blindly onward.

When conducting a Satanic ritual, there is never a particularly good candidate to raise from the dead. But Saul's decision to conjure up Samuel qualifies as a decidedly dangerous move (v. 11). Samuel had never shrunk from declaring the harsh judgments of God to Saul, so there is no reason to think he would bring sugarcoated news from beyond the grave. Still, Saul is a religious man, and Samuel was the religious leader he knew and trusted. So when he found himself in a pinch, he fell back on his religion, despite the utter foolishness and sheer danger of it. To the very last, as we see with his homage toward Samuel, Saul is meticulous with his religious details.

Samuel dutifully appears at the woman's summons, apparently to the woman's surprise (v. 12). (She may not, it seems, have been accustomed to her rituals actually working.) Regardless of her expectations, the clairvoyant is now seeing clearly. As she stands face-to-face with Saul and Samuel, she rightly recognizes that she has gotten herself into an enormous mess. On one hand she has Saul, the man who made her profession punishable by death. On the other hand she has Samuel, a man known to hack the enemies of God into pieces before everyone's eyes. The situation looks bleak, with no sign of hope on the horizon.

The End Foretold

Fortunately for the medium, Samuel refrains from immediately punishing her and Saul. Maybe as a ghost he literally had no way of touching them. Maybe he was a little groggy from having just woken up. Who knows? In any case he hardly seems pleased by the arrangement Saul and the medium have cooked up, as he makes immediately plain (v. 15).

"Let me get this straight," Samuel fires at Saul. "God has turned from you and become your enemy. But rather than reconciling with Him, you're looking for favors from me?" Then Samuel gives Saul a promise no one ever wants to hear from a ghost: "I'll be seeing you and your kids real soon" (v. 19). I doubt this is how Saul envisioned this scenario playing out.

The key to Saul's imminent collapse lies in the heart of Samuel's speech. The answer to Saul's problem was not to be found in a magical ceremony but in the much more obvious (and much more difficult) path of repentance. As Samuel reminds him, Saul never really owns up to his disobedience (v. 18). Throughout his life Saul shows sorrow when his disobedience leads to disastrous results; but instead of letting that lead him to true repentance, he glosses over any accusation of wrong and refuses to confess. He wants the blessing of God, but he plugs up his ears any time he hears the correcting voice of God.

What Samuel says to Saul he says to us all: A "repentance" that would not change you in life will never save you when death threatens, either.

Saul is seeking God here because his life is in crisis. We all do that. But crisis is not always the best time to seek God because crisis moments push us to be desperate, gullible, and deceitful. We will do or say any-thing to get ourselves out of a jam. As proof, look at the many prom-ises people make to God during times of crisis that they never fulfill once the crisis passes. They may "repent" but only until the catastrophe dissipates.

Is it wrong to seek God during a crisis? Absolutely not! God often uses those moments to shake us up and open our eyes to our true need. Many people trace their first steps with Christ to a major crisis in their lives. The danger, however, is that we are prone to see God as a vehicle to avoid pain, suffering, or hell. In that case we do not want God on His terms; we want whatever He can give us. But God will not be our spiri-tual pimp. If our only motivation in seeking God is avoiding hell after we die, we still do not understand repentance. We are still Saul.

Before looking at Saul's actual demise, one last point here bears mentioning. Several chapters back, when Saul refused to destroy Amalek as God had commanded, Samuel had made the strange state-ment, "Rebellion is as the sin of divination" (1 Sam 15:23 ESV). At the time that probably seemed like an odd comparison for Saul. All Saul had done was keep a little of the spoils of war for himself. Was that really worth comparing to witchcraft and sorcery? Yet here Samuel stands before Saul again, and the comparison has proven literal. Samuel's warning was not just a poetic image or a hyperbole. Saul's small compromises have grown into full-orbed dependence on the demonic.

We tend to resist this lesson because we cherish our little areas of compromise, but rebellion always works this way. We may never pray to Satan or visit a witch, but if we compromise in the small areas, we are set-ting in motion a pattern that will inevitably lead toward more compro-mise. Every act of rebellion separates us from the security of knowing we are in God's will, so we seek another source of security to fill that void. In the absence of God, an idol emerges.

This is true for all of us, whether we identify as religious or not. Something will be ultimate in our lives, acting as the source of our hap-piness, fulfillment, and security. Every step we take away from God's filling those roles is one we take toward another source of worship. What Saul shows us is that every form of idolatry, whether religious or irreligious, pushes us toward the original author of self-worship, Satan. Either God is our God—with no conditions or qualifications—or we are idolaters on the path of Satan. There simply is no middle ground.

The End of Saul and His House

Just as Samuel predicted, Saul meets his end, sees his sons die before his own eyes, and loses nearly everything that had belonged to Israel in battle to the Philistines (1 Sam 31:1-10). The rout was so total that even the cities Israel had previously occupied are abandoned. And the last image we have of Saul is his headless corpse shamefully lifted and fastened to a wall.

This is the dismal note on which the entire book of 1 Samuel ends. Israel's earnest desire for a king has led them to a tragic dead end. As Alfred Edersheim vividly summarizes this scene,

> And now it was night; and the headless bodies of Saul and his sons, deserted by all, swung in the wind on the walls of Beth-shan, amid the hoarse music of vultures and jackals. (Swindoll, *David*, 204)

Saul had such promise. Israel looked to him to give them triumph over their enemies, to guide them with courage and wisdom. Yet in the face of the Philistines, he loses ground instead of gaining it. In times of trouble, Saul shows himself to be a coward. His colossal potential dwindles into a life of utter disappointment. It is impossible to imagine a more devastating end to a person's life.

To add to the insult and shame of Saul's demise, the temple of Ashtaroth lies in the same region as the place where Saul was crowned. Within eyeshot of Saul's dangling body, Samuel had proclaimed over him, "You shall reign over the people of the LORD and you will save them from the hand of their surrounding enemies" (1 Sam 10:1 ESV). In place of those glorious promises hangs a lifeless carcass—childless, defeated, forsaken by God.

Lessons from Saul, a Religious (and Lost) Man

Saul's problem was not the Philistines. Saul's problem was not Goliath. Saul's problem was Saul. God could have conquered all his enemies— He had promised it—but Saul refused to trust God. At every turn he trusted in himself. How can we learn from a tragedy like his? How can we keep ourselves from ending our lives in the same disgrace? Saul's death points up three truths about his life and death, truths that serve as warnings for us.

Saul Kept Up Religious Practices without Ever Knowing God

Saul accomplished a lot during his life. He fought battles against the Philistines, as God had commanded him. He eliminated the witches and sorcerers from the land. He even prayed to God—and earnestly!—when he was in trouble. He was, to modernize the imagery, a churchgoing man who volunteered on the weekend and went on mission trips.

Yet despite his religious activism, Saul was lacking the two essential elements to actually knowing God. First, Saul lacked *trust in God.* We see this every time he is given an opportunity to obey but follows his own path instead of God's. Never fully convinced that God's ways were trustworthy, he could never yield his life to Him. As 1 Chronicles notes, Saul "did not inquire of the Lord" (10:14). In all his prayers, consultations with prophets, and use of the Urim, Saul was after a solution, not after the Lord. He wanted to use God to make his life work. Many of us follow the same pattern.

Saul's lack of trust stemmed from the second critical element that was missing: *satisfaction in God.* God was never really enough for Saul. So when God told him he should refrain from enriching himself off the Amalekites, Saul effectively answered by saying, "Being God's king is not enough. I also need to be rich. I need a few monuments." When David arose as the next king of Israel, Saul effectively answered, "Being God's anointed now is not enough. I need to ensure that I never have to share the praise I am due."

Trust in God and satisfaction in God—these two elements are indispensible if we are going to know God truly. Saul teaches us that those who do not grasp those two elements do not know God, regardless of their religious fervor.

All of our spiritual problems can be traced back to a lack of trust or a lack of satisfaction in God. Either we do not know God's gracious love for us, or we do not grasp the value of that love. When Jesus sends people away from Him on the last day, His rebuke will not be, "You didn't perform enough religious activities." His rebuke will be, "I never knew you" (Matt 7:21-23). To know Christ is to know how He feels about us and to rest in His work on our behalf.

Saul Never Learned How to Repent

Saul may have looked like a repentant man: he said he was sorry, performed religious rites to absolve himself from past mistakes, and even wept bitterly over his sins. Yet at the end of his life, Samuel points the finger at him and says, "You never repented."

Saul may have fooled a lot of people around him that he had repented. Tragically he may have even fooled himself since he repeatedly expressed surprise at God's growing distance from him. Saul was just going through the motions of repentance—confession, prayer, religious activity—but he had never dealt with the root issues of idolatry. He never trusted God enough to fully surrender to Him, nor did he value God enough to be satisfied in Him. Repentance is full trust in God and complete satisfaction with God that leads to unconditional surrender to God.

Saul's failure to repent raises the question for us: Do we know how to repent? We might feel terrible. We might vow to change. And yet we may, like Saul, be missing the heart of true repentance. Thankfully, we have the capacity to discern true repentance from the charade. False repentance is always accompanied by one or more telltale signs.

First, false repentance often manifests in rationalization or blame shifting. We will admit that our actions are not upright. We crossed lines. We made mistakes. But we also point out that our wrongdoing was justified if viewed under the right light. I may have taken some money from the company, but I'm really hard up right now, so I needed it. I may have had that brief fling with the woman at work, but my wife isn't showing me the love I deserve. I may be refusing forgiveness toward a friend, but I've just been hurt so much before. The excuses are endless, but the heart behind them is the same: I was justified in what I did. And a rationalizing, self-justifying attitude leaves no room for repentance.

Second, false repentance manifests in unchanged behavior. Real repentance is not shown in an emotional catharsis (as nice as that may feel) but in a life that looks different. So, if our mouth confesses Jesus, does our life back up that claim? The most certain test to discern whether we have really repented is to look at our lives. If there is no change—not perfection but change—then there is no Jesus.

Third, false repentance produces the wrong kind of sorrow. As the apostle Paul says, "For godly grief produces a repentance not to be regretted and leading to salvation, but worldly grief produces death" (2 Cor 7:10). Worldly sorrow and godly sorrow both cry over sin, but only one leads to salvation. The difference between the two is the cause behind the sorrow. Godly sorrow grieves because it has hurt an eternally loving, kind, good God. But worldly sorrow reacts to consequences. It arises out of fear of getting caught, out of shame for what others might think, or out of self-pity. Until our repentance and confession are motivated by a desire to return to our God, the most elaborate display of emotion will be utterly fruitless.

Fourth, false repentance sometimes manifests in conditional obedience. We start to bargain with God, as if we could assuage Him with a clever deal. The folly in this should be self-evident. God is hardly impressed with our obedience to Him under the conditions we set ourselves. He is after an entirely different sort of obedience—that of a doting child. So long as we try to buy God off with promises of obedience, we are still miles away from true repentance.

Fifth and finally, false repentance manifests in partial obedience. This is a close cousin to conditional obedience. We begin to obey God passionately in one area, but we refuse to let Him exert His lordship over our entire lives. So we read our Bibles diligently and tell others about Jesus but won't give a cent to the church. Or we continually say no to the call of God to engage in missions. Or we nurse a secret pornography habit we think is "no big deal."

Repentance results in obedience—not conditional obedience and not partial obedience. Anything less than this is simply offensive. Think of it like this: imagine a husband who was having multiple affairs, a different woman every day of the week. As often happens, his wife finds out and confronts him. What if he were to respond, "Oh, I'm so sorry! What was I thinking? I'll quit sleeping with the girl on Tuesday . . . and the one on Friday. And you know what, to show you I'm serious, I'll even call it off with the one on Thursday." We can all anticipate what kind of response he might get.

A man cannot be "mostly faithful" to his wife. She is either his one-and-only or she is not. This is one of the key analogies God uses to describe our relationship to Him. He wants to wed Himself to us. Our response cannot be halfhearted approval. If Jesus is actually Lord, then that lordship is either total or it is a complete sham. As it is often said, Jesus is either Lord *of* all, or He is not Lord *at* all.

Saul Died the Sinner's Death

Saul died as all sinners do. He was hung up in shame on a wall, forsaken by God. The Philistines mocked God at Saul's death because it appeared as if they had conquered Yahweh's king. Here was Saul, stripped of his armor and displayed ignobly for the whole world to see. Without God death truly is a tragic end to a beleaguered life.

There is, however, a faint glimmer of hope in the dark cloud of Saul's demise. With the death of Saul comes the rise of another king, one who was being prepared for this role even as Saul was flailing in his downward spiral. Silently in the shadows God has been preparing a man named David, who would bring salvation to the nation in the wake of Israel's moment of immense shame.

David's ascension to the throne teaches us how a later king, God's ultimate King, would take the throne. Jesus, like David, would assume His throne only after the faithless ones had stirred up shame and rejected God. The part of Saul would be played by us, humans who refused to fully trust and delight in God. And like Saul we would be condemned to die the death of the sinner.

The twist in Jesus' kingship, however, is that He would go to the place of death in our place. He would die a shameful death, fastened to a tree, and put on display for all to see. The enemies of God would triumph at His death—not ours—as they stripped Him of His armor and mocked Him. "Was this not the King of the Jews? He could not even save Himself!" Yet through that shameful death, salvation came to us all. Just as salvation could only come to Israel through Saul's death, so eternal salvation could only come to humanity through Jesus' death. Jesus was killed like Saul so He could reign like David.

Contemporary minds struggle to accept this counterintuitive method of salvation. When modern Jews are asked why they do not believe Jesus was the Messiah, for instance, they will inevitably respond, "The primary promise for the Messiah was that He would end all wars and bring peace to the earth. That has not happened, so Jesus could not have been the Messiah." This is not just a stumbling block for Jews, either. Ask ardent skeptics what it would take to believe in Jesus, and many will say, as Bart Ehrman did during a recent debate, "If Jesus had brought peace on earth, I'd believe he was who he said he was."

What the rabbis and Dr. Ehrman fail to see is that our deepest problem in the world is never the Philistines. We do not only need "peace on earth" in regard to famines or poverty or nuclear weapons. The peace we need lies within the reach of each of us. We need a Savior who can remove the spirit of Saul that is lodged in the heart of every last one of us. Until God deals with the sin within us, no government, however savvy, resourceful, and beneficent, will bring peace to our broken world.

The cultured experts of our society desire a savior. But they desire a savior like Saul. God cannot build His kingdom and fill it with people like Saul, like us, who refuse to acknowledge God as our King. His rescue project is much more radical, creating new people altogether. So before Jesus can solve problems "out there," He has to solve the problems "in here." Before David can sit on the throne, Saul has to die.

Reflect and Discuss

1. How does this passage help you understand God?
2. How does this passage of Scripture exalt Jesus?
3. Does it make sense that someone can be in the vicinity of God but not experience intimacy in relationship with Him? Why or why not?
4. In what ways did Saul know or not know God? Where did he go wrong?
5. Does this story resonate with you? Are you guilty of associating with Jesus at church but not really knowing Him as your Savior and Lord?
6. Saul lived a life of fear. Do you live a life of fear like he did? Write down your thoughts.
7. If you resonate with the story of Saul's tragic end, would you like to commit once and for all to Jesus and allow Him to forgive you?
8. In what ways does the notion of "false repentance" ring true in your life? Do you see false repentance in the lives of those around you?
9. Take time to ask the Lord to grant a heart of true repentance.
10. Who in your life do you know like Saul, dying without really knowing the Lord? Take time to pray for their salvation and commit to share the good news of Jesus with them.

David as King: Conflict Leads to Gospel-Centered Worship

2 SAMUEL 2–6

Main Idea: In the midst of conflict and as he experiences divine favor, David moves the ark to Zion and reveals the substance of gospel-centered worship.

I. God's Favor in Conflict
II. The Punishment from an Offensive God
III. The Problem of God's Presence
IV. The Gospel According to the Ark
V. David's Response to the Gospel

Introduction

The more a person steeps himself in the stories of 1 and 2 Samuel, the more he may suspect that the author rather enjoyed the bizarre and risqué. Folks get hacked to pieces, ghosts come back from the dead, sexual exploits (and their graphic consequences) are described in disturbing detail. True to form, 2 Samuel 2–6 does not disappoint.

We have battle where hundreds die, betrayal and murder, political intrigue and assassination, and even a coronation. To top that off, the text records a story where David gets naked and dances before the Lord! Awkward. Cue the snickers from the middle-school crowd—and the middle schoolers at heart.

Second Samuel 6, however, gives contemporary readers a glimpse into the true nature of worship. While we may not strip down to our skivvies and dance our hearts out like David, we have much to learn from this shepherd king about the way the gospel informs proper worship.

Worship has always been a contentious aspect of church services, and contemporary theological arguments prove that this debate has hardly subsided. On one hand, many Christians from Reformed and Catholic traditions prefer worship that is predictable, time-honored, and orderly. They find overly expressive forms of worship uncomfortable, possibly even arrogant and showy. On the other hand, many Christians from the Pentecostal tradition find this type of worship stiff and lacking the

Spirit. We yell like madmen at basketball games, for crying out loud, so why should we come before God with less enthusiasm?

There is more to the debate, of course, than these two sides—which we've oversimplified to heighten the point. But it is sadly true that worship *style* tends to divide Christians more than unite us, while far too few of us consider the core of biblical worship—in other words, worship *substance*. Whether we are Presbyterian hymn singers or Pentecostal back-flippers, David has something to teach us. Before we get there, however, we need to understand how God maintains his favor for David in the midst of terrible conflict.

God's Favor in Conflict

After the death of Saul and Jonathan (1 Sam 31–2 Sam 1), David has a window to step into the authority God had already granted him. So God gives David the go-ahead to move to Hebron, and the men of Judah anoint David the king over Judah (2 Sam 2:4). David then begins to consolidate his authority and reign (vv. 5-7). It looks like things are going well until conflict comes.

Abner, who was the commander of Saul's army, takes Ish-bosheth and makes him king over Israel. Ish-bosheth was Saul's son, and he has a terrible name. His name literally means "Man of Shame."[9] He reigned over Israel, and David ruled over Judah. This is to provide a glimpse of the division that will take place in the book of Kings, where the northern kingdom of Israel is primarily wicked, but the southern kingdom of Judah maintains its faithfulness slightly longer than the north.

Ish-bosheth's kingdom and David's kingdom inevitably engage in conflict and civil war. The battle lines derive from those who are loyal to Saul and those who are loyal to David. We should know by now God's perspective on the matter: Saul's kingdom was doomed, so anyone who follows him will be brought to shame; but David's kingdom is favored and chosen by God to be the instrument through which God will bless the nations. As God's plans cannot be thwarted, we see the power of divine favor on David:

---

[9] According to 1 Chr 8:33 his name was originally Esh-baal, "Man of Baal," but that was even worse, so the author of Samuel refused to write it.

The war between the house of Saul and the house of David was long and drawn out, with David growing stronger and the house of Saul becoming weaker. (3:1)

Eventually even Abner comes to David's side. This was short-lived because through a set of circumstances recorded in 2 Samuel 3, Joab (who was David's commander) did not trust or like the fact that Abner came to David's side. Part of this, no doubt, was personal and stemmed from the fact that Abner had killed Asahel, Joab's brother. As a result and in an act of revenge, Joab murdered Abner. David mourned the loss of Abner, the short-lived ally, because he was a king who wanted unity rather than disunity.

The conflict between Israel and Judah finally came to an end when Ish-bosheth was assassinated (2 Sam 4). And he is not just assassinated; he is humiliated. Two men called Rechab and Baanah perform the grisly deed. They stabbed him in the stomach, decapitated him, and then brought his head to David at Hebron. David is not impressed. Instead of greeting this news with joy, he recognizes it as an affront. He has the two men executed, has their hands and feet cut off, and hangs them. He took the head of Ish-bosheth and buried it in the same tomb in which Abner was laid.

Some immediate questions arise from this story:

- Why do the two men cut off Ish-bosheth's head?
- Why does David react so badly, to kill and mutilate these men?
- Does God approve of these actions?
- Do these actions have the stamp of God's favor?

Each of these questions is important, but they can be grouped into pairs: the first two go together, and the last two go together. So taking them in turn, the bodies are mutilated and Ish-bosheth's head is severed most likely because these were shaming acts. In other words, both were unnatural deaths and involved a shaming of the man. Remember, this is an honor-shame culture. Rechab and Baanah wanted not just to defeat Ish-bosheth but also to shame Saul and his dynasty. As a result, they mutilated Ish-bosheth and thereby brought shame to his entire household. Likewise, David responds by shaming the two men and their household. Mutilating the bodies with hands and feet cut off recalls the fate of the Dagon idol in the Philistine temple (1 Sam 5). David, with utmost sincerity and resolve, denounced the actions of the men by shaming them. Displaying their bodies would ensure that anyone who saw what they did would know it was disgraceful. In a backhanded way David honored the house of Saul with his actions against Rechab and Baanah. He was appalled that they would do this to Ish-bosheth while he was alone, defenseless, and in his bed—no man should die like that (2 Sam 4:11).

But does God approve of these actions, and do we gain God's favor by doing such horrific and violent things? These last two questions go together. We do not believe God was necessarily pleased with any of these horribly violent acts.

- There is no divine command demanding these actions.
- There is no mention from the narrator (who often presents the perspective of God) that these actions were good in the eyes of God.

Because of this, we are comfortable saying God did not love the actions of David, Rechab, or Baanah. The text *describes* the actions but does not *prescribe* the actions. Just because these actions of violence happened in the past, it does not follow that these actions serve as blueprints or patterns for our actions as we follow God today. In fact, quite the opposite! Jesus said we are to love our enemies and those who slander us (Matt 5:44). We are not to repay evil for evil (Rom 12:17). We are to be known, as the apostle John says, by our love (1 John 4).

Still, the chapters present the gritty, real, raw, and horrific realities of people on the ground, trying to figure out how to live their lives before God. God does not lift Himself out of these dirty realities, but He does condescend in His grace to work redemptively in those less-than-ideal circumstances. This passage is a hallmark example of how the Scriptures present not the best world or the ideal world, but they do present the real world. That is good, because in the horrific presentation of reality, we can still see a God who maintains favor with an imperfect king like David to achieve His purposes through him. This is good news for you and for me. If God only worked with perfect people, then we would be out of luck (and God would not have anyone to work with)!

After the horrible assassination of Ish-bosheth, all the tribes of Israel made pilgrimage to Hebron to see David and install him as king. David's installation as king was followed by his defeat of the Jebusites and the establishment of Jerusalem as his capital (2 Sam 5:6-10). The Phoenecians honored him as he was installed as king (vv. 11-12). David brought rest to the people as the Lord defeated the Philistine threat

that had plagued Israel for so many years (vv. 22-25). After his installation the question arises as to what kind of king David will be. As we will
see, he will be by no means perfect. But David would still receive divine
favor since he would be the instrument through which God would bring
blessing to all peoples. David would be a man who worships the Lord.

The Punishment from an Offensive God

*David again assembled all the choice men in Israel, 30,000. He and
all his troops set out to bring the ark of God from Baale-judah. The ark
is called by the Name, the name of Yahweh of Hosts who dwells between
the cherubim. They set the ark of God on a new cart and transported it
from Abinadab's house, which was on the hill. Uzzah and Ahio, sons
of Abinadab, were guiding the cart and brought it with the ark of God
from Abinadab's house on the hill. Ahio walked in front of the ark.
David and the whole house of Israel were celebrating before the Lord
with all kinds of fir wood instruments, lyres, harps, tambourines,
sistrums, and cymbals.*

*When they came to Nacon's threshing floor, Uzzah reached out
to the ark of God and took hold of it because the oxen had stumbled.
Then the Lord's anger burned against Uzzah, and God struck him
dead on the spot for his irreverence, and he died there next to the ark of
God. David was angry because of the Lord's outburst against Uzzah,
so he named that place an Outburst Against Uzzah, as it is today.
David feared the Lord that day and said, "How can the ark of the
Lord ever come to me?" So he was not willing to move the ark of the
Lord to the city of David; instead, he took it to the house of Obed-edom
the Gittite.* (2 Sam 6:1-10)

The ark, we recall, was the wooden box God had instructed Israel to
build shortly after the exodus from Egypt. It was overlaid with gold,
inside and out, and topped with a "mercy seat" that had two golden
angels facing each other. This ark was placed in the innermost part of
the tabernacle, in what the Jews called the most holy place, which was
intended to be the place where God's presence would dwell.

Remember, however, that at the start of this story the ark is not in
Israelite possession. As we saw in 1 Samuel 5, their disobedience led
them to lose massively to the Philistines, and part of the Philistine spoil
was the ark. The Philistine leaders, at first, were thrilled to have such
a lucky weapon in their new arsenal. But through a series of strange

events, beginning with the decapitation of the Philistine idol Dagon and culminating in an outbreak of tumors, mice, and death, the Philistines decided the ark was more trouble than they could handle. They strapped it to an oxcart and pointed it back to Israel.

The oxen made it most of the way but took a pit stop at the house of Abinadab. Abinadab, for his part, was in no rush to do anything with this volatile piece of furniture, so it sat in his back room for 20 years. Until David. David, unlike Saul before him, was jealous for the presence of God, so he did what any type-A leader would have done: he made a plan and followed it through.

The journey begins well enough: David and his retinue have brought out just about every instrument they had on hand, and they are busy having a raucous worship service on the road when suddenly tragedy strikes. The oxen pulling the ark trip, and as Uzzah reaches out to make sure the ark doesn't fall in the mud, he suddenly drops to the ground, dead. It doesn't matter what worship tradition you come from, when someone drops down dead, the worship service is over.

Uzzah's death represents a thread of the biblical narrative that contemporary Westerners find particularly odious. Here we see a picture of an angry God, one who lashes out and kills for what seems to be a trifle. Uzzah wanted to keep God's ark from hitting the dirt; what is so sinful about that? And even if it were wrong, did God have to levy such a harsh punishment?

What makes this story unique, relative to other biblical texts, is the window we are given into David's response. He responds just like we do. David looks at God and says, "God, this guy was trying to do You a favor! What gives?" There is no shred of demure acceptance here. David responds with raw, unbridled anger. God has offended him, and he lets God know it.

We in the twenty-first century tend to assume we are the first to encounter truths about God in Scripture and be offended by them. We assume—whether we articulate it in this way or not—that we have only recently achieved a measure of enlightenment sufficient to critique God for His judgmental ways. Previous generations might have simply accepted these truths, but we are savvy enough to see them for what they are.

David's anger, however, blows that assumption out of the water. David was offended at the way God acted. Nor is he the only one. God is, as has often been said, an equal opportunity offender and has been for as long as people have interacted with Him. Scripture does not show us ignorant men and women blindly following God but pilgrims who struggle to follow God when He offends their sensibilities.

The Problem of God's Presence

To overcome our offense, we must pause and consider this scene with Uzzah further. What precisely was Uzzah's crime? How does it relate to this mysterious and dangerous gold-plated box known as the ark?

The ark, we mentioned, represents God's presence. Throughout much of Israel's history, the ark brought blessing, security, and power. This is precisely why David wants it back, because he, like all of us, wants to know that the all-powerful Creator is part of his life. But this ark seems rather volatile. The presence of God can bring blessing, but as the Philistines have learned, it can also bring massive destruction. This is no lucky rabbit's foot its owners can wield for their benefit. This is God's presence, dynamic but dangerous.

God's presence, however, is not absolutely mysterious. That was the pattern of the ancient Greek gods, who were so capricious that no one could ever tell what they would do. God's ways may seem arbitrary to us, but they never are. God did not lash out at Uzzah as a whim but because Uzzah was guilty.

What was Uzzah's crime? God had given specific instructions about how to transport the ark (Exod 25:10-22). The priests were to use poles that slipped through four rings on the ark so that their hands would never touch the ark itself. But here they were carrying it around just like the Philistines did—on an oxcart. This story alone should tell us how God feels about the attitude that says, "I worship God in my own way. It doesn't matter how one worships God or what you do, as long as it's sincere." God does not take kindly to worship that disregards His standards.

Uzzah, however, was not the only one involved in this faulty worship service. What set him apart was the touch. And why did this matter? Uzzah's touch represents a failure to understand his own sinfulness. Uzzah saw the ark headed toward the dirt, and he reached out because he assumed his hand was less dirty than the ground. Most of us would have done the same. But think of this: the earth has never committed the blasphemy of rejecting God's authority. The earth has always obeyed the commands of God. Dirt could never pollute the ark. But the touch of a sinful man could.

Uzzah did not understand this so he tried to do God a favor. David did not understand this so he got upset with God. Chances are, we do not understand this so we join David in his frustration. But the reason we do not understand the judgment of God is that we do not understand the wickedness of our sinfulness.

Scripture offers this truth without apology: that the punishment God gives to sinners is not more severe than the crime. Most of us think that hell, for instance, is too severe a punishment for sin. How can even a full lifetime of sins—say, 70 years—merit an eternity apart from God? We tend to think that God's justice is an overreaction.

Or think of the cross. Our sin was apparently so heinous that Jesus, the Son of God, had to come to earth and be torn to shreds. Crucifixion was an unspeakably brutal process, meant to inflict maximum pain and to showcase a person's shame to anyone watching. The crucified person, with holes in his hands and feet, would have to pull up to even breathe in, forcing pressure on these wounds. The utter torment was nearly unbearable even to watch. The Roman author Cicero, for instance, says that when the Romans crucified women (yes, they did), they would crucify them backwards so people were not forced to watch their agony.

This was the punishment God Himself took for our sins. It was brutal. It was unbearable. It was disgusting. And that is precisely the point. The reaction we have to an event as horrific as crucifixion is the reaction we ought to have toward sin. The cross should remind us that our sin is unspeakably wicked. At its core sin is not merely transgressing a boundary. It is a delight in the wrong, accompanied by a hatred of God. And God simply cannot allow an attitude of treason against Him into His presence.

The usual rejoinder to a line of reasoning like this is to point out that God is "a God of love." But on some level we understand that love itself requires boundaries. If, for instance, an unrepentant, active sexual predator came to our church and offered to volunteer with the children's ministry, would it be loving to allow him? "Brother, we are so glad you are here! Feel free to roam about. We accept you as you are." If that is love, it is a narrow and warped view. For the sake of our children, love demands that we also act with wisdom.

What if this sexual predator repented? We would probably still maintain boundaries with our children, but we would have a more welcoming stance. The problem with those in hell, however, is that they refuse to repent. They are not down in hell, begging God for mercy. No, they rush headlong away from God because they resent and resist His authority in their lives. They may hate the pain of hell, but they hate the rule of God even more.

It bears repeating: the punishment is not too severe for the crime. God is so holy that He cannot tolerate impurity. Just as we would rightly resist a blood infusion with "just a little" of the HIV virus in it, God resists sinners who think they are smitten with "just a little" sin. The difference between Uzzah and us is that God gives us time to repent of our callous attitude. If He were to strike us down for picking up His Word with the same nonchalance as Uzzah, who among us would still be alive? Do we realize the magnanimity of His grace toward us, that we can come into God's presence, day after day, year after year, and not be struck down?

The Gospel According to the Ark

The ark of the LORD remained in his house three months, and the LORD blessed Obed-edom and his whole family.
  *It was reported to King David: "The LORD has blessed Obed-edom's family and all that belongs to him because of the ark of God."
So David went and had the ark of God brought up from Obed-edom's house to the city of David with rejoicing. When those carrying the ark of the LORD advanced six steps, he sacrificed an ox and a fattened calf.*
(2 Sam 6:11-13)

God would be within His rights as a just God to allow our story to end in verse 10, with Uzzah's funeral. Yet the love of God breaks through once more, not as a result of any Israelite obedience but by the sheer mercy of God. Obed-edom, the newest landlord for the ark, has seen a change of fortune. Unlike several of the previous takers—for whom the ark only meant tumors, mice, and death—his household has seen the blessing of God.

We risk missing the sweetness of God if we rush too quickly past this point. David's last interaction with God led him to a crisis of faith, one that caused David to be angry and afraid. David had seen God in action and had pushed Him away. We might expect God to confront David for his disobedience. What we see instead is a slow process in which God woos David back to Himself. David has said to God, "Please leave me alone." And God has gently responded, "I love you too much to do that."

David hears the news of Obed-edom as a sort of promise for himself. God's intention is not to be wrathful forever. So David ends the radio silence between him and God, determined to bring God's presence back to his city with him.

These three months have been instructive for David, too. He must have done some reading because now, instead of using an oxcart to pull the ark, David has ensured that people are "carrying" it (v. 13). The poles are back in place, and David is attempting to worship God the way God has revealed.

The poles, however, are just the start. The caravan has not even taken a dozen steps before David calls a halt and offers up the chief picture of worship in all Scripture—sacrifice. The Israelite people were familiar with animal sacrifice, harkening back to the great sign of Passover. In the Passover, God had provided a way of salvation for His people: through the death of a spotless lamb, God's wrath would "pass over" the households of Israel. And Israel's worship centered on rehearsing this scene, reminding them that God's presence with His people could only come at the cost of substitutionary death.

The pinnacle of the Israelite calendar was the Day of Atonement, in which a priest took the blood of a sacrificed lamb and sprinkled it on the ark. This was both a reminder of what God had done and a promise that He would one day send an ultimate sacrifice to pay sin's penalty of death. We now see what Israel only looked forward to—that sin's penalty of death would be paid by Jesus, the spotless Lamb of God who alone could take away the sin of the world.

Like Uzzah, Jesus would die the death of a sinner, struck down by the wrath of God. But His death would not be the punishment due Him for His own sins; instead His death would be the result of our sins. Just as the Passover lamb shed its blood in place of the Israelite people so they could live in God's presence, so Jesus, the true Passover Lamb, shed His blood in our place so the presence of God would not be fatal but sweet to us.

Sin requires death. There is no getting around this. And there are only two options: either we reject God and pay the steep price ourselves, or we accept the sacrifice Jesus dearly made on our behalf. His grace is a gift, but it is a gift that must be received. David knew this, and he responded the only way people ever respond in light of God's gracious love—with overwhelming praise.

David's Response to the Gospel

Even though chapter 6 is full of worship—and lessons for us about worship—few contemporary readers find these scenes in verses 14-23 normal. David's first worship service ended with a man being struck dead; his second worship service, although more conventional, involved the slaughter of an animal four times David's size; and this last worship service finds David stripping down half naked and dancing like a madman (v. 14). Say what you will, but worship with David around was anything but mundane.

David's dancing, however, irks his wife Michal (v. 20). Unrestrained dancing in your underpants might communicate passion, but it did not—in her mind—communicate dignity. It was conduct unbecoming of a king.

Michal, we recall, is Saul's daughter, and it seems that the apple has not fallen far from the tree. King Saul was undone because he insisted on preening and peacocking so that others would think highly of him. As a result, he lost the Spirit of God. Now Michal, following her father step for step, prioritizes public image above all else. We ought to seriously ponder whether we find Michal's reaction in our own heart. We know, of course, that we should defend David. But how often do we consider our image above our devotion to God?

We might have been intimidated by Michal's attack, but David certainly was not (vv. 21-22). He fired back, "Look, God is finished with Saul and his house. He's chosen me, but not because of my might. He chose me to put His glory on display, and that is just what I plan to do." David understood what Saul consistently missed—that God wanted to make a big deal of Himself, not of the king. So if exalting God meant that David needed to be humiliated, David was on board. What is true for David is true for us as well: Only one person can be large in my life. It is either me or God.

David's worship made clear who was the most valuable person in his life. So what does our worship tell others about the value of God to us?

It is unfortunate how often the word *worship* gets reduced to singing. Worship includes singing, of course, but biblical worship encompasses so much more. Worship is, in essence, our response to the gospel. It is less about what we sing and more about how we live. The word itself hints at this, since the original meaning had more to do with *worth* than with songs. People offer "worth-ship" to something because it demands it, because it has inherent worth.

Seen this way, it becomes clear that our entire lives speak volumes to the world about who has the most worth in our eyes. Worship becomes clear in how we spend our free time, where we spend our money, and what we teach our children. Worship comes out in moments of frustration or anger or in the activities we seek for solace. Worship is seen in our lives when we come face-to-face with sin, injustice, and suffering. Will our responses say, like Saul, that we care more for our image than for God's priorities? Or will we worship God like David, putting ourselves in humiliating positions so long as we make much of Him?

Understanding worship as whole life, however, does not exempt us from applying that attitude to our singing. When we come together as a body of believers and sing praise to God, we are putting on display God's greatness and glory in our lives. Our worship should put our hunger for God on display. Our physical response should demonstrate admiration, awe, gratitude, and wonder.

Most of us have a lot to learn from our more expressive brothers and sisters in this regard. Granted, we may acknowledge (in some measure rightly) that our personality plays a role in our singing. Yes, be yourself. But think of this: If someone handed you an envelope with one million dollars in it, would your response really be to smile and flatly say, "Thank you. I appreciate it"? Chances are you would show some emotion, regardless of your personality. Could it be that the problem is not personality but the value we are putting on the priceless gift of salvation? Those who are forgiven much love much, and throughout Scripture that love frequently overflows in embarrassing ways. Many of us simply need to admit that our dignity is more important to us than responding to the gospel. And we need to repent.

On the other hand, however, singing in worship need not always be raucous and exciting. There is indeed a time when, like David, the only appropriate response is to shout and dance like a crazy person. But the Bible presents a range of emotions that are appropriate in worship. Sometimes we need to stand in the presence of God in stunned silence. Sometimes we need to sit in awe. Sometimes we need to bow our heads and weep over sin. And sometimes we need to be flat on our face. What we never need is to pretend that what we do with our tongues and our bodies is irrelevant. Worship starts as an attitude of the heart, but it never stays there.

All the teaching in the world, however, will make little difference if our attitude toward worship remains steeped in works. Most of us have had the experience of hearing from the worship leader, midservice, as he castigates the congregation for not being enthusiastic enough. That may work for a little while, but the natural end of it is burnout. David was not dancing because someone told him to; he was dancing because he understood the gospel.

The gospel, and the gospel alone, holds the power to make our worship fruitful. Notice that little detail in verse 19, about "a raisin cake." Raisin cakes were the aphrodisiac of the ancient world. David ended his worship service by handing out some raisin cakes and saying, "Go home and be fruitful!" There is an illustration here for us. Natural fruitfulness—the kind that results in babies—does not occur through to-do lists. It is the natural end of a process of intimacy. Spiritual fruitfulness works the same way. We cannot drum up emotions of gratitude and awe on our own. They are the fruit, and they only come as we are caught up in the spiritual intimacy of knowing God and knowing what He has done for us.

True worshipers—both in singing and in life—are those who know the character of God, who know His love for them, who feel deeply that they were once lost and are now saved, were once blind but now see.

The opposite side of this coin, though, is tragically true as well. Those who fail to accept the grace of God bear no fruit. Michal, as verse 23 shows us, ended her days childless. Her mocking led to barrenness. This is a serious punishment for what we might consider a relatively minor mistake. In just a few chapters, we will see David travel the road of adultery, cover-up, and murder. Yet David remains fruitful, while Michal does not. Was Michal's sin worse? Not necessarily. But her dignity was dangerous because it prevented her from throwing herself on God's mercy. Ultimately, it is not our bad deeds that keep us from God. They can be forgiven. It is our good deeds—that which we take pride in—that keep us from God because they prevent us from knowing how desperately we need a Savior.

Reflect and Discuss

1. How does this passage help you understand God?
2. How does this passage of Scripture exalt Jesus?
3. How have we confused authentic worship with music styles, liturgical styles, and preferences? How have you done that in your own experience?

4. In what ways does this text about God's punishment of those who touched the ark create frustration, confusion, or even anger among those who read this text? Why do you think that is the case?

5. In what ways does this text reveal the power of a wild and holy God?

6. How do you respond to the fact that God will not tolerate impurity? Write down your thoughts.

7. What impurity and sin in your life do you bear right now? What does it do to your heart to know that on the cross Jesus bore the impurity associated with sin and made us holy and pure by His shed blood?

8. In what ways does your attitude toward worship need to change?

9. How does the gospel once again change us in worship?

10. How does the gospel engender in us love to God and those around us? Write down your thoughts and be specific.

David as King: Who Is Giving to Whom?

2 SAMUEL 7

Main Idea: The Davidic covenant reveals that Yahweh has blessed David to be a blessing; those who bless him will be blessed, and those who curse him will be cursed.

I.   Who Needs a House, Anyway?
II. The Davidic Covenant and God's Everlasting House
III. David's Response: Humility and Gratitude in the House of God
IV. Four Principles for House Building
  A. The Grace Principle
  B. The Giving Principle
  C. The Disappointment Principle
  D. The Kingdom Principle

Introduction

One of the most troubling words in the English language is the word *enough*. Many of us are plagued by whether we've been good enough, worked hard enough, or loved our families enough. And if we start applying that tricky word to our relationship with God, things get even messier. How much is enough for God?

Here's a confession you won't often hear from a pastor: I (J. D.) spent a lot of my Christian life feeling overwhelmed by guilt over what I was not doing in the kingdom of God. It's not that I wasn't committed to Jesus, living a sacrificial life, or intensely busy for the kingdom. I was. There was just always so much more to be done, and the needs of the world were crushing me. I would start off really zealous but end up feeling paralyzed, toggling between summers of feverish activity and winters of guilt and fatigue.

Speakers would come along talking about the needs in the world, telling me how people who really care about Jesus would be involved meeting those needs. I heard about the sex trade and decided to do everything I could to free those poor kids. I heard about more and more unreached people groups so I went on mission trips—a lot of mission trips.

But it never seemed to be enough. There was always one more child to rescue, one more people group to reach. And the more I poured myself out for cause after cause, the more I felt guilty.

How could I keep any money for my own enjoyment when so many in the world remained lost? If the price of a cup of coffee could really feed an Indian orphan for a week, was it ever right for me to have a cup of coffee? And why did I need a hot shower? Should I take only cold showers and free up another $20 a month to house another refugee?

I used to think I was alone in this, but I've grown to see that many, if not most, Christians feel like this. It may not be as extreme as my experience, but many believers are asking, "Is it possible to know what God specifically wants from me? Is it possible to know I've done enough? Can I even know—for sure—how to get back on good terms with God?"

None of these questions are new. In fact, they are precisely the questions that prompt the story in 2 Samuel 7, one of the most famous Old Testament prophecies about the Messiah. There is no need to separate "deep doctrine" from "real-life questions." As Scripture shows us, our most pressing, heartfelt questions are answered by the deepest biblical truths.

Who Needs a House, Anyway?

At this point David is now—finally—established as the king of Israel. He hasn't had much time to sit back and ponder until this point, since he was busy challenging oversized Philistines to rock-throwing contests, running away from Saul, and hiding in caves. But now the kingdom is stable, David's enemies have been routed, and the land is prospering and at "rest" (v. 1).

So one night after dinner, David is sitting out on his back porch, chatting with Nathan, the priest—essentially, the nation's pastor. And as they sip on their decaf coffees, David looks over the city of Jerusalem. His eyes fall on the tabernacle, just outside his palace. The tabernacle, we recall, was the tent God had told Israel to build so that His presence could dwell with them. By this point, however, the tabernacle was a few hundred years old. It wasn't as swanky as when Israel first built it.

So David gets an idea (v. 2). "You know, Nathan, this doesn't seem right. I live in this ridiculously nice house. But God lives in a dingy old tent. Can we do something about that?" Well, how do you think Nathan responded? Exactly like any pastor would when a wealthy man comes to him, ready to do something for the kingdom of God. "Sounds great, king! Drop a check off, and we'll start building!"

The next part, however, doesn't usually happen (vv. 4-11). If nothing else, this little story proves the existence of God. That's the only thing I can imagine that would explain a pastor going back to a wealthy donor and saying, "Don't bother giving me your money." At least, I've never seen it happen.

So God explains why He rejects David's offer with three points.

First is what theologians call "the incarnational principle." God wants to be in the same condition His people are in. If God's people are in tents, God will be in a tent, too. And when they are wandering or homeless or in pain, He wants to be among them. He wants to dwell with them and share in their condition.

Second, God pokes a bit of fun at David, pointing out that He doesn't particularly need a physical residence. "You think I'm worried about My accommodations down there, David? Cedar doesn't much impress Me. My streets, after all, are made of gold." Or, as God says in Psalm 50, "If I were hungry, I would not tell you, for the world and everything in it is Mine" (Ps 50:12). In other words, "David, if I needed a nicer place to live, I wouldn't have to come asking you for funding."

Third, and most important, God flips David's script. Look at that passage and see who the actor is. David isn't in the driver's seat; God is. David was concerned about God's house and wanted to build Him a new one. Like many of us today, he thought of God as a cause in need of good supporters (and financial backers). So he was going to give and give big. But God won't have it. "I am the giver," God declares, "and you are the receiver. I am never the debtor; you will always be indebted to Me." The house of God's salvation, in other words, will be constructed entirely by God.

But at this point God lifts David's eyes to see something greater than a house. David had been thinking of building God a house. But what God offers to do instead would never have entered David's mind to ask.

The Davidic Covenant and God's Everlasting House

In the introduction to this volume, we saw that 2 Samuel 7 demarcates the covenant God makes with David and his household. The Davidic covenant appears in 7:8-16. Although "covenant" language does not appear here, it does in 23:5, where David rehearses the fact that God made with him an "everlasting covenant" (*berit 'olam*), which no doubt draws us back to 2 Samuel 7. Finally, David's son, Solomon, reiterates the covenant in 1 Kings 3:6-9 and 8:23-24, highlighting the point that both David and his dynastic successor understood the divine promises recorded in 2 Samuel 7 as nothing short of an eternal covenant.

The Davidic covenant clearly builds from the Abrahamic and Israelite covenants, as we have seen in the introduction (pp. 23–27). Some similarities between the Abrahamic, Israelite, and Davidic covenants draw them together, revealing how God's redemptive story progresses:

Similarities between Covenants

Abrahamic Covenant	Davidic Covenant
Great name (Gen 12:2)	Name (2 Sam 7:9)
Children (Gen 12:2-3)	Dynastic succession (2 Sam 7:12)
Land (Gen 15:7)	Land (2 Sam 7:10)
Curse on enemies (Gen 12:3)	Rest from enemies (2 Sam 7:10-11)

Israelite Covenant	Davidic Covenant
God's "firstborn son" (Exod 4:22)	King is God's son (2 Sam 7:14)
Royal and holy nation (Exod 19:4-6)	Priest-king (Ps 110:2,4)
Stipulations to follow (Exod 20:2-17)	Stipulations to follow (Deut 17:14-20)
Divine promises (Exod 23:20-33)	Divine promises (2 Sam 7:8-20)

The Davidic covenant, then, continues the story of God's redemption. God's kingdom will be manifested most clearly under the rule of the Davidic king. The king will only be successful in so far as he rules in accordance with, and under, the rule of the Lord God. And how he knows if he is following God's rule is by virtue of the stipulations of the Israelite covenant! David himself recognized as much. He wants to make a temple where God's people can worship the Lord forever (following the pattern of Exodus and Leviticus).

He pensively asks the prophet Nathan how he can live in a palace when God, the Creator of the universe, lives in a tent (2 Sam 7:2). David wants a place of worship for his people so that all can come to adore the true King of Israel and the God of creation.

William Dumbrell highlights the significance of the verse as it leads into the heart of the Davidic covenant. King David understands "that his own kingdom will not be established nor will his own line endure, unless divine rule is acknowledged appropriately within Israel" (Dumbrell, *Covenant and Creation*, 219). So the Davidic king becomes, at his best, an exemplar for worship and piety among God's people. Moreover, when he is successful, the Davidic king drives God's people to worship the true God of the universe. So it is not surprising that the book of Psalms regularly returns to the feature of Israel's Davidic king as a leader in worship of God.

The book of Psalms also emphasizes the rule of the Davidic king over all nations with justice and equity. This international flavor of the Davidic covenant is best seen in Psalm 2 (specifically Ps 2:7-11), but it appears throughout the Psalter as well (see Pss 18:40,43-49; 72:8; 89:35-36; 132:11-12; see the discussion of Wenham, *The Psalter Reclaimed*, 161–86). The Davidic reign over Israel and the nations, however, in the final analysis indicates nothing less than the reign of God (or the kingdom of God). As McCann summarizes, "The Psalms proclaim God's reign and invite persons to live under God's rule" (*A Theological Introduction*, 49). The Davidic covenant is God's way in which He will achieve His kingdom among all nations.

But note the title the text gives to David. God appoints David as a "prince" (v. 8 ESV) who rules over all peoples under the authority of the great King, God Himself.[10] The language of "prince" is important. God's people wanted a "king" (*melek*) like all the other nations (1 Sam 8:5). But what does God actually give them? He gives them a *nagid*, translated "ruler" or "prince" (1 Sam 9:16; 2 Sam 7:8). The "king" whom God and Samuel conceived always and ever remained a "prince." This "prince" lived in service to the real and true King of Israel, Yahweh. The narrative presents the real King as Yahweh, and the king of Israel is His *nagid*. Who is the true King of Israel? God. Who is the *nagid* of Israel? It is the appointed and anointed servant. This is, according to the narrative, not Saul (1 Sam 10–15). Saul's fall opens the reader up for the rise of the true prince, the Davidic ruler.

---

[10] For Yahweh as the great King, see Ps 48:2. I [Heath] am not fully convinced with Dumbrell that v. 19 teaches that the Davidic covenant is not only for the good of Israel but also a "charter for humanity," in Dumbrell, *Covenant and Creation*, 227. The words that indicate this are difficult and may refer to the future royal line of David. For the latter view, see McCarter, *II Samuel*, 232–33. Still, the psalms recognize the benefits of the Davidic covenant for the whole of humanity as described above.

One of the key terms God uses to describe the Davidic king is the Hebrew word *mashiach*, "anointed one" (or "messiah"). It stems from David's "anointing" in the shepherds' fields in and around Bethlehem (1 Sam 16). There God anoints David (through the prophet Samuel) for kingship (see also 2 Sam 12:7). The anointed king of Israel has a sacred role among God's people as their leader and exemplar in fidelity to God (see 1 Sam 24:6,10; 26:9-23; 2 Sam 7). The special role of the messiah-king is captured in David's words: "[God] is a tower of salvation for His king; He shows loyalty to His anointed, to David and his descendants forever" (2 Sam 22:51). David's words echo the Davidic covenant and Israelite covenant, but they highlight the special place of Israel's messiah who stands in relationship with God.

Israel's messiah brings the promised "rest" of creation to fruition. We consider it interesting and significant that God promises David "rest" in the land of promise (2 Sam 7:10-11). The importance of this connection lies in the fact that the goal of the seventh day (the kingdom of God!) will come to fruition at least in part through David and the Davidic line. The development of the theme of rest, which we have seen in Genesis 2 and 6, finds its way through David. This is good news because it shows God's commitment to bring the kingdom to bear through David's lineage, which we will see is fulfilled in Jesus Christ (Heb 4).

But until the advent of Jesus, how well did the Davidic kings do with their special role and responsibilities? Overall, not so well, as we saw with the reign of Israel's first king, Saul! By the mid-sixth century BC, no Davidic king sat on the throne, which indicated a terrible reality. The writers of Samuel and Kings suggested that the failure of the Davidic line was not the failure of God but rather the failure of the king in terms of his fidelity to God. Despite this, God would preserve the Davidic line well into the future, leading to a Good Shepherd to rule over God's kingdom.

In later books like 1–2 Chronicles, the biblical writers anticipated that there would be a king who would not be like the old kings. He would be, true to the Davidic covenant, in the line of David. But He would not be like David or Solomon. He would be a good king who ever lived to pray, to worship, and to lead God's people with justice and equity. The good king was like all God's people: those who would know and love and worship God in His kingdom. This king would rule over

Israel and, indeed, over all nations. Together, both Israelite and non-Israelite would serve the Lord with gladness.[11]

As time went by, the Davidic king became more and more important for Israel. The reason is probably because there really was no king that was perfect in justice and righteousness, so God's people looked for a king that would meet God's requirements for justice and righteousness. Indeed, God's people began to anticipate a coming king that would deliver them from oppression, even from their sin.

When we understand the failure of Israel's kings and the promise of the coming king who would rule under God's authority, read once again:

> "When your time comes and you rest with your fathers, I will raise up after you your descendant, who will come from your body, and I will establish his kingdom. He will build a house for My name, and I will establish the throne of his kingdom forever. I will be a father to him, and he will be a son to Me. When he does wrong, I will discipline him with a human rod and with blows from others. But My faithful love will never leave him as I removed it from Saul; I removed him from your way. Your house and kingdom will endure before Me forever, and your throne will be established forever." (2 Sam 7:12-16)

In the light of the broader look on the Davidic king in the Bible, it becomes clear that this is one of the most famous messianic promises. But one little detail immediately strikes a lot of readers as odd. It's that phrase, "When he does wrong . . ." If we're talking about Jesus here (which we are), what is this about wrongdoing? Jesus never sinned!

It is helpful to remember here that most biblical prophecies have a dual meaning. There is an *immediate* meaning, and then there is an *ultimate* one. From the perspective of the prophets, of course, it was often difficult to untie the two, but they remain distinct. Think of it like the experience of seeing a mountain range in the distance. When you first spot it, you might see two peaks, seemingly right next to each other. It's only as you get closer that you discover that these peaks are miles apart.

The first fulfillment of this prophecy was David's biological son, Solomon. Solomon's reign was marked with rest from enemies and a

---

[11] See the wonderful discussion of Hahn, *The Kingdom of God as Liturgical Empire*, 23–41.

time of prosperity, so in many ways he would exemplify this promise. His reign would extend rest throughout Israel, and on his watch Israel constructed the temple. Yes, Solomon would do some patently foolish things—some Saul-like acts, as God puts it here—like having 700 wives and worshiping idols. But even so, God keeps His promise and doesn't strip the kingdom from him.

But Solomon is not the forever king God had promised. Perhaps people expected that he would be. But his reign ends in disappointment, with his sons sinning so badly that the nation would descend into civil war.

This prophecy points through Solomon to another King: Jesus. He was the descendant of David whose kingdom would last. He was the descendant who would establish a real temple—not a building constructed with human hands but the temple of His own body. And after His ascension He would send His Spirit to make us, His people, the temple of God.

Unlike Solomon, Jesus would not need to be disciplined with the stripes of men. Instead, He would be bruised for our iniquity, and by His stripes we would be healed. The real Son of David would build the real temple of God and establish God's real presence with His people forever. And He would not just be David's son. He would be God's own Son, building the house of salvation for God's people on earth all by Himself. Wrap your head around that: God would build His own house, and He would become the house He promised to build. In Jesus, God would be the fulfillment of His own promise.

David's Response: Gratitude and Humility in the House of God

The Messianic promise is astounding—so astounding, in fact, that we may be tempted to miss David's response. But here in verses 18-26 we see the story come full circle. David began this discussion wanting to go and build for God. But he ends it sitting, wondering, knowing, pondering, adoring.

This is the key to salvation. Asking, "How much is enough for God?" is the wrong starting point. Instead, salvation always starts with knowing what God has already done—which leaves us sitting in stunned awe in the presence of God. Yes, trusting Christ will lead you to do things for God. But everything you do is only ever a grateful response to what He's done for you.

We often think the world is supposed to look at Christians and say, "What impressive works they've done! They must really love God." But that aspiration can be crushing. And it's not the biblical picture. As God shows us here, our witness to the world should leave them saying, "Wow, what great things God has done for them!"

We Christians are not primarily role models. We are trophies, works of art that demonstrate God's saving power. No one admires a trophy for having done *something* great; they recognize that the trophy represents *someone* great. Our lives are supposed to burn brightly with evidence of God's miraculous greatness. And ironically, the more we steep ourselves in the finished work of Christ, the more we will find His Spirit rising up within us. The fire to *do* in the Christian life comes only from being soaked in the fuel of what He has *done*.

Four Principles for House Building

The Grace Principle

David's desire to build God a house might seem odd to contemporary readers, but it was actually a pretty common practice in the ancient world. King Tut, for instance, built a temple for the Egyptian god Amon-Ra. In exchange Amon-Ra allegedly proclaimed that King Tut would rule a kingdom that would span the globe and last for millions of years. (He fell just a few thousand miles, and a couple million years, short.)

The order is significant: (1) king builds temple for god; (2) temple makes god famous; (3) god thanks king by blessing kingdom. That's the order of every religion in the world: work hard for me, and I'll work hard for you. But God rejects that and reverses it. "My power establishes you, and you will always be My debtor. Your life will be lived in grateful response to Me." The house God builds does not bear the inscription "Built by David for God" but "Built by God for David."

Grace: it seems so simple. It's a gift, costly for the giver, but free for the recipient. And yet this is where so many people stumble. We're hardwired to ask, "How much is *enough*? How often do I need to come to church? How much money do I have to give?" Those questions will never get you to the gospel. The gospel begins with God's extravagant gift. Jesus' blood, and Jesus' blood alone, is *enough* for your starving and dying soul.

Christianity is not about you living a good life and then giving your record to God but Jesus living the perfect life and then giving His record to you as a gift. He lived the life we were supposed to live and died the death we should have died. His life is ours but only if we receive it.

The Giving Principle

There are three main aspects to the "giving principle."

First, God doesn't need you. Never has. Never will. For anything. Ever. God is not now, nor was He ever, looking for "helpers" to assist Him in saving the world. That doesn't mean He isn't calling us to give ourselves generously to that mission, just that He's not looking for people to supply His needs. He's not short on money, talent, or time. He never commands us to go save the world for Him; He calls us to follow Him as He saves the world through us.

So He says to David, "Thanks for the offer, but I don't actually need you to build Me a house." And He might as well say to us, "I appreciate the thought, but I can get along just fine without your donation." Salvation, from start to finish, is from God, and He requires nothing from us in the process.

Remember, Jesus went to the cross alone. It wasn't a team effort. All His closest friends—even His heavenly Father—abandoned Him. And He walked out of the grave without any human assistance, too. There was no crash cart, no team of disciples laying on hands and praying fervently. It was just Jesus. It still is.

Consider this: Jesus' presence was apparently so vital to our mission that He told His disciples not to even lift a finger toward the Great Commission until Jesus had sent His Spirit. Wait in Jerusalem, He said, until you receive the Holy Spirit (Luke 24:49). Millions of people around the globe are dying and going to hell; you are the only ones who know what to do about it; but I want you to sit in a room and do nothing until the Spirit comes. Jesus said, "You can do nothing without Me" (John 15:5).

Second, we should want to give back to God. We have to balance the truth that "God doesn't need us" with this truth: God still wants us to give back. After all, David wasn't rebuked for his attitude. God commended it: "Since it was your desire to build a temple for My name," God says, "you have done well to have this desire" (2 Chr 6:8). David wasn't trying to buy God off; he wanted to do something great for God because of God's great love toward him. And if we think "God doesn't need us" means we can just spend all our time and money on ourselves, that only proves we haven't met the real God.

David's heart wanted to give of itself back to the God who had given so much to him, and his heart overflowed with that. That's precisely how we should be in response to the gospel. How can we see the riches God has poured out on us and not want to share that with others? A heart touched by the gospel will become like the gospel: overflowing with grace.

In Christ, God has given us the most precious thing in the entire universe. In Christ, He has rescued us from eternal death. We don't give to God to earn anything. We give to God because we just can't help but give our lives to the One who gave His life for us.

Third, we should offer ourselves to God and do what He tells us to do. When we think the weight of the world lies with our abilities and our decisions, it leads to paralysis. But when we instead offer ourselves to God, we can do what He calls us to and rest in that. As I once heard a pastor say, "Not everything from heaven has your name on it." Our job is to figure what does have our name on it and follow the Spirit in that.

When we allow the Spirit to guide us, we can finally avoid the pressing guilt of not doing everything. We can throw ourselves into that corner of God's mission that He leads us to instead of being torn apart by all the causes in the world.

People make two key mistakes when it comes to giving. On one hand they act like the salvation of the world lies on their shoulders. But it doesn't. God is building the house, so grab a trowel and ask Him where He wants to build through you. On the other hand, though, are those people who have never offered themselves to God. They want to pay God off and get on with their lives, to give a 10-percent "tax" to God as a salve for their soul. But that misunderstands the great grace God has poured out on us. It puts us in the position of builder, when we need to let God set the terms.

The great saints of old didn't try to buy God off. Nor did they try to save the world on their own. They realized they served a miraculous God who lacked for nothing. That vision gave them the courage to dream great things for God and then to attempt great things for Him.

The Disappointment Principle

David had a dream to do something for God. And God responds by saying no. Have you ever had that experience? You were pursuing a godly passion, attempting something great for God, and instead of blessing you ran into adversity. The door you thought was open slammed in your face. And unlike David you didn't have a "Nathan" to explain to you why.

We may not always see them, but God always has reasons for our disappointments, even for our failures. Much of the time disappointments and failures act as a way of reminding us of who the real Savior is. It's a humbling thought, but it is worth considering: God ordains many failures in our lives so that we—and other people—will make a bigger deal out of God than out of us. God knows our hearts better than we do: He knows that certain success in our lives would actually make us more full of our own pride than full of gratitude. So He lets us fall on our face because He knows it's far more dangerous for us to be swelled up with pride than it is to suffer through the most difficult adversity in this life.

None of us likes disappointment. It's not comfortable to be weakened and humiliated. But the path to God's glory often comes not through our successes but through our weakness. So when God weakens us to remind us to depend on Him, it may not be easy, but it's certainly for our good.

Or it may be that our disappointments are God's way of shaking us out of a faulty identity. We are all tempted to find our identity in idols, in something other than God. It might be success, financial security, or family. And when we've built something we think is beautiful and sturdy, we think God must be pretty pleased. So God lets a room or two cave in to remind us that what defines us isn't the house we're building but the house He has given to us. He smashes our idols to prevent us from getting too attached, not because He wants to ruin our fun but because He knows the road of idolatry has only one end: death.

Once we accept disappointment as a tool God can use, we find both the strength to endure and the audacity to pray boldly. We can endure anything, knowing that God is a loving Father. If He tells us no, we can trust that He knows better than we do and that He cares more about our well-being than we do. But at the same time we can approach Him with boldness because we are no longer seeking victories for our sake but for His. When "Your kingdom come, Your will be done" shapes our disappointments, everything begins to change.

The Kingdom Principle

This story is all about God's house, God's kingdom, God's unfolding drama. But the wonder of it all is that we are invited to share in that story. God calls us first to behold Him in wonder, but He also commissions us to go and tell. He is, as Tim Keller puts it, a spiritual cyclone, pulling people close in order to hurl them back out.

This raises the question, Are you a part of that eternal kingdom? What God told David is just as true for us. Our kingdoms will fail. Our businesses will fail. Our loftiest ambitions will fail. Even our families will not last forever. Jesus is the only thing that will last forever. And the greatest privilege of our lives is asking God to show us where we can join Jesus. He doesn't need us, but He will use us for eternal value. He can make our miniscule lives into something beautiful, precious, and everlasting.

What greater purpose could you have than to be used in the story of God? What higher calling could there be than to follow Christ as He moves throughout the world? For far too many of us, our lives are just so small. We think of God as a personal assistant, someone to get us out of a jam. What He desires for us is so much bigger, so much richer, so much more profound than any of us realize.

But that greatness begins in humility. It is one of the extraordinary paradoxes of Christian faith: if you desire greatness for yourself, God will oppose you; but if you desire God to be great, your life will have eternal value and miraculous power. Don't waste your life building houses for yourself, or even building houses for God. Rest in His all-sufficient work, and answer Him when He calls. Your life will never be the same.

Reflect and Discuss

1. How does this passage help you understand God?
2. How does this passage of Scripture exalt Jesus?
3. Consult the introduction of this volume once again, particularly the theological theme of covenant (pp. 23–27). How does this text fit within the story of the covenants in Scripture?
4. In what ways is the Davidic covenant related to the other covenants? Write down your thoughts and be specific.
5. In what ways does God "outbuild" David?
6. In what ways have you seen God "outbuild" you, whenever you make the effort to do something great for Him? Write down your thoughts.
7. What does this passage teach us about God's plan, God's grace, and God's love?
8. How does this passage help us understand that God opposes the proud but gives grace to the humble?

9. Have you, like David, completely offered yourself to the One who can and will build your house? Why or why not?

10. Do you believe disappointments in life are a tool God can use to change you? What disappointments are you experiencing today that He can use? Ask Him to transform your disappointment to joy and purpose.

David as King: Victory and Honor

2 SAMUEL 8–9

Main Idea: God blesses His covenant King, and the covenant King blesses others.

I. **"The Lord Made David Victorious."**
II. **David Brings Honor to the Shamed.**

Introduction

Second Samuel 8–9 reveals God's blessing of David. God's blessing is a gift that is not earned in any way. It is much like the gospel of Jesus Christ: a gift given but never earned. When one considers the expansiveness of the Davidic covenant, one sees the gracious heart of Yahweh, the high and holy King. In the biblical presentation David is now the undershepherd of the divine Shepherd, Yahweh. Because of this, David will rule the kingdom of God. Under the rule of David, 2 Samuel 8–9 records his military victories and the extraordinary kindness he displays to undeserving peoples.

"The Lord Made David Victorious"

2 SAMUEL 8

In business it is not uncommon for issues of "turf" and "credit" to be sources of consternation and competition. What do we mean by this? *Turf* refers to the region of responsibility for which one is responsible; if anyone steps into another person's turf, then conflict inevitably ensues. Stay off my turf: that's my project, my client, my department, my responsibility! In reality the issue of credit is closely linked to turf. People guard their turf because they want credit for what happens on it. Getting credit means that someone acknowledges something good that has happened on your turf: that project went well, that client paid out, that department turned a profit, or you handled your responsibilities well (now you get a raise!). Credit and turf go hand in hand in business.

But credit and turf do not go together in kingdom business. When we turn to 2 Samuel 8, we see that God has made David king, and the king gains victory over his adversaries. The military report in this passage is pretty astounding! Little, puny, runt David tackles and conquers nations far stronger, wiser, and older than his kingdom. He conquers regions in the north, south, east, and west and expands the Israelite territory significantly. It is no wonder that 2 Samuel 7:1 says that in the reign of David Israel experienced "rest" from all other enemy nations. David is amazing!

But we must keep in mind that if David ever wanted to take credit for what happened on his turf, the word of the Lord keeps him in touch with reality. Twice the text reads, "The LORD made David victorious wherever he went" (8:6,14). Why does the narrative say this twice? The reason is simple but profound. We are supposed to understand that Yahweh is the only reason David is where he is and is doing what he is doing. In short, the text highlights the true hero of the story: Yahweh the King! The divine King grants His human king victory. In short, God blesses David.

But for what reason does God bless David? Sometimes we act as though God blesses us so that we can just sit back, relax, and revel in His goodness—so that we can pat ourselves on the back as we drink a margarita and think, *Wow! I am so blessed. Great to be me.* But that is the wrong perspective on divine blessing. The biblical view of divine blessing is this:

Blessed by God to be a blessing to others.

God's blessing is meant to flow to us and through us. The Lord gives David victory and blesses him, to be sure. But what does David do with that gift? He blesses others. Second Samuel 8:15 says, "So David reigned over all Israel, administering justice and righteousness for all his people." God granted David victory and success so that he could rule God's kingdom in "justice and righteousness for all his people." God blessed David so that the blessing would flow to him and through him.

This is true for you and for me. God's victory and blessing to David is a picture of what God would do through Jesus. God put all enemies, including sin, death, and hell, under the feet of Jesus. God gave Jesus victory wherever He went. And He did this so we might be forgiven and brought into God's kingdom. But those who are blessed in the forgiveness of Jesus are meant to share the blessing. We are blessed by God to be a blessing to others.

David Brings Honor to the Shamed
2 SAMUEL 9

"Beauty for Ashes" is one of the most famous and beautiful praise songs that I (Heath) was able to sing while we lived in England (Bennetts, "Beauty for Ashes"). Our worship pastor, Neil, wrote the song, and its opening lyrics go like this:

> Beauty for ashes and garments of praise,
> you come and adorn me with joy once again,
> and pour oil of gladness in instead of despair;
> bringing your mercy again like sweet, spring rain.

The words speak of the restoration, forgiveness, and transformation that occur when we are saved by the blood of Jesus. Jesus brings a reversal of the despair, gloom, and drought that gripped our lives prior to knowing Him. Of course the song derives from Isaiah 61:3, where God promises the reversal of shame and dishonor and reveals that joy, gladness, liberation, and forgiveness come in His salvation. But experiencing such a reversal is also the turnabout from shame to honor. God provides beauty instead of ashes, honor instead of shame.

In 2 Samuel 9 we see God's son, the Davidic king, give beauty for ashes and honor from shame. Almost "out of the blue," verse 1 begins with David asking his officials if there is anyone he can bless from Saul's family (if anyone is left!). The officials find one of Saul's servants, Ziba, who is the one who shares that Mephibosheth is still around. Mephibosheth is Jonathan's son, who is lame in both feet, a disabled individual. The name "Mephibosheth" in Hebrew is linked to the concept of shame (*bosheth* in Hebrew means "shame"). The text indicates in two places that Mephibosheth was "lame in both feet" (vv. 3,13 NIV 1984). This detail is emphasized for a specific purpose. In the ancient world, if someone was disabled or was born with a birth defect of some sort, they often were ostracized or thought of as sinful.

We remember this from the New Testament as well, when the disciples encountered a person with a disability. The event is recorded in John 9:1-3: "As He was passing by, He saw a man blind from birth. His disciples questioned Him: 'Rabbi, who sinned, this man or his parents, that he was born blind?'" Of course, Jesus responded, "Neither this man nor his parents." God's glory would be revealed through that man and his disability.

The reality was that Mephibosheth was not disabled due to a specific sin he had committed; he was just disabled. But in that culture, disability prevented one from experiencing the same kind of life a fully healthy individual could. Now we might not like that, but that is how it was at that time. That fact is what makes this passage so powerful. David brought the disabled/shamed Mephibosheth to the king's banquet table in a place of honor.

The story of David's blessing of Mephibosheth is a story of God's glory. The text records that David wanted to show some form of kindness to Mephibosheth because he was Saul's family member. God had chosen, anointed, and appointed David to be the king over Israel and all peoples. What kind of king would God's chosen messiah be? He would be the one who brings honor from shame. Those who are broken and shamed, either by circumstances or self-inflicted wounds, would be brought to the table of honor in the messiah's kingdom.

In the narrative of David's reign, this story reveals that kindness, justice, and a reversal from shame to honor will characterize God's messianic kingdom. All people will be welcome at the Messiah's table.

The extravagant kindness of the messiah and his table is one of the ways this passage reveals to us Jesus, the true Davidic Messiah. Jesus is the Davidic Messiah whose kindness, generosity, and reversal of shame to honor stand as the banner for His rule. At His table all come to enjoy the feast, whether Jew, Gentile, lame, poor, sinner, or outcast. He draws all to Himself (Luke 13:28-29; Matt 8:11-12) (see Pitre, "Jesus, the Messianic Banquet, and the Kingdom of God," 145–66).

What about David? He was a type of the Messiah to come. His actions toward Mephibosheth transformed him from shame to honor. Because of David, Mephibosheth had a seat at the messiah's banquet table. But because of the true Messiah and His act of kindness and love—giving His own life for ours—we who are washed by the blood of the Lamb now will share in the banquet of Jesus forever. Jesus truly gives us beauty for ashes and garments of praise. He comes and adorns us with joy and gladness instead of despair.

Reflect and Discuss

1. How does this passage help you understand God?
2. How does this passage of Scripture exalt Jesus?
3. How does this story help us understand God's choice of David?

4. According to this passage of Scripture, who is the ultimate source of victory in life? Do you take credit for your victories, or do you have a grateful heart that recognizes God as the source of all victory?
5. How have you experienced shame? How did you handle it?
6. Why specifically did you handle that situation in that way? Write down your thoughts.
7. What does it do for your heart to know that God sent Jesus to give you "beauty for ashes"?
8. Identify the ways Jesus has transformed shame to honor in the past year. Write down your thoughts, and as you compile your list, express gratitude to God.
9. Read Luke 13:28-29 and Matthew 8:11-12. What does it do for you to know that we will dine at the King's table for eternity just as Mephibosheth dined at David's table?
10. How can you love others as Jesus has loved you?

The King Who Needs a Savior

2 SAMUEL 10–12 (PSALM 51)

Main Idea: David took God's blessing for granted and as a result fell into sin. The passage tells the story of the king who needs a Savior.

I. **A Shift toward Shame (10:1-9)**
II. **Slavery of Slaveries: David's Captivity to Sin (11:1-5)**
   A. David was blessed.
   B. David was disengaged.
   C. David was in a place where he could be tempted.
III. **The Road to Destruction: David's Cover-up of Sin (11:6-27)**
IV. **Gospel-Centered Repentance: David's Confession of Sin (12:1-31 and Ps 51)**
   A. Gospel-centered repentance makes its sole hope the mercy of God.
   B. Gospel-centered repentance owns that the sin we committed is deeply inherent in who we are.
   C. Gospel-centered repentance is directed first toward God.
   D. Gospel-centered repentance cries out for the gospel.

A Shift toward Shame

2 SAMUEL 10:1-19

The story in 2 Samuel 10 reveals a subtle move away from the overarching power and honor of David we saw in 2 Samuel 5–9. David is king and in covenant with Yahweh; he exerts his authority over all rivals. David defeats Saul and is the chief leader and worshiper of God's people. He brings honor to Mephibosheth in 2 Samuel 9, a magnanimous gesture that shows David's rule will be kind and generous, bringing honor to the shamed. In many ways it is a picture of what Christ does for those who place their faith in Him: He gives beauty for ashes, life out of death, and a song of praise where there was only the sound of mourning.

But something changes in 2 Samuel 10. The old allegiances erode after the Ammonite king, Nahash, dies. Nahash's son, Hanun, decides that David is untrustworthy and so instigates a war with the people of Israel. This leads, of course, to a battle between Ammon and Israel, which of course Israel wins. Ammon conscripted some Aramean soldiers to their aid (10:6-10). In the long run the rebellion against David and the people of God was ill conceived folly. However, for the alert reader, the shift to highlight the shame brought on David and his house signals something is about to change for David.

This chapter exposes the honor-shame social structure mentioned in the introduction (pp. 15–17), as Hanun shaves half of the beards of Israel's emissaries and cuts their clothes in half (10:4). David recognizes that this act was designed to shame both the Israelite emissaries and the Davidic house because David encourages the emissaries to remain in Jericho until their beards grow back and their honor is restored. The honor-shame dynamic is important because, if God's people had seen David's emissaries shamed, then they would know that David's honor and power in the wider world was diminished. The people would not see this because David commanded the emissaries to stay in Jericho. However, as readers we see this reality: shame has been brought on David and his house.

Consider the shift between chapter 9 and chapter 10. In 2 Samuel 9, David is kind to the son of Jonathan, Mephibosheth. As we have seen, Mephibosheth was lame or deformed in both of his legs, an unnatural condition in that day. The name "Mephibosheth" is related to the concept of shame, as *bosheth* in Hebrew means "shame." So David's magnanimous behavior in chapter 9 of bringing honor out of shame is contrasted with chapter 10, in which shame is brought to David's honorable actions. The winds of favor in David's reign are going to shift direction, and shame will reign instead.

As we have seen in the structure of the book, 2 Samuel 10 launches a fundamental change in the narrative of David. This chapter tells a story of sin that leads to the exile of David. The great king, as good as he was, was not the One who would provide the ultimate peace and rest God's people desired. God would provide this coming King "when the time came to completion" (Gal 4:4), and His name would be Jesus, for He would save His people from their sins. David was not, and could not be, that salvation. In reality the great king David still needed the Savior.

Growing up, I (J. D.) remember an old country preacher who used to come to our youth group and warn us about the dangers of sin. A favorite tactic of his was to point his finger at us and shout, "Sin ain't fun!" I never corrected him, but even at the time I thought, *Well, if sin ain't fun, you ain't doing it right.*

Let's be honest: sin can be a lot of fun. We don't rush toward sin because it's painful but because it's so promising. Sin almost always begins with a thrill, with a rush, with fun. And the more we Christians talk about sin, the more we risk sounding like that old country preacher, warning people about sin because we want to ruin other people's fun.

But we have to warn people. Why? Because while sin starts off with the excitement of endless possibility, it always leads to the same place: brokenness, agony, disappointment, and despair. And what is true of sin generally is especially true of sexual sin. Sexual sin is so powerful, so destructive—and yet so easy to access—that it can bring the strongest believer to utter ruin. After all, it did so for David, a man after God's own heart.

In David we see sin in all its predictable ugliness—its capacity to enslave us and to motivate us to cover it up. But we also see the possibility of renewal through confession. We'll get to the renewal. But first we have to walk the dark road with David for a few paces, into the captivity of sin.

The Slavery of Slaveries: David's Captivity to Sin
2 SAMUEL 11:1-5

Sin doesn't exist in a vacuum. It takes place in specific times and in specific ways. But Satan isn't as creative as God, so by taking a look at David's temptation and sin in 11:1-5, we see a paradigm for all temptation and sin. I see three relevant details.

David Was Blessed

Life is actually pretty good for David at this point. The kingdom is established; everyone loves him. Go back and read 2 Samuel 10, and you'll see that David has just emerged the victor of a whole slew of battles. If there were stock in David, Inc., it would be through the roof. In short, David was living a blessed life.

It may seem surprising to us that David's sin comes at a moment of extreme blessing. In times of adversity, sure, sexual sin is appealing. It acts like a savior, an escape, something to give us the quick fix we think we need. But what's so dangerous about blessing?

The danger in blessing is that we tend to forget just how dependent we are on God. When life showers us with goodness, we assume we have caused it. So God gets pushed to the periphery. This is why the author of Proverbs 30 prays to God, "Give me neither poverty nor wealth," but rather "feed me with the food I need. Otherwise, I might have too much and deny You, saying, "Who is the LORD?'" (Prov 30:8-9). The more self-sufficient we feel, the closer we are to disaster. As the apostle Paul says, "So, whoever thinks he stands must be careful not to fall" (1 Cor 10:12).

David Was Disengaged

It's no random detail that David had just sent Joab and the whole army out to battle. But where was David? At the time of year when kings go out to battle, David was back at home. David the warrior had become David the vacationer, and his lack of engagement made him susceptible to cheap thrills.

The way to successfully resist the enticements of this world isn't merely to have a strong will to say no. It's to be busy with a higher purpose. For many people their lives are so empty, so pointless, so devoid of something more, that the excitement of sex promises a fulfillment they desperately crave. It's not always that sin is incredibly alluring; it's often that we're so unbelievably bored.

We simply weren't designed to live our lives on the sidelines. God created us to engage in battle, to pursue His ministry with zeal and courage. Only a vision of what God wants to do *in* you will give you a sense of purpose strong enough to free you from the boredom that leads to sin. Only a vision of what God has done *for* you in the gospel will keep you from giving your souls away to idols. If we had that perspective, sure, we'd still sin, but we'd find so much less space for it. Bathsheba sure is tempting if we're sitting around, staring off into space. David would have found it a bit more difficult to sleep with her if he had been 50 miles away, in Rabbah with his troops.

David Was in a Place Where He Could Be Tempted

David is wandering around on the roof, alone, peering over at one roof after another. This is the ancient equivalent to staying up late and browsing the Internet. Is it any surprise what happens next? David had put himself in a place where he could be tempted. Deep down he wanted to be tempted.

One thing I (J. D.) have learned, from painful experience and through years of ministry, is this: it is far easier to avoid temptation than it is to resist sin. Don't get me wrong: resisting sin is important, immensely so. We must cultivate a habit of coming face-to-face with temptation and still resisting sin. But the world throws enough temptation our way; do we really need to go seek out more of it?

Dietrich Bonhoeffer says it perfectly:

> In our members there is a slumbering inclination toward desire which is both sudden and fierce. With irresistible power, desire seizes mastery of the flesh. All at once, a secret smoldering fire is kindled. The flesh burns and is in flames. In this moment, God is quite unreal to us. And Satan does not here fill us with hatred of God, but with a forgetfulness of God. The lust thus aroused envelops the mind and the will in deepest darkness. It is here that everything in me rises up against the word of God.
>
> Therefore the Bible teaches that in times of temptation to our flesh there is one command—flee. Flee youthful lust. Flee worldly temptation. If you're feeling under pressure and on the verge of something—an emotion is welling up within you—what does the Bible say? Run. No human being has within them the strength to resist such overpowering emotions. (*Temptation*, 116–17)

Some people will call this legalism. I just call it knowing the power of sin and the weakness of me. I know the consequences of toying with temptation, and I'm just not willing to play Russian roulette with my soul and my family.

In verses 3-5 David's dark road continues. His descent into sin wasn't immediate, and even here we see how he was given a chance to escape. "This is Eliam's daughter," someone tells him. "This is Uriah's wife." Why these details? This is the author pointing out to us—even if David didn't catch it—that Bathsheba wasn't just an object. She was someone's wife, someone's daughter. The anonymous person who answered David was trying to say, ever so subtly, "David, I know what you're thinking. And someone is going to get hurt."

It doesn't matter what the venue is. It doesn't matter what the sin is. Sin hurts people. It affects someone's mother, someone's daughter, someone's son—even if that someone is just you. God's rules, we have to remember, are never arbitrary. They are given to us for our good, to show us the most life-giving way of interacting with others. God doesn't want to keep us from sinning because He's out to ruin our fun. He wants to keep us from sinning because He knows how deeply it will wound us. Sin disintegrates. It wounds. Every time. Without fail.

One last point: note the hypocrisy of religion in this passage. Bathsheba had been "purifying herself." That was part of the Levitical law, a religious observance. It's as if she and David are able to ignore their adultery because they are going through the motions religiously. Don't we do the same? Aren't we tempted to think God is willing to overlook what we do on Saturday night as long as we show up for church on Sunday? God doesn't want our religiosity. He wants our hearts, our repentance. We'll get to that in a moment. But things are about to get much worse before they get better.

The Road to Destruction: David's Cover-up of Sin
2 SAMUEL 11:6-27

Second Samuel 11:6-27 records David at his most ingenious . . . and his most devious. David hatches a series of plans in order to hide the result of his sin. Plan A is an obvious one but a tricky one to accomplish: David attempts to trick Uriah into thinking the baby is his (vv. 6-11).

At any other time of year, this might not have seemed too difficult. But Uriah, you'll recall, is miles away fighting David's battles. So David needs to "create a moment." He invites Uriah home from battle, asks for a briefing on the war, and then sends him home. Uriah hasn't seen his wife in a while, and we already know she's a knockout. So David thinks he's got it covered.

Wrong. Uriah is a noble guy, and he's thinking of all his comrades sleeping in the field. They don't have the pleasure of sleeping in their own bed and enjoying their wives. So Uriah camps out with the palace guards for a night. Imagine how convicting that could have been for David if his conscience was not already suppressed.

David, however, isn't a quitter. He plots Plan B, which is really just an upgrade on Plan A (vv. 12-13). It now includes a previous step of getting Uriah hammered. Uriah, apparently, despite his nobility, likes a good Corona and walks right into David's plot. Uriah was just a few short steps away from his house (and David just a few short steps away from apparent freedom) when the alcohol overcame him. He passed out right there on his front lawn. Strike two for David.

So David starts Plan C (vv. 14-27). By this point he's desperate. He writes a note to Joab that tells him to put Uriah in the front of the battle and to abandon him. It's a death sentence for Uriah, and Uriah himself carries the plan to Joab. In the end David's plan succeeds. Uriah dies in battle, and it looks like David is going to get away with it.

But then comes the chilling end to the chapter: "However, the LORD considered what David had done to be evil" (v. 27). No one else may have seen what truly happened. David himself may have convinced himself that it was all behind him. But God's eyes were watching. They always are.

And David's life, from this point forward, begins to unravel. His family starts to fall apart. His newborn son dies. His children rebel against him. All because of sin. What does this show us but that sin has an enormous capacity to destroy?

Sin can always be forgiven. As we will see in a moment, David came to God and received healing for what he had done. But we can't always undo the damage caused when we freely walk into sin. Sin is a plague: by its very nature it destroys.

I hesitate to hammer this point too heavily because I never want people in sin to feel condemned. But some of you are on the brink of making an enormously foolish decision, running headlong into a situation you know you shouldn't touch. It might be an adulterous affair. It might be pornography. It might be cheating in school, or dishonest business practices, or a grudge you've been nursing that is consuming your heart. Whatever it is, you need to know that sin's whispers that promise joy are lies and that the end of that road is disaster. As John Owen said, "Be killing sin, or it will be killing you."

Gospel-Centered Repentance: David's Confession of Sin
2 SAMUEL 12 AND PSALM 51

For the choir director. A Davidic psalm, when Nathan the prophet came to him after he had gone to Bathsheba.

Be gracious to me, God,
according to Your faithful love;
according to Your abundant compassion,
blot out my rebellion.

Wash away my guilt
and cleanse me from my sin.
For I am conscious of my rebellion,
and my sin is always before me.
Against You—You alone—I have sinned
and done this evil in Your sight.
So You are right when You pass sentence;
You are blameless when You judge.
Indeed, I was guilty when I was born;
I was sinful when my mother conceived me.
Surely You desire integrity in the inner self,
and You teach me wisdom deep within.
Purify me with hyssop, and I will be clean;
wash me, and I will be whiter than snow.
Let me hear joy and gladness;
let the bones You have crushed rejoice.
Turn Your face away from my sins
and blot out all my guilt.
God, create a clean heart for me
and renew a steadfast spirit within me.
Do not banish me from Your presence
or take Your Holy Spirit from me.
Restore the joy of Your salvation to me,
and give me a willing spirit.
Then I will teach the rebellious Your ways,
and sinners will return to You. (Ps 51:1-13)

Few of us have sinned as egregiously as David did, in open adultery and murder. But we all sin. And every one of us is capable of David's heinous crimes. I know this because that's the nature of unconfessed sin. It changes us. When confronted with the results of our sin—as David was when Bathsheba got pregnant (11:5)—we can hide it, rationalize it, or shift blame. And that may work for a season. But there's only one true remedy for sin, and that is to repent. The question is not, Do you sin? The question is, What do you do after you sin? The answer to that question is a matter of life and death.

Fortunately for David, God chose to expose what David had covered up (ch. 12). He sent the prophet Nathan to remind David that although he thought he had gotten away with everything, God wouldn't let it end there. And in a moment of profound humility, David finally came clean. The result was one of the most beautiful and exemplary songs in Scripture: Psalm 51. In this psalm David shows us four keys to gospel-centered repentance and confession.

Gospel-Centered Repentance Makes Its Sole Hope the Mercy of God

David begins precisely where he should, by centering on God's grace. He prays "according to Your faithful love" and "according to Your abundant compassion." This is actually a rather risky thing to say. What if God decides not to be merciful? Shouldn't we make our case with God first? At least this is how many of us approach God.

But that's not repentance. Repentance begins where blame-shifting, bargaining, and rationalization end. Nothing in this prayer suggests that David comes to God looking to make a deal. He's not bargaining with God, trying to commute his sentence. He's not reminding God of all the great things he did in the past ("Remember Goliath?"). He's not trying to explain away his sin. He's not even promising to do better in the future. No, David appeals to God on the only ground that won't crumble, the ground of God's grace.

This is the heart of the gospel, and the reason so many people turn away from it. Religions, after all, are good at teaching people to seek mercy. Do this, say this, pray this, avoid this . . . and maybe God will be merciful to you. But only the gospel says, "I will rely on the mercy of God based on nothing about me." That can be a scary place to be, but here's the good news: no one who has ever made the mercy of God the sole basis of their plea has ever been turned away. Jesus turned many people away and for many reasons. He never turned someone away for trusting Him too deeply and relying too exclusively on His grace.

Gospel-Centered Repentance Owns That the Sin We Committed Is Deeply Inherent in Who We Are

When we're caught in our sin, our natural inclination is to explain it away. "I'm not really as bad as all that," we want to say. "It was just a moment of weakness." But David goes the complete opposite direction. "I am conscious of my rebellion," he says. "It isn't a mistake I made; it's at the core of who I am." In verse 5, he takes this about as far as it will go: "Indeed, I was guilty when I was born; I was sinful when my mother conceived me." In other words, "Hey, you think I'm bad? You don't know the half of it. This sin stuff? It's in my blood."

The theological term for this is "original sin." Our culture hates the idea, of course, and is deeply afraid to ever say anything like this. We try to convince ourselves that we're basically good people who make mistakes from time to time. The entire idea of having "deeply inherent" sin seems backward, repressive, and unhealthy. It's actually the only healthy way to live, as we'll see in a moment. But as G. K. Chesterton put it, original sin is "the only part of Christian theology which can really be proved."

This is the truth about all of us, if we'd ever admit it. No one ever taught me, for instance, how to be a lying, cheating, manipulative, selfish jerk. I'm just naturally good at all that. Or take, for example, our children. Children are precious, yes, but any parent will tell you that they are just plain good at sin. We don't need to send them to "sin camp" to pick it up. Their favorite words are usually *no* and *mine*, symbols of defiance and willfulness. And while we grow more sophisticated as we grow up, we don't naturally grow less rebellious. Every one of us is born a rebel against authority, especially against God's authority.

Gospel-Centered Repentance Is Directed First toward God

We might need to take off our Sunday school hats for a second to realize how bizarre verse 4 is: "Against You—You alone—I have sinned," David says. Really? Against God alone? What about Bathsheba? Or Uriah, for crying out loud? On the face of it, this doesn't make sense, but it's actually the heart of David's entire prayer. David's sin really was primarily a sin against God for two reasons.

First, David realizes that his sin began as a sin against God. What was it about Bathsheba that David wanted? Was it the feeling of power? her beauty? a moment of physical pleasure? Ultimately, David wasn't swept away because he wanted something specific. David was seduced by Bathsheba's beauty because he was no longer captivated by God's.

All our sin starts as a dissolution in our relationship with God. It begins as we grow dissatisfied with what God has given us, as we doubt His goodness toward us. So we start to feel God's boundaries as restrictive, not life-giving. This means the way to deal with sin in our lives isn't merely to suppress the sin; it's to increase our delight in God so that we love Him more than we love the sin. The only way to overcome sinful urges is not by learning to love them *less* but by learning to love God *more*.

Second, David realizes that God was the most significant One he had offended. What he did to Bathsheba was shameful; what he did to Uriah was despicable; but what he did to God was the most heinous of all. God had created David, had raised him up from the position of shepherd to that of a king, had given him every good thing in his life. In light of God's goodness toward him, as David reflects on his sin, all he can say is, "God, have I really done this . . . to You? After all You've done for me, this is my response?"

I fear that many of us don't realize how large and majestic is our God. But think: the bloody cross was the price for our sin. Jesus didn't have to die because of what we did to one another, but because of what we did to God. Have you ever sensed how much He has done to create you, to save you? He took you and me, His enemies, and brought us close to Himself, calling us His friends. That should change how we think of sin against God—not merely as treason against a mighty king but as a betrayal of a close friend's trust.

We need to see afresh the hammer in our own hands, driving nails into Christ's hands and feet. We need to hear our voices joining with the crowds, yelling, "Crucify!" We need to feel upset not just because of sin's consequences but because of what our sin has done to God. Until we do, our repentance will only be a smoke screen.

Gospel-Centered Repentance Cries Out for the Gospel

Throughout this psalm David points out that our repentance needs to flow from the heart. But there's a problem: our hearts are wicked. We can't change them, and David knows it. So he cries out for God to cleanse him: "Purify me with hyssop, and I will be clean; wash me, and I will be whiter than snow." Hyssop is only mentioned two other times in Scripture: once in the Exodus story, as the Jews were supposed to dip hyssop in a lamb's blood and spread that blood on their doorposts; and once as a means of cleansing leprosy. To a Jewish reader the connection David was making here would have been obvious. David is saying he needs something to free him from sin's slavery (like the slavery in Egypt), something to heal him from sin's disease (like the leprous disease). But literal hyssop wouldn't be enough. What David is crying out for is the hope of the gospel.

David needed someone who could "blot out all [his] guilt." That someone was Jesus, the true Passover Lamb, dying in our place so God's wrath would pass us by. David needed someone to "create a clean heart" for him. That someone was Jesus, who came to cleanse our leprous souls, souls so deeply sick that no amount of reformation or incentive could cure them. David needed someone to "renew a steadfast spirit" within him. That someone was Jesus, who imparted His Spirit to us as a sign of God's grace toward us.

Here's what is so beautiful about the gospel. David was crying out to God, asking God to purge him and cleanse him. But he also knew how deep his sin was. To be truly purged, truly cleansed, he would need to pay far more than what he possessed. The penalty for his sin—and ours—was death. But in the gospel God takes the penalty of our sin on Himself, absorbing it in the cross. The cross is God's promise to us that there is no sin so heinous, no heart so wicked, that He cannot cleanse it. And the resurrection is God's promise that there is no situation so dead that He cannot renew and restore it.

Reflect and Discuss

1. How does this passage help you understand God?
2. How does this passage of Scripture exalt Jesus?
3. How does this passage transition the story toward David's failure as king?
4. Why is it important to recognize that David is not the perfect king?
5. Why is it often so much easier to identify the sin of others and blame them rather than owning up to sin ourselves? Write down your thoughts.
6. In what ways do you understand that God supremely is the offended party by our sin? Write down your thoughts and be specific.
7. Does the point above somehow let us off the hook in our accountability and confession to others?
8. Identify the major ways you set yourself in places to be tempted. Be specific. Why do you think you set yourself in those places?
9. We have asked this before, but is your satisfaction in God alone? Why or why not?
10. In what ways do you think ease and comfort create a terrible context for temptation?

Consequences: The King in Jeopardy

2 SAMUEL 13–14

Main Idea: King David, unfortunately, has much in his life to teach us about the painful consequences of sin.

I. David's Sin: The Headwater of Family Dysfunction
II. From Family Dysfunction to Family Destruction (13:1–14:24)
III. From Family Destruction to National Unraveling (14:25-33)

Introduction

The doctrines of sin and redemption can be complicated—for non-Christians, of course, but also for many Christians. One problem nearly every pastor can attest to encountering is the confusion of sin's *punishment* and its *consequences.* When sin creates a rift in our lives or in the lives of those in our congregations, the response is often bewilderment. *Hasn't Jesus conquered sin?* we think. *Why is this still so damaging?* What we are struggling with in those moments is distinguishing the punishment for our sin from the natural consequences of it. And while Jesus absorbs sin's punishments, He does not always remove every consequence.

This may seem obvious enough, but it is remarkable how frequently the consequences of sin catch us by surprise. But how could it be otherwise? Imagine getting in a fight with your friend—over, say, a sports feud—in which the altercation came to fisticuffs. After a few days both of you calmed down, came together, and forgave each other. But your busted lip and black eye are testament that forgiveness doesn't automatically remove the consequence of sin.

King David, unfortunately, has much in his life to teach us about the painful consequences of sin. What we see throughout the later years of his life is a series of excruciatingly painful episodes that grow out of his sin with Bathsheba in chapter 11 and God's verdict on it in chapter 12. And while David found grace, the consequences were still real.

David's Sin: The Headwater of Family Dysfunction

Having been called out by the prophet Nathan for his sinful affair with Bathsheba, David responded with repentance. His prayer of confession

223

in Psalm 51 stands as a beautiful paradigm of godly grief over sin and confident hope in God's redemption. Nathan even confirms that David's prayer has been answered, telling him, "The LORD has taken away your sin; you will not die" (2 Sam 12:13). After David's blatant adultery, series of lies, and mass murder, this was certainly good news.

Yet Nathan also brings some bad news. Because of David's sin, three negative consequences will emerge. First, "the sword will never leave your house" (12:10). David had previously enjoyed military victory and a measure of peace, but his sin would now mean a lifetime of war, anxiety, and strife. Second, his wives will be unfaithful to him (12:11). This is a fitting, albeit gut-wrenching, consequence for a man who was unfaithful to his own wife. Third, the son born to him from this affair will die (12:14). We may wish that our sin did not have ripple effects into the lives of other people. But even the most cursory of reflections reveals that this is true. The alcoholic who chooses liquor over his family, the porn addict who chooses an online thrill over marital fidelity, the troubled youth who one day acts on his violent fantasies—sin harms not only us but also the lives of innocent others.

Losing a newborn child is tragic, nearly beyond the capacity of human words to express. But to lose a newborn because of your sin is devastating. This is what David is faced with and what comes to pass by the end of chapter 12. Sadly this one death was just the beginning of a precipitous spiral into family dysfunction.

From Family Dysfunction to Family Destruction
2 SAMUEL 13:1–14:24

The following five chapters depict a level of family strife that would top that of most American households. The litany of sins is disgusting—incest, sexual abuse, murder, rape, adultery, murder, substance abuse, theft, and more murder. Destruction follows destruction, violence begets violence, until the entire thread of God's grace seems to disappear. God is still at work in this dark time, but the consequences of sin are running their due course.

By chapter 13, David's oldest son, Amnon, develops a perverse crush on his stepsister Tamar. The text tells us that he wants her so badly he can't even eat. Eventually his lust gets the better of him, and he hatches a plot to get Tamar alone. Despite Tamar's protests, Amnon rapes her. The scene that follows conforms to a familiar pattern in sexual abuse.

"Amnon hated Tamar," the text tells us, "with such intensity that the hatred he hated her with was greater than the love he had loved her with" (2 Sam 13:15). The man (or woman) driven by lust is not consumed with desire for a person but for a selfish pleasure. Once the pleasure is grasped, the person is discarded. As C. S. Lewis put it, "How much he [the lustful man] cares about the woman as such may be gauged by his attitude to her five minutes after fruition (one does not keep the carton after one has smoked the cigarettes)" (*The Four Loves*, 94).

Sure enough, after getting the sexual pleasure he was after, Amnon cannot even bring himself to refer to Tamar by name. "Throw this woman out and bolt the door behind her!" (13:17). *This woman.* Not only is this an insult to Tamar's personhood, but it should also be a familiar phrase to the reader. When David saw Bathsheba from his roof, literally he inquired about "the woman" (ESV). When David's servants tried to remind David that what he saw was not merely a beautiful woman but Bathsheba, a woman with a name, a father, and a husband, he brushed them aside. What David saw was an object for his pleasure. And now Amnon, David's son, is repeating David's sin. The sin sown by the father is harvested in the child.

Where is David in all this? He seems completely disconnected and not because he's off in battle with his troops. He is actually right there in the city with his children—he unwittingly helps orchestrate the fateful meeting between Amnon and Tamar. But when it comes to the life of his kids, David is clueless. Even when David finds out about Tamar's rape, he does nothing. The man who had stood up to the giant Goliath does nothing to avenge his little girl.

David's passivity sets the scene for the next outbreak of familial damage. Another of David's sons, Absalom, finds out about what happened to his sister Tamar. He responds as David should have, by showing compassion on Tamar and welcoming her into his home after her rape (13:20). But he also watches as his father responds to horror with silence (v. 21). What a disappointment that must have been! Absalom had grown up hearing stories of David's heroism and courage. His father was his hero. And at this crucial moment, when courage and heroism were most required, David was nowhere to be found. So Absalom decides he will take matters into his own hands. Amnon must die.

Absalom's plot to kill Amnon is remarkably patient (13:22-29). He must have known Amnon might suspect violence initially, so instead of attacking Amnon in the immediate aftermath, he plans a scheme that will take a full two years. He believed back then what they say nowadays: revenge is a dish best served cold. But in the end the result was the same as if Absalom had assaulted Amnon the next day. He got Amnon drunk and had him murdered. Note again the parallels with David's story. David had tried (unsuccessfully) to cover up his affair by getting Uriah drunk. And when that did not work, he had Uriah murdered. Once again the sin sown by the father is harvested in the child.

After Absalom murders Amnon, he flees for his life. For three years he remains in exile. David knows where he is this whole time but never once goes to him or even sends word to him. Eventually Joab, the captain of David's army, reaches out to bring Absalom back (14:1-23). But even then, when Absalom was in the palace itself, David refused to see him. "He may return to his house, but he may not see my face" (v. 24).

David's family is in shambles at this point, but each successive tragedy is preventable. Had David been more involved, he could have prevented Amnon from acting on his perverse desires. Had David gone to Tamar after her assault, he could have prevented Absalom from avenging his sister's death. Even now, with all this death and destruction in the rear view, David could still stem further damage. If he would reach out to Absalom, he could prevent him from descending further into darkness. Sadly, once again, David does nothing.

The greatest temptation men face, then as now, is not to outright wickedness but to the smoother—and equally destructive—path of apathy and inaction. When we look around at the family situation in the United States today, we are grieved by the failure of fathers to fulfill the role God has given them. In some instances this manifests in outright abuse. But far more often it manifests in absent dads, men who would rather know what is happening on ESPN than in the lives of their sons and daughters. Were most of the men in our churches to show the same level of apathy in their jobs as they do in their home lives, they would have been fired long ago.

From Family Destruction to National Unraveling
2 SAMUEL 14:25-33

Unfortunately, David remains stuck in passivity. Perhaps he was nursing old wounds, wallowing in self-pity. Perhaps he was busying himself with other kingly duties. Either way, his failure to act would result in further destruction. Now, instead of just watching his own family unravel, his apathy would lead to the unraveling of a nation. Absalom is a ticking time bomb, and the question is not *if* but only *when* and *how* he will explode.

It begins, in 14:29-30, with a seemingly petty act of vandalism. Absalom, frustrated that his father continues to give him the cold shoulder, decides that he will act up to get his dad's attention. So he takes a few torches and goes after the fields of Joab, David's right-hand man. In short order Joab's fields are ablaze. David may not have much cared to reconcile with his son, but at this point Joab has been given renewed motivation. Joab becomes, once again, the primary agent attempting to get David and Absalom to settle their feud.

Joab is able to get Absalom back into King David's presence, but all is not well in Jerusalem. Like most dysfunctional families these two never address the five years of silence or the heinous acts that precipitated them. They gloss over the deeper issues—a tactic that never ends well.

David, for his part, should have known better. His failure to address Tamar's rape enraged Absalom to begin with. Now he is confronted with the same hotheaded son, a son who is still seething and liable to do tremendous violence. But David's response is the same. Sadly so is Absalom's.

Absalom begins to plot an armed revolution to take the kingdom from his father (ch. 15). We have already seen how savvy Absalom can be when hatching a devious plot, and his coup proves once again how resourceful the young man is. He parks himself outside David's palace and gradually begins to steal away devotees to King David by adjudicating their disputes for them. Absalom's silver tongue disparages David's capacity to rule with justice while simultaneously implying that, if he were in charge, he would set things right. Thus, right under David's nose, "Absalom stole the hearts of the men of Israel" (15:6). When the time was right, he rose up and took the capital by storm. David and his loyalists were forced to flee. As we will see, this is the red-eyed beast of ambition rearing its ugly head in Absalom's life and is the outworking of David's passivity.

Reflect and Discuss

1. How does this passage help you understand God?
2. How does this passage of Scripture exalt Jesus?
3. How does this passage reveal David's failure as king?

4. How does David's sin with Bathsheba produce even more significant rotten fruit in David's family?

5. What does it do to your heart to read and hear of Tamar's violation? What do you think of the way David handled that violation?

6. Is Absalom's action understandable, even if not justified? Why or why not?

7. How does David's passivity in his family affect his entire nation?

8. Many readers will experience the story of Tamar with painful memories. Take time to reflect that pain and hurt back to God in prayer.

9. Do you believe Jesus gives honor and healing? Give thanks that Jesus restores honor and beauty and brings joy back into battered and wounded lives.

10. Is the dangerous trait of apathy creeping into your life? Take time to repent of this and turn once again to Jesus.

The Red-Eyed Beast: Ambition

2 SAMUEL 15

Main Idea: Absalom's revolt against David reveals the horrifying monster of ambition in lives when we live for our kingdom rather than Christ's kingdom.

I. **Unhealthy, Sinful Ambition**
II. **For Whose Kingdom Do You Live?**
III. **Ambition Assessment**
   A. Are people a means to your end?
   B. Do you make memorials to yourself?
IV. **Taming the Beast of Ambition**

In Oliver Stone's classic movie *Wall Street* (1987), the tycoon Gordon Gekko said, "Greed is good." Greed keeps you sharp. It helps you satisfy your ambition. In the sequel to the classic, *Wall Street: Money Never Sleeps* (2010), Gordon Gekko is released from prison. He is somewhat of a figure on Wall Street once again. He says now, "I once said greed is good. Now it appears it's legal." Wall Street, both in fantasy and in reality, is one of America's golden shrines to pay homage to the god of ambition.

If envy is the green-eyed monster, then it's fair to say that ambition can be called the red-eyed beast. Ambition is a character trait that is celebrated in our culture. It is something we use to achieve greatness, or at least so the story goes. But in this section we are going to take a hard look at one of our culture's deepest idols. What is ambition? Ambition is the desire for notoriety or rank, often at the expense of others.

Unhealthy, Sinful Ambition

In the book of Samuel, ambition is the desire to create and cultivate one's own kingdom rather than live under the reign of God in His kingdom. And any time God's people live for themselves rather than live under the reign of their Lord, bad things happen. So 2 Samuel 15 reveals a disturbing picture of ambition gone awry. This destructive picture of ambition solidifies the overall narrative of David's failure as a leader.

Notice the following actions of Absalom from 15:1-6. These give a chilling picture of ambition.

1. Driving the chariot with horses and 50 men to run before him (v. 1)
2. Sitting at the city gate, stopping people as they went to the king, and settling their disputes for them (vv. 2-6)

Driving chariots and hearing disputes at the city gate are common practices of ancient Israelite leaders and kings. If Absalom enacts these practices, he is enacting the office of the king. The question we must ask is this: Why is Absalom doing the things that normally are reserved for kings?

In these actions we see the heart of his ambition. Absalom wanted to be king.

Interestingly enough, that desire is not necessarily bad. After all, he was David's son. He was the son-in-law to the king of Geshur. So Absalom was a royal figure; he was a prince. In this way a prince aiming at kingship is not so far-fetched or inappropriate.

But the problem of Absalom's ambition lay in this point: Who was God's appointed king in Israel at that time? It was King David. And for all David's faults (there is a laundry list!), God had made him king in Israel, as 2 Samuel 7 shows. Through this king God was leading Israel at that time.

Absalom's ambition for kingship, although natural, was here not a good thing. Why? He wanted to make his own name great at the expense of his father. He wanted to dethrone his dad.

For Whose Kingdom Do You Live?

If we think about this in terms of God's plan, then we must say that Absalom was working against God's design for His people. Absalom wanted to discard God's design with David and create the world in his own image, God's design be damned.

We see the heart of Absalom's ambition. It was not directed for the glory of God. Absalom's ambition was to build his own kingdom, not God's kingdom.

Some of us who know the story may think, *Well you can't blame him. David's a bad king, a bad dad, a bad husband, and a horrible friend. We've just been reading about his failures. He can't rule well and puts some heavy taxes on the people, he didn't defend his daughter when she was raped, he cheated on his first wife, and his second wife, and third, and fourth, etc. And finally, he let some of his best friends (like Jonathan) die. What a despicable person. No wonder Absalom did what he did. David deserved it!*

But it is precisely at that point where we find the difference between God and us.

God does not relate to us on the basis of what we deserve. He relates to us on the basis of His love for us. Despite his faults and sin, David appreciated God's gracious love for him and returned that love by pursuing God's plan. Absalom, however, thumbed his nose at God and God's plan. Absalom was not interested in what God wanted. Absalom was interested in what Absalom wanted.

The text of 2 Samuel presents Absalom in an interesting way. Absalom drove the chariots. He judged at the gates. But Absalom did not do any of the heavy lifting God empowered his father to do. Absalom did not fight battles like David and did not give wise counsel like David. When we see David, he is king, and he earned the right to sit up in the chariot. He spent years fighting tough fights. He was a warrior and a king. When he went about with his army, it wasn't for show; it was for action. What about Absalom? He wanted to look the part of king without having to experience any of the hard knocks. As one scholar says, Absalom "has the accoutrements of regality before he has the inner and outer qualities" (Goldingay, *Men Behaving Badly*, 278).

When we see David, he gives counsel to people. He devotes himself to "justice and righteousness" (2 Sam 8:15) in his reign. What is "justice and righteousness"? In the Bible it does not mean what we may think it means. It does not mean "treating everyone the same." Rather, "justice and righteousness" in the Bible means the king works for the people and their well-being rather than his own well-being. Goldingay states "justice and righteousness" is a "concern to do right for your people that expresses itself in decisive action on their behalf" (*Men Behaving Badly*, 279).

But what about Absalom at the gates? Notice his response to all who come to him. He is essentially a "yes-man" trying to get folks on his side. He says, "Well, your complaint is a good one. Someone needs to hear this. Wow! I completely agree with you!" You see, Absalom says yes to everyone. Why? He wants to be king in the place of his father.

The narrative presents Absalom as one who apes at kingship without experiencing divine anointing, undergoing tough battles, or being tested in the fire. We have a name for Absalom in today's language: a "wannabe." He wants to be king, but he has neither the maturity nor the wisdom to do so.

Attempting to be someone or something we are not ready or equipped to be leaves us frustrated and exposed. Such a charade does not satisfy, but it does reveal someone acting silly. Attempting to be someone we are not actually exposes our lack of understanding of both God and ourselves. We aren't satisfied with who we are because we don't know who God has made us to be.

This was Absalom's problem. He wanted what he wanted but didn't want what God wanted for his life or his people. He was not satisfied with his father David (warts and all!), and as a result he ended up trying to pretend to be David, the king. He was a wannabe. There are some basic ways we can assess whether we are wannabe believers. It may be helpful to run your life through the following assessment:

Ambition Assessment

Are People a Means to Your End?

When we look at Absalom in the narrative, we see immediately his view of people. When he is at the gate, he stops people from going to the true king (David) for just judgment. He sits at the gate and says, "Oh hello, my dear, dear friend, my brother! What ails you? My, my, that is a fix, and someone should do something! Yes, of course you are in the right! Well, I wish I could do something for you, but you know, David's on his throne, and well, things don't really get done with him. If only I were a judge here, I could help you out" (cf. vv. 3-6).

The narrative in the original language makes pretty clear that Absalom is being disingenuous. He does not care one whit about the people to whom he speaks. As chapters 15–20 make clear, much less verses 7-12 in this chapter, Absalom did what he did for three reasons: (1) to steal allegiance from David, (2) to make people think he cared, and (3) to build support for his eventual coup. Frankly, the people of the city—we might add they were real people with real problems—remain unimportant to Absalom except insofar as they are a means to help him achieve his ends. Do you know what people are as far as Absalom is concerned? People are tools. Tools for him to use as he wants. But once he has finished using them, he can toss them aside. Do you know anyone who treats others in that way?

Maybe we use people in the same way. (God forbid!) This could take place at work, where we use people to get what we want rather than treating them as real, genuine people who are created and loved by God.

Maybe this message hits home with parents who use the behavior of children to make others think what great parents we are. Or we use the sports or academic achievements of our children as trophies for others to admire. The joy in those situations lies not in what the children have achieved; the joy lies in the acclaim we receive from those who are impressed. In this scenario our children become tools that feed parental ego.

For those in the workplace, we could use people in various ways. As an employer we might be tempted to overwork our employees (sometimes with little or no pay!) so that the employer can get the promotion or save a dollar for maximum profit. In this case employees are not real, live people created by God and worthy of dignity and respect. By contrast our actions reveal that we view them as tools we can use and throw away, like a screwdriver or paper cup. Why do we do this? We want our kingdom rather than God's kingdom!

Do You Make Memorials to Yourself?

Memorials testify to a person or event. Absalom was set on erecting a memorial for himself rather than pointing to Yahweh and His plan through the Davidic king. In verse 6 we discover some chilling words: "So Absalom stole the hearts of the men of Israel." The question we must ask is this: In what way did Absalom "steal" people's hearts? To steal on a biblical reckoning means to take from someone something that does not belong to me. So if that is true, then Absalom has stolen the minds and wills of the people, which do not belong to him.

To whom do the hearts of the people belong? In the immediate context the hearts and minds of the people belong to David, Yahweh's anointed and appointed king. But we must take this further. The book of Samuel, particularly from 2 Samuel 7 onward, reveals that God's reign and His kingdom flow through His anointed and appointed king. As we have seen, 2 Samuel 7 confirms that Yahweh established David as king, the one who rules under the authority of the Lord. The king and his family, then, are to point the people back to Yahweh, His reign, and His ways. So David is not just a political leader; he reminds the people who God is.

When Absalom steals the hearts and minds of the men of Israel, he does more than just a political act. He draws the people away from their devotion to God and God's ways.

Absalom was more concerned with his own name being known and remembered than with God's name being known and remembered. That plan always ends in disaster. For Absalom it meant losing his father, his friends, and eventually his life. More than that, he led people away from God's plan. Yahweh chose King David to rule, and from his family and royal throne, Jesus would come. Absalom, by trying to make his name known rather than God's, showed himself to be in direct contrast to what God was up to.

Henri Nouwen, that distinguished Christian thinker, said this in his wonderful book *In the Name of Jesus: Reflections on Christian Leadership*: "It seems easier to be God than to love God, easier to control people than to love people, easier to own life than to love life" (58–59). This is so true for those of us who have faced down the red-eyed beast of ambition. We use people, and own them, and attempt to be God to set up a memorial to ourselves. We think of how our actions impact and increase our own name before we think of how our actions increase and impact the name of the Lord. Absalom's life is an example of a tragic life where ambition has gone terribly wrong.

Taming the Beast of Ambition

So if we want to "tame" the beast of ambition, what do we do? We must discover the clue to real life: Jesus Christ. God is not a cosmic killjoy. God is the one who brings us life and forgiveness. He provides this forgiveness and life in Jesus. *In Jesus, like a treasure amid darkness, we discover our true selves.* In Jesus the apostle Paul describes who we become as "a new creation" (2 Cor 5:17). What does that mean? It means that in Jesus we are forgiven of sin and find our real life and purpose in life. The mark of the "wannabe" is replaced with the confidence and peace of knowing who we are in Jesus. *In Jesus, we discover the wonder of real relationships—loving people and treating them as we would like to be treated.* People then are not resources for us to use but rather individuals of intrinsic worth, worthy of friendship and relationship. In Christ we can overcome using people for what we want and instead learn what it means to partner with people in building life together. Finally, *in Jesus, we discover the satisfaction that comes from living for something greater than yourself—for a NAME greater than your own.*

Henri Nouwen, whom I mentioned earlier, is an immensely fascinating person. He hit the heights of the academic world. He taught at Harvard, Yale, and Notre Dame. He was a brilliant man, but he discovered that achieving these ambitions left him empty, restless. He discovered, however, a home and joy in life not in the heights of human achievement but rather in the difficulty of what is called a L'Arche community. L'Arche communities are little groups of people living all over the world. They are communities of people with disabilities, both physical and mental.

On a media program from 1989, Nouwen spoke about his journey to L'Arche, and he said this:

> One of the things that I am becoming aware of more and more is that from the very beginning of my life there have been two voices. One voice saying, "Henri, be sure you make it on your own, be sure you can do it yourself, be sure you become an independent person. Be sure that I can be proud of you." And, another voice saying, "Henri, whatever you are going to do, even if you don't do anything very interesting in the eyes of the world, be sure you stay close to the heart of Jesus, be sure you stay close to the love of God." You can sort of guess which voice was whose. But, I guess we all hear these voices to some degree—the voice that calls you upward and says, "Make something of your life, be sure you have a good career." Then, a voice that says, "Be sure you never lose touch with your vocation." There is a little bit of a struggle there, a tension. ("Journey to L'Arche")

The key to killing the red-eyed beast of ambition is this: to be captured by the gospel and to stay close to the heart of Jesus. Set Jesus on display. We must make it our ambition that "He must increase" and we must decrease (John 3:30).

Reflect and Discuss

1. How does this passage help you understand God?
2. How does this passage of Scripture exalt Jesus?
3. In what ways do you see unhealthy ambition present in your life? Why do you think that is the case?
4. As you do an ambition assessment, do you find that you have a tendency to use people? Why do you think that is the case?

5. Are you willing to allow God to shape you into the person He wants you to be? Another way of asking this is, "Are you comfortable with who God made you to be, or do you fantasize about being someone else?" Take time and be honest. Confess your thoughts and feelings to the Lord.

6. Why specifically do you feel this way? Write down your thoughts.

7. In what ways do you think you need to be captured by the power of the gospel to understand that your worth is first and foremost who you are in Christ and who He has made you to be?

8. In light of the extended Henri Nouwen quote at the close of the chapter, which voice sounds loudest in your ear right now: the voice of selfishness or the voice of Jesus? Why do you think that is the case? To whose voice do you need to listen?

9. In what ways do you see your life as a part of God's great kingdom? In what ways do you see your story in His story?

10. God does not relate to us on the basis of what we deserve. He relates to us on the basis of His love for us. How does this statement about the gospel impact your heart?

The King in Exile

2 SAMUEL 16–18

Main Idea: Rebellion against God's Messiah is painful and destructive, but such rebellion will not last.

I.   A Blessing and a Curse
II. A Tragic Victory
III. From David and Absalom to You and Me

Absalom is not finished. Fresh off of his triumphant victory, he stages an X-rated scene atop the palace, sleeping with several of David's concubines "in the sight of all Israel" (2 Sam 16:22). This was not an act of voyeurism so much as a statement of power. Absalom wanted to publicly humiliate David, to make patently clear that he had stolen his father's kingdom. In so doing, he reenacts—and heightens—David's sin with Bathsheba, stealing everything from another man and sleeping with that man's wife. Even the location is identical.

A Blessing and a Curse

Meanwhile, David is fleeing from Absalom, weeping as he goes. The confident warrior who stood up to Goliath is now a self-pitying shell of his former self. Two figures emerge in David's flight: Ziba and Shimei. Ziba has no business being a blessing to the defeated David. But he recognizes the authority of the Lord's anointed and helps him.

But David receives cursing as well as blessing. During his retreat David endures the curses and physical abuses of Shimei, who taunts David over his fresh wounds. "The Lord has handed the kingdom over to your son Absalom," Shimei screams at David, all the while hurling stones at him. "Look, you are in trouble because you're a murderer!" (2 Sam 16:8). David accepts the scorn, wondering if perhaps this is God's lot for him: "He curses me this way because the Lord told him, 'Curse David!'" (v. 10).

There may be a sliver of humility in David's admission, but David's comment here flies in the face of God's previous declarations. We ought not commend David for trust in God's sovereignty so much as castigate him for forgetting God's promises. After all, God had promised blessing, not cursing, to David. In no uncertain terms God told him that his kingdom could never be taken away—that, in fact, it would be an everlasting kingdom. David's sin, though it would lead to brutal consequences, was taken away, and his soul was washed with hyssop, made whiter than snow.

At this point, however, David seems to have forgotten this. Or, if he remembers it, he simply does not believe it. The truth of God's promises carries less weight in his life than the guilt complex he continues to nurse as he plods away from the city, the throne, and the kingdom God had promised him.

A Tragic Victory

Revolutions rarely end well, and Absalom's is no exception. What follows in 2 Samuel 17–18 is a scene of David's victory but a victory that is soured by tragedy and regret.

Largely due to the support of other generals and leaders, David is encouraged to turn back and fight for his kingdom. As swiftly as Absalom ascended the throne, he was forced to abandon it, running for his life through the wilderness. David's men, eager to avenge their king and their own humiliation, naturally desire to kill Absalom the usurper. But David is beginning to see Absalom less as a usurper and more as a son. "Treat the young man Absalom gently for my sake," he tells his soldiers (18:5).

The orders are clear, but they prove powerless. While fleeing through the forest, Absalom gets stuck in a tree by his hair, suspended in full view of the oncoming soldiers, completely vulnerable. Joab, knowing full well that David had given orders to spare Absalom's life, flouts David's command. For years he had been the chief advocate of reconciliation between the two, but he had reached a breaking point. So even while the other soldiers beg him to stop, Joab runs Absalom through with three javelins. The revolution is over, and David is once again king.

But there will be no rejoicing in this victory. News of Absalom's death reaches David, and it seems, for the first time, David realizes what he has lost.

> The king was deeply moved and went up to the gate chamber and
> wept. As he walked, he cried, "My son Absalom! My son, my son
> Absalom! If only I had died instead of you, Absalom, my son, my son!"
> (18:33)

It is almost impossible to represent the intensity of emotion in this verse. Throughout this entire episode David has not once called Absalom "son." And now, only now at his death, the word comes pouring out from his lips again and again and again. David is finally feeling the emotion of a father, but it is too late. All he has left are memories tainted by bad decisions, regret, and missed opportunities.

And so ends the tragic story of David and his son Absalom.

From David and Absalom to You and Me

Whenever reading through the narratives of the Bible, it is helpful to regularly stop and ask, "Why is this story in here?" One answer to this question, of course, is always, because this actually happened. But Scripture does not merely give us history lessons. It also demands that we learn from them. So what is there for contemporary readers in this dark and tragic cycle of destruction?

We must not be too quick simply to moralize David and Absalom. Yes, it is true that men should be proactive in their families. Yes, it is true that sin is so damaging we should avoid it at all costs. But before those pieces of good *advice* can be helpful, they have to be situated within the context of good *news*. We must see David's story in the bigger picture of Jesus and the gospel. King David was not the perfect king that Israel—and we—needed. Jesus was.

Absalom's rebellion may fill us with disgust, but spiritually speaking, we are all Absalom. We have rebelled against a God and Father more pure and holy than David, stolen His kingdom for ourselves, and publicly humiliated Him on the rooftops of our lives. We deserve the shameful fate of Absalom.

And yet God does not dole out what we deserve. Absalom returned to his father, but his father refused even to meet him at the gate. How different is our Father's response to us! Jesus told a story about a son, much like Absalom, who had sinned against his father and publicly shamed him. But when that son returned home, the father ran to meet him. The prodigal son could not even finish his apology before his father was pouring out forgiveness. This is our God, pouring out forgiveness even before we fully see the stain of our sin.

The Father's forgiveness, though freely given, came at enormous cost. When Absalom died, David cried out, vainly wishing he could have died in his place. What David longed to do for Absalom, God accomplished for us. Jesus Christ went to the cross to die in our place, an act of love that should remind us of David's heartfelt cry, "My son, my son!" In the death of Christ, God was saying to us, "My son! My daughter! Do you know how much I love you? My child, I am dying in your place!" Jesus did for us, His sons and daughters, what David could not do for his own. Absalom died hanging in a tree with a spear for his rebellion thrust through his heart; Jesus died on a tree with a spear for our rebellion thrust through His.

Seeing this, the gospel of Jesus' sacrifice for us, is the only vision that can change us. Warnings about following David's footsteps may frighten us; words of advice about raising the right family may equip us; but only seeing Christ on the tree gives us the power to break the cycle of sin. What is more, the cross gives us the capacity to hope in the midst of painful circumstances, even if we caused those circumstances ourselves.

God, you see, was not finished with David. The promise of an eternal kingdom had never ceased being true. And despite his many failings, despite tragedy on tragedy, God would use David to raise up the greatest King and Savior Israel would ever know. The consequences of David's sin ran deep, but the plans and promises of God ran deeper.

Nor is God finished with us. Many of us are suffering from the direct consequences of our sin—a broken marriage, an estranged son or daughter, a body crippled from drug use. Sin's effects are strong in our lives, but the grace of God is stronger. And while He may not remove those consequences, we can say with David, "Only goodness and faithful love will pursue me all the days of my life" (Ps 23:6). Our sin, if we are in Christ, is not the final word for us. So to the thief, the abuser, the divorcee, the adulterer, God says, "And some of you *used to be* like this. But you were washed, you were sanctified, you were justified in the name of the Lord Jesus Christ and by the Spirit of our God" (1 Cor 6:11, author's emphasis). Our past sins may plague us, but in Christ they have no more power to define us.

David knew God's goodness in his life. He knew God had a plan for him, a plan to prosper him and not to harm him. He knew, albeit dimly, the majestic love of the gospel. But he allowed the contrary words of his circumstances to be louder in his life. God had spoken forgiveness and healing to David, but he was all too quick to believe Shimei's curses. He need not have ignored his past sins to answer Shimei. There was no need to pretend that the Bathsheba incident never occurred or that David was sinless. He could still have spoken with strength and conviction, the conviction that comes from a sinner saved by grace.

Our sin may lead to devastating consequences, but we must never let it shut our mouths. Many of us feel that because we sin—and others know it—we can never speak into their lives with moral authority or conviction. This would be true if our authority rested on our righteousness. But we speak as ones redeemed. Thus our words are not, "Be like me!" but rather, "Look to Christ!" And the more we see our sin, the more we can say to others, "Join me, and let's run to Christ together." The grace-saturated soul is the only one that can speak both with authority and without arrogance. Grace frees us from the paralysis of guilt to the possibility of true community.

All of us are Absalom. But it is no foregone conclusion that we end where he did. God's grace is available to break the power of cancelled sin, to set the prisoner free. We know this because we have felt it ourselves: "His blood can make the foulest clean, His blood availed for me" (Charles Wesley, "O for a Thousand Tongues to Sing," 1739). The cross forgives our past; the resurrection re-creates our future. And this gospel delivers us in the present to the power of new life.

Reflect and Discuss

1. How does this passage help you understand God?
2. How does this passage of Scripture exalt Jesus?
3. Ziba and Shimei both offer words to David. What is the difference in their speech?
4. In what ways do we use the language of Ziba or Shemei to bless or curse others? In what ways do we use our words to bring honor or shame to our Savior?
5. In David's flight from Jerusalem, how did he fail to trust in God's provision? Does God desire to curse the messiah or bless him?
6. Why do you think Absalom rebelled and caused a revolution? Be specific in your response.
7. In what ways does the failure of the Davidic family press us to see the grace of God despite human frailty?
8. How do Absalom's death and David's dirge help us see Jesus?
9. If you are in Jesus but are facing the consequences of sin, what does it do for your heart to know that those adverse consequences are not the final word on your life? Jesus has spoken a better word for the future!
10. How can our experience of sin and consequences be brought to the church as gifts God can use to build His people?

The King's Return and Continued Conflict

2 SAMUEL 19–21

Main Idea: David returns to the throne, but continued conflict marks the final days of his reign. The unsettled reality of his last days looks beyond his reign to that of the true and coming King.

I.   **A Broken Father and Politician**
II. **A Conflicted Kingdom**
III. **Abiding Consequences of Sin**
IV. **Waiting for the King**

A Broken Father and Politician

The sin of David with Bathsheba, coupled with the lack of parental care and action with Judah's abuse of Tamar, led to Absalom's revolt. The threads of sin, sex, and selfishness weave together into a bloody and awful tapestry from 2 Samuel 11 through 18. David's sin echoes through these chapters, as does Yahweh's rebuke through Nathan, the prophet:

> *"Now therefore, the sword will never leave your house because you despised Me and took the wife of Uriah the Hittite to be your own wife."*
> *This is what the LORD says, "I am going to bring disaster on you from your own family: I will take your wives and give them to another before your very eyes, and he will sleep with them publicly. You acted in secret, but I will do this before all Israel and in broad daylight."*
> (2 Sam 12:10-12)

David would never again have "rest" from all sides. Sin does that. It causes us to be unsettled, unsatisfied, and in conflict. David's kingdom survived Absalom's insurrection not because of David's righteousness or power but certainly because "the LORD has delivered him from his enemies" (18:19).

Still the victory would be, at best, bittersweet. The opening verses of chapter 19 reveal the interior life of David, and he is completely distraught. We might think David should be happier that his kingdom has been restored. We might think he is a weak king that mourns over a no-good and rebellious son. But that would be a harsh and compassion-less judgment. As Robert Gordon says, "Even in times of crisis and high drama a king may be a father" (*I & II Samuel*, 287).

David's mourning signals that all is not well. While the Lord did give David victory and deliverance, the consequences of sin still sting. A son is dead. A father is bereaved. A family is torn apart, and a nation is ripped to shreds. This is not a clean return to the throne for David by any stretch of the imagination. God's speech of 2 Samuel 12 rings true: disaster has come, and the sword is present in David's reign the remainder of his days.

Still, David is the consummate politician. Recognizing that Absalom has swayed many to his side, David is conciliatory in his approach to return to Jerusalem's royal palace. He wooed the elders of Judah with words of kindness (19:9-12). He places Amasa, a general from Judah, as commander of his army to replace Joab (vv. 13-14). He knows that many followed Absalom and so now are not with him. He needs to bring them back to his side. Instead of triumphantly marching into Jerusalem, he moves from his base at Mahanaim (17:24) only as far as Gilgal (19:15). From there he begins to meet with people who were loyal to Absalom.

From David's slow and steady march geographically (from Gilgal into Jerusalem), we see his deliberate and political march into the hearts of those who formerly swore allegiance to Absalom. Shimei, Ziba, and Mephibosheth are reconciled to David. David also consolidates his power with those who were loyal to him in exile, particularly Barzillai the Gileadite and Chimham. The text records, "All the troops of Judah and half of Israel's escorted the king" (19:40). David had consolidated power with those in Judah through cajoling and through kinship. He brought those allied with Absalom to his side. He was a powerful politician.

A Conflicted Kingdom

Still, the text reveals that David's restored kingdom was not a peaceable kingdom. As quickly as David returns (finally) to Jerusalem, another Benjaminite (like Saul!) starts wreaking havoc. Sheba denounces David, effectively mounting a rebellion against the king and his house:

> *We have no portion in David,*
> *no inheritance in Jesse's son.*
> *Each man to his tent, Israel!* (2 Sam 20:1)

This statement provides an ominous foreshadowing of what will play out in 1–2 Kings, a nation divided between Israel and Judah. At Sheba's words, "all the men of Israel" withdrew from David, while the men of Judah staunchly supported their king.

David charged Joab with quashing Sheba's insurrection. Instead of helping things, Joab made them worse. We are not exactly sure why Joab did it, but he disemboweled and murdered Amasa (2 Sam 20:11), David's new military commander (19:13). Amasa, you will remember, was loyal to Absalom. As a result, those who are loyal to Amasa now turn on David! The point is that David's political savvy proved to be a temporary bandage on an incurable wound.

Joab and his men track down Sheba to a little village called Abel. They lay siege to it, which means they surrounded the city, cut off food and water supplies, and waited for everyone in the village either to die of thirst and starvation or to die from disease. Either way, not a good way to go! Instead of suffering in those ways, the people of Abel caught Sheba, cut off his head, and threw it over the wall to Joab. Joab then released the city from siege and went back to David in Jerusalem (with Sheba's head, of course).

What a mess! David's return to the throne in Jerusalem cannot be described as "ideal." And that is, no doubt, the point. The Scriptures give the raw and real. And it is important to remember once again that just because the Bible *describes* certain actions does not mean God *prescribes* those actions. Disembowelment, murder, beheading, revolt, and intrigue do not carry divine sanction here. But they do reveal the horrific and sometimes hauntingly real world in which we live.

Second Samuel 21 carries the realism further with a story of David's settling things with the Gibeonites. The Gibeonites, we remember, have a rather checkered past with Israel. At the time of the conquest and entrance into the promised land under the leadership of Joshua, they deceived Israel in a treaty (Josh 9). The Gibeonites also experienced terror at Saul's hands in the early monarchy. It is unclear when this event happened, but at some stage Saul slaughtered the Gibeonites because the Lord says to David that Saul had done just that (2 Sam 21:1).

Yahweh tells David this information after the king inquired of Him. And David had inquired of the Lord because "there was a famine for three successive years" (21:1). When famine strikes God's land, there is usually a reason for it, at least according to the biblical account. Both Leviticus 26:20 and Deuteronomy 28:24 indicate that Yahweh sends famine to His land as a result of the infidelity of His people. It is a way for God to snap His people out of their apathy, lethargy, and rebellion so they would turn back to Him. Although the narrative never clearly tells us that the famine is divine discipline, the sharp Israelite reader would certainly not miss it. It reveals that all is not well in Israel under David's reign.

At any rate, when David inquired of the Lord as to why they experienced such a terrible famine, Yahweh informed David, "It is because of the blood shed by Saul and his family when he killed the Gibeonites" (21:2). David went to the Gibeonites to determine what restitution could be made. Their response? David should give seven remaining sons from Saul's family for execution and display: "Let seven of his male descendants be handed over to us so we may hang them in the presence of the LORD at Gibeah of Saul, the LORD's chosen" (21:6). David did as they requested, only sparing Mephibosheth.

Finally, the text reveals that the Philistine problem kicks up again in David's reign (21:15–22). Not only that, the Philistines who appeared at this time all descended from, get this, Goliath! David defeated the giant at the birth of his reign, and now in his dotage giants enter into the land once again. Although David did defeat these Philistines, as the text records (21:22), the fact that they appear in the narrative at this juncture draws attention to impending and continuous conflict and threat. All told, this casts a long, dark shadow on the reign of the once promising king.

Abiding Consequences of Sin

In so many ways 2 Samuel 21 serves as a fitting conclusion to chapters 9–20: David's rise, and fall, and return. But the return is complicated, bloody, and ambiguous. What are we to learn from this chapter, and what does the narrative want to communicate? Over and above all, we are to learn the abiding consequences of sin.

Firth is one of the best commentators on the narrative of Samuel and notes the importance of this lesson (*1 & 2 Samuel*, 506–7). Sin takes us much farther than we want to go, and its reach is far greater than we ever could have imagined. The sins of both Saul and David are like stones thrown in the middle of a pond. The initial plunge into the water makes a big splash, but the ripples move from the middle of the pond, to the shore, and then back to the middle in innumerable waves and mini-collisions. This is the nature of sin. One never can calculate its fallout.

Saul's sin impacts not only himself but also his family. The death of Saul's lineage (2 Sam 21) almost appears out of nowhere. However, it appears as an exclamation point on the failed, faithless reign of that feckless king. But before we go too hard on Saul, the narrative reminds us that both kings are equally offensive.

David's sin impacts not only himself but also his family. His accession to the throne is anything but peaceful. Although the death of Saul's lineage appeared out of nowhere, David's troubles are plainly foreshadowed. The text has hinted and shown that David's sin impacted the king, his family, his kingdom, and the nations around him. David's sin brought horrific consequences one after another in an unending succession of pain.

As biblical narrative is designed to instruct its readers, we should not miss the lesson here. The fallout of sin is like that of a nuclear disaster: its impact is immeasurable. As Christians, we like to think that Jesus forgives our sin and takes the blame of guilt away. And this is, without doubt, true. Jesus delivers us from the guilt and blame of sin. The stain of sin is washed away. We stand holy and righteous before a holy God because Christ's blood covers us.

However, on this side of eternity, consequences of sin still remain. Imagine that a student became intoxicated and drove his vehicle drunk. As he is driving, he loses control and strikes a family in an SUV in an oncoming lane. The family is killed. The student lives. Now imagine that the student confesses his crime, accepts responsibility, and takes his punishment from the state. We would say that the punishment fit the crime and that the student should understand that actions have consequences.

Now imagine that this student is a Christian. Let's say he confesses his sin and repents of it. Is he forgiven? Yes. But do the consequences remain? Yes. He is freed from the stain of sin and the blame that comes with it. He is not condemned for his sin before God because the blood of Jesus covers him, and he is hid in the cross of Christ. And yet the fallout of sin still remains. A family is dead. A student is in jail. And parents are deprived of their son. Sin has consequences that abide long after the sin is committed.

Second Samuel 19–21 depicts in awful detail the fallout of sin. There is some hope despite the fallout. The good news in the midst of the fallout is that sin does not have to be the final word on our lives eternally. We can be freed from the blame of sin before God even if we face consequences of sin and wrestle with them day in and day out. The consequences of sin do not determine our eternal destiny, but they do affect our days now.

This is why it is important to keep the good news of Jesus before our eyes. Jesus gives us hope to endure today and confidence that we will endure for eternity. The blood of Christ tells us that our today, whatever our circumstances, does not determine our tomorrows. Jesus has given a word on our future if we are in Him: we will be with Him. This confidence that Christ gives us for tomorrow actually gives us strength for enduring today.

Waiting for the King

Finally, the close of the king's return to the throne of Israel reminds us that David will not be the Savior the world needs. By the close of his story, the giants have returned, sin's stench wafts through the halls of the palace, and his dynasty has been tattered by a royal coup and political intrigue.

If the kingdom of God is God's rule over God's people in God's land, the kingdom of David was decidedly not a faithful presentation of that ideal. The world would wait for another Davidic king to bring in that kingdom.

Only in the advent of Jesus do we have the announcement of the kingdom. Jesus' words are crystal clear: "Jesus went to Galilee, preaching the good news of God: 'The time is fulfilled, and the kingdom of God has come near. Repent and believe in the good news!'" (Mark 1:14-15). Jesus would bring God's kingdom at the fullness of time.

In the meantime God's people would wait. They would wait for the King to come. They would wait for God's reign to be brought to reality in the real world.

Reflect and Discuss

1. How does this passage help you understand God?
2. How does this passage of Scripture exalt Jesus?
3. Summarize the steps David took to get to the place of mourning in 2 Samuel 19. How does David's journey to mourning impact you? Do you experience compassion for him, or is your response to David's journey more in tune with the phrase "he made his bed; let him lie in it"? Why do you think you respond the way you do?

4. Why do you think the text presents David as the consummate politician, even after Absalom's death?

5. In what ways does the failure of David's political strategies in 2 Samuel 19–21 reveal that David is not the king for whom Israel ultimately longs?

6. Why does Joab murder Amasa? Write down your thoughts and share them with someone you trust. In what ways do Joab's motives reflect the dark side of the human heart?

7. What is the significance of the return of the Philistine giants in 2 Samuel 21?

8. List how many ways God's word in 2 Samuel 12:20 comes to pass in David's life in chapters 13–21. What does this say about the certainty and reliability of the Word of God?

9. Can you identify with how sin carries with it a lot of unintended consequences? Reflect on the consequences you have experienced in the past or are experiencing now.

10. Allow God to challenge you to trust Him and spurn sin. But also allow God to encourage you in the gospel: The consequences we experience today are not eternal for tomorrow! The blood of Christ provides a future where the consequences of sin will have no bearing on life in the new creation. Allow God to encourage you in that hope.

The King's Final Praise

2 SAMUEL 22–23

Main Idea: David's final songs teach of the glory of Yahweh and the anointing of Yahweh's king; they help us see Jesus.

I.   **Yahweh the Deliverer**
II. **Is David Righteous?**
III. **The Majesty of Yahweh**
IV. **He Trains My Hands for War**
V.   **The Reign of the Messiah**

Introduction

Second Samuel 22:1-51 and 23:1-7 mark the final songs sung by David. They parallel Hannah's Song of praise in 1 Samuel 2:1-11 in major themes. As such, they provide the "bookends" of the entire story of 1–2 Samuel and establish the major themes of the book. The hero in both Hannah's and David's songs of praise is none other than the incomparable Yahweh. We should not miss this all-important point. Yahweh is the hero of Samuel!

But many would object: surely Jesus is the hero. Some have argued that in preaching and teaching surely Jesus is the one we sing—Yahweh plays second fiddle. Actually, we should not drive a wedge between Jesus and Yahweh. This would lead to a division of the triune God for our people. Sidney Greidanus helps us avoid this pitfall by reminding us that to be Christocentric is necessarily to be God centered. Another way to say it is this: to preach Christ will mean to preach the fullness of God, including the Father, the Son, and the Holy Spirit. Greidanus reminds us that "the first New Testament principle to remember is that Christ is not to be separated from God but was sent by God, accomplished the work of God, and sought the glory of God" (*Preaching Christ*, 179).

When David and Hannah exalt Yahweh in all His glory, they are by necessity exalting Christ. For Jesus is always there in the Godhead. And Yahweh's redemptive plan and work through the earthly messiah are gloriously fulfilled in the ministry of Jesus, the Son (John 6:57). Jesus lives to do the will of the One who sent Him. And we know who He is through the Old Testament. So how do David's words glorify Yahweh and His divine Messiah?

Yahweh the Deliverer

Verses 2-3 of 2 Samuel 22 pile up first-person pronouns one on top of the other (11 in all) to present the extraordinarily personal tone of the entire song. This is not a recounting of a God that David does not know—Yahweh is his God! Through the entire journey from his anointing to the later years of his life, Yahweh is eternally "my God" for David.

And what is the nature of Yahweh for David? Yahweh is the deliverer:

> The One who protects from external threat: He is the rock and fortress.
> The One who protects from enemy arrows: He is the shield.
> The One who hides David from harm: He is a refuge.
> He is the One who anoints David for purpose: He is the horn of salvation.

In all this Yahweh is "my deliverer." David has seen his fair share of enemies. His own father-in-law wanted him dead and tried to kill him multiple times! David learned that Yahweh delivers. He encountered enemy nations like the Philistines! David learned that Yahweh is his salvation. He learned that revenge is not his but in the hands of the Lord. He learned from Nabal that God is the One who rights wrongs. In this, David discovered that Yahweh is the One who saves him from violence. Verse 4 crystallizes David's praise in verses 2-3: "I called to the LORD, who is worthy of praise, and I was saved from my enemies."

Verses 5-7 take the image of God's salvation from personal distress further. In these verses Yahweh delivers at a cosmic and eternal scale. David says that death, destruction, and Sheol threatened to swallow him whole. But he called to Yahweh in his distress and the Lord heard his voice. Verse 7 says that God heard David's cry from "His temple." Why is this significant, and why does David say this? In the Old Testament the temple (particularly the throne of God) is the place where God hears cries of distress and issues divine verdicts. From the temple God moves to act in justice. We see this in other passages as well. In the Minor Prophets, for example, the prophet Jonah longs for this place in his time of trouble; his petition goes up "toward Your holy temple" (Jonah 2:4,7). Jonah's prayer goes before the Lord in the temple so that he could receive the divine verdict on his prayer of distress. In Micah 1:2, from the "holy temple" Yahweh is a witness against all the peoples and all the earth. As a witness against the lawlessness of His world, God renders judgment from the temple against His people and land (Mic 1:3-7). Yahweh's faithful ones look to the temple because it is there He will give His divine decree. This is the place where God vindicates the righteous and punishes the wicked. So from the temple God hears and responds.

Yahweh's response is deliverance. Verses 9-16 present the earth responding to Yahweh marching out to deliver His anointed, David. Similar presentations occur in the Old Testament—Habakkuk 3:3-13 is a good example (see Thomas, *Faith Amid the Ruins*, esp. ch. 4, "Habakkuk's View of God"). David summarizes the deliverance in verses 17-20. Why did Yahweh do this? Because David had prayed for help (v. 7), but the text also says that Yahweh delivered for another reason: "He rescued me because He delighted in me" (v. 20). The connection of Yahweh's delight in David has to do with the fact that David was a man after God's own heart (1 Sam 13:14) but also the fact that David is Yahweh's chosen leader. David has found favor in Yahweh's sight, and Yahweh has brought him back to rule in Jerusalem, thus answering his prayer from 2 Samuel 15:26 (see Firth, *1 & 2 Samuel*, 519).

Is David Righteous?

Verses 21-27 read strangely to many, no doubt. David says some seemingly crazy things:

He is righteous and has clean hands (vv. 21,25).
He has "kept the ways of the LORD" (v. 22).
He was "blameless" and sinless (v. 24).
He is "faithful" and "pure" (vv. 26,27).

After reading the story of David from 2 Samuel 12 through 21, in what world can David say these things with a straight face? Well, David is telling the truth. Readers often like to read a song like this and think David is speaking in vague generalities about his spiritual state. The opposite, however, is true. David is speaking about specific ways he has been righteous (which is probably better translated "innocent"), cleanhanded, and sinless. To Saul's descendants, for instance, he did not bring shame in the case of Mephibosheth, Ziba, or even Ish-bosheth. David twice spared Saul's life (1 Sam 24; 26). He can say that he followed the Lord. The point is that he is not making *general statements* about his spiritual state but rather identifying *specific and important moments* of fidelity to

Yahweh. Still the statements carry an ironic twist. As Firth rightly says, it is important to remember that in the book of Samuel

> the claim is that David received the reward of the kingdom because he refused to seize it. Yet even as this is highlighted, placing this poem after the events concerning Uriah is an ironic reminder of what David has also done. There is a positive statement by and about David and an ironic criticism of him, criticism that knows David has been both punished and forgiven. (*1 & 2 Samuel*, 519)

David can praise God for his fidelity to Yahweh. This is good and right. David has exercised faithfulness *to* Yahweh. But we see, in turn, that at every turn the faithfulness *of* Yahweh stands out again and again. It is not the righteousness of David that is primarily in view but the righteousness of Yahweh. And it is the righteousness of God to which he clings. In this way, strangely, these verses point us to the gospel: only those who run to the Lord and Christ's righteousness will be saved.

There is another word for this kind of people: the "afflicted"—those who know their desperate need for the Lord. And this is the term David uses in verse 28: Yahweh saves the "afflicted." God saves people who are not proud, those who know how wicked and broken they actually are. God saves those who are absolutely and utterly dependent on the Lord. Or as the apostle James says, "God resists the proud, but gives grace to the humble" (Jas 4:6).

The Majesty of Yahweh

Verses 32-34 remind us of the incomparable majesty of Yahweh. He is once again a "rock." But the comparison is taken further to the form of a question: "For who is a god besides Yahweh? And who is a rock besides our God" (22:32, authors' translation). In verse 32, David uses two names of God: Elohim and Yahweh. Yahweh is the covenant name of the Lord. To know Yahweh is to know the covenant Lord of the patriarchs, of Israel, and of David. Elohim is the name used in contexts when creation is mentioned. So David combines both names of God: Yahweh and Elohim. He is the God of creation and Lord of the covenant. No other being can claim the power of deity as can Yahweh. There is no other. David's words here express the majesty and sheer otherness of Yahweh. There is no god but the true God, and He has a name: Yahweh-Elohim.

He Trains My Hands for War

Verses 35-49 depict how Yahweh enables His messiah to vanquish all rivals. Yahweh strengthens and protects the messiah (vv. 35-36). He gives the messiah stability and stamina to pursue, overtake, and defeat enemies. The idea is that David's enemies are on the run and now David just has to finish off the final skirmishes. As there was irony present in David's "righteousness," we can see there is a certain irony in David's "victory" over enemies as well, in the light of 2 Samuel 19–21. Although David has defeated specific enemies, it appears that they keep cropping up again and again! And giants like Goliath seem to hang around (21:15-22). Nonetheless, the hero of the text is Yahweh, who strengthens His messiah to defeat all rivals and reign over all peoples (vv. 44-46). The Davidic messiah, then, is king over Israel, but David says something more: that the messiah is the king over all nations.

The Reign of the Messiah

Second Samuel 22:50-51 and 23:1-7 present the reign of the messiah. Although Yahweh trains the messiah's hands for war, the closing statement in the praise of 2 Samuel 22 is not that of a warrior. David closes his psalm with praise:

> *Therefore I will praise You, Lord, among the nations;*
> *I will sing about Your name.*
> *He is a tower of salvation for His king;*
> *He shows loyalty to His anointed,*
> *to David and his descendants forever.* (22:50-51)

The final image of David is that of a worshiper. He is the leader who praises Yahweh and draws all other nations to sing the praises of Yahweh as well. The reign of the messiah, David instructs us, is not marked by war but praise. The personal way the psalm of praise began also now closes the song. David sings the praises of Yahweh's name. There is power in the name of Yahweh. As David calls on the name of Yahweh, the true God delivers. As David appeals to Yahweh by name, Yahweh does wonders on David's behalf. So David draws all nations to celebrate and revere the name of the God who is above all others: Yahweh! And Yahweh is revered because of the covenant kindness and loyalty Yahweh shows to the messiah (anointed) and his dynasty. This last statement in verse 51 confirms the Davidic covenant recorded in 2 Samuel 7. Yahweh will not abandon the dynasty of David. They may rebel and be wayward, but Yahweh will discipline them and bring them back. The Davidic messiah is the one through whom Yahweh will bless the world.

It is no wonder that 2 Samuel 23:1-7 follows on the beautiful affirmation of 22:51. In this psalm the Davidic covenant and the Davidic messiah stand central. In this psalm a number of interrelated topics proceed one to the next:

> The Davidic messiah is imbued by the Holy Spirit to speak
> good words (v. 2).
> The Davidic messiah will rule justly over his kingdom (v. 3).
> The Davidic messiah's just rule is like sun and rain, refreshing
> the kingdom (v. 4).
> The Davidic messiah is bound to Yahweh's everlasting
> covenant (v. 5).
> The Davidic messiah's enemies will be cast away forever
> (vv. 6-7).

David speaks more than he knows. In fact, his words are prophetic. Although he speaks words of praise about the favor of Yahweh on the Davidic house and the Davidic covenant, his words speak toward God's continuing work with the family of David. David's words are not just retrospective about what Yahweh has done with him in the past, David's words anticipate the kind of rule his children should strive toward and their commitment to this Yahweh.

David's words do apply to his own experience and his hopes for the coming Davidic kings. But the song pushes forward to the ultimate Davidic King, Jesus. We like the way Peter Leithart describes 23:1-7. We would apply his thought to the entirety of 1–2 Samuel:

> The king described [in 2 Sam 23:1-7] applies to some degree
> to David, but the idea of the king as the rising sun is ultimately
> applied to the Messiah. 2 Samuel 23:1-7 is a full-length portrait
> of Jesus. He is the one who rules righteously and in the fear
> of the Lord, who brings the light of the new creation in His
> coming, who causes the land to flourish like a garden, and
> who takes up armor and spear against the thorns. But, as
> the next section makes clear, a righteous king also inspires
> imitation in his subordinates, and Jesus does the same, so that
> leaders of the church should aspire to approximate Him. All
> pastors and elders would do well to place 2 Samuel 23:1-7 on

the doorposts of their houses, on their wrists, on the frontals of their foreheads. (Leithart, *A Son to Me*, 309)

Reflect and Discuss

1. How does this passage help you understand God?
2. How does this passage of Scripture exalt Jesus?
3. Read through 2 Samuel 22–23. How do these songs speak to you and encourage you? Why do you think you respond the way that you do?
4. In what ways have you experienced God as a "refuge" and "rock" as David did?
5. In what ways does the description of Yahweh in 2 Samuel 22 encourage and challenge you? Write down your thoughts and share them with someone you trust.
6. Do you think you drive a wedge between Yahweh and Jesus, or do you see them united in the Trinity? Have you ever thought about how Jesus relates to Yahweh? Why or why not?
7. What is the significance of the Davidic covenant in 2 Samuel 22–23?
8. Reflect on the names of God in the songs: Yahweh and Elohim. How do we see different attributes of God through His names?
9. Read Luke 4:16-21. What similarities can you see between Jesus' words in Luke 4 and the reign of the King in 2 Samuel 23:1-7?
10. Reread 2 Samuel 23:1-7. Allow God to encourage you that we have a Messiah, Jesus. He brings justice, pleasant words, refreshment, forgiveness, and ultimate healing.

Still Searching for the King

2 SAMUEL 24:1-25

Main Idea: David's census reveals that God's people still search for the true King that is found in Jesus the Messiah.

I. **A Senseless (and Costly) Census**
   A. What was David doing exactly?
   B. Why was this census wrong?
II. **The Deep Waters of Sovereignty**
III. **God's Response and Ours**
IV. **The Gospel According to David**

Introduction

It should not surprise us that King David was a deeply flawed man whose life was full of foolish decisions and outright sinful behavior. He was, after all, simply a man and, like all of us, was liable to fall. What should surprise us, however, is how candidly Israel deals with David's sin. This is Israel's hero of heroes, the paragon of Israelite might and faithfulness, the man "after [God's] own heart" (1 Sam 13:14 ESV). And yet David's shortcomings are not covered up; in fact, they often take center stage in the biblical drama.

Perhaps no other story illustrates Israel's strange way of honoring their national hero than the way the book of Samuel ends. David does not exactly end his reign as a failure, but what we see is certainly not the "happily ever after" we might expect.

A Senseless (and Costly) Census

Modern readers are liable to quickly lose their way through a passage like 2 Samuel 24:1-10. The order of events is clear enough (though the ancient city locations can muddy the waters some), but the motivation behind these actions is what confounds us. What was David doing exactly? Why was it wrong? And didn't God initiate all this anyway? Let us tackle each of the first two questions in turn. The third, and most troubling, question we will return to once we have watched the entire story play itself out.

What Was David Doing Exactly?

Our first question is probably our last simple one: David was conducting a census of his entire country. Specifically he was concerned with counting the number of men who were (1) already in the army or (2) old enough to be drafted in the near future. There may have been other statistics the census workers gathered, but the only relevant detail we are given about the census results concerns the military: Israel and Judah have 1.3 million soldiers (v. 9). Quite an army.

The savvy reader will notice that the numbers mentioned in the parallel account (1 Chr 21) do not match the numbers here. Chronicles puts Israel at 1,100,000 and Judah at 470,000, while Samuel gives 800,000 and 500,000, respectively. While many contemporary critics assume the accounts are merely contradictory, a plausible reconciliation is at hand. First Chronicles 27 gives a detailed list of the Israelite standing army, numbering 288,000. The standing army seems to have been included in the 1,100,000 figure of Chronicles but omitted in the Samuel number. Thus Samuel outlines the number of prospective soldiers while Chronicles outlines the number of total soldiers—those already enlisted as well as those ready for drafting. Even compensating for this difference, of course, the numbers are not precisely identical. Accounting for the standing army, the Chronicles count sits at 812,000 and 470,000, while the Samuel count is 800,000 and 500,000. But the trailing 0s should serve to highlight that these numbers are obviously rounded figures. It is hardly a contradiction if the author of Samuel, knowing the precise figures, chose to use 800,000 and 500,000, much as we use broad figures in everyday speech today. When discussing the population of the United States, for instance, given differing circumstances, it may be equally valid to say that the current population of the United States is either 321,362,789 or 320 million.

Why Was This Census Wrong?

Most nations, modern as well as ancient, conduct censuses regularly. It is simply a matter of prudence: the government can only serve the interests of the people if they know who those people are. God had even given Israel regulations about census taking (Exod 30:11-16), so we cannot assume from this story that God is inherently anti-census. Something about this census specifically is out of order.

We get hints of this even from the dialogue between David and his commander, Joab. Joab does not provide us with reasons for his reluctance, but he lets David know that he finds the request troubling. In the end, however, David flexes his kingly muscles, and Joab is left with two options—follow orders or defy the king. He duly obeys. Ten months later the census is complete, but now David has come around to Joab's opinion. Instead of congratulating everyone on a job well done, he cries out in distress, "God, have mercy on me for my sin!"

Before we examine the specific reasons David's census is wrong, there was ultimately one reason: God did not want David to do it. Whether the issue is an ill-advised census or something more immediately relevant—like sexual ethics or financial stewardship—when God says no, our response must be to yield in submission. We may understand His restrictions. We may not. But we must always follow.

Our culture finds this kind of obedience unbearable. We assess God's rules and decide that we will follow His laws if and only if we understand and agree with them. This is arrogance of the highest order. If there is a God, we must come to the point where we accept that He makes the rules, even if we fail to understand them at first. He knows better than we do, so humility demands that if we are unsure, we submit to the One whose knowledge far exceeds our own.

Don't many of us intuitively know this from our own experience as parents? When one of our children grabs a fork and reaches to place it into the tiny slits in the wall that seem perfectly suited for that fork, how do we respond? "Don't do that. Forks don't go into the electric socket." When the reply inevitably comes, "But why, Dad?" how often do we go into specifics? "Well, son, you see, at the subatomic level, there are tiny particles called electrons jumping between orbits. This creates what is called an 'alternating current' that travels through the wires in the wall. And if that current enters your body, it disrupts your central nervous system, burning your skin and possibly stopping your heart." Go ahead and try that on a two-year-old and see if it does the trick. (We're doubtful.) There should come a day when they understand electricity enough to know why fork-in-socket is a bad idea. But for now we are all content to say, "Don't touch." Why? Because we, the parents, love our children. And while they are young, we know much more than they do.

The gap between a toddler's knowledge and ours, however, pales in comparison to the gap between our knowledge and God's. Far too many of us have deceived ourselves into thinking that God is only a slightly stronger, slightly wiser version of us. He is not. He created every cell in our bodies. He made the blazing sun in the sky—not to mention the billions of other stars throughout our galaxy and the billions of galaxies in the universe—with a single word. Isaiah tells us that He stretches the heavens out as effortlessly as a man drawing back a curtain (Isa 40:22). In the face of such power, do we not feel powerless and weak? And yet we too often forget that not only is God's *power* immeasurably greater than ours; so also is His *wisdom* far greater than ours.

God has reasons for every restriction, for every law, for every bit of wise counsel. Just because we fail to grasp those reasons does not mean they do not exist. Let us have the humility to follow God until we see as clearly as He sees. If we only obey God when He makes sense to us, then He has no business being called "Lord." He is merely our advisor.

Now, back to David. The problem with his census hinges on a key word—*delight*. When Joab asks, "But why does my lord the king *want* to do this," he uses a word that means "delight." In 22:20 David rejoiced that God "delighted" in him. In Psalm 40:8 David said, "I delight to do Your will, my God." But here in 2 Samuel 24 David apparently delights to know how many soldiers he has. His drive to number his people comes not from a desire to serve his nation but from delight in the size of his army. Behind this are three critical issues.

First, David's delight is a manifestation of pride. He is trying to rejoice in how strong he has made the institution. We mentioned above how a census can be a reasonable act of service for a nation. But it can also be an act of hubris, a way for a king to prove to the world that he has become somebody. Thus, for instance, when Caesar Augustus desired to show the world just how mighty he was, his vehicle for showing this might was to conduct a census of the entire Roman world. Ironically, at the same time Caesar was "proving" how great he was by counting his people, God was demonstrating His greatness by counting Himself among Caesar's people through the birth of His Son.

Second, David's census betrays a lack of faith. He wants to see how well Israel might fare in a battle against their enemies. Once again David has forgotten the promises of God, who told him that victory would come not through Israel's military size but through faith in their God. As David's friend Jonathan had said, "Nothing can keep the LORD from saving, whether by many or by few" (1 Sam 14:6). David believed this as a teenager standing toe-to-toe with Goliath. But now that he has grown up, his trust is no longer in the God of his youth but in the size of his military.

Third, David's census hints at a plan of military aggression. One of the main reasons you figure out how many fighting men you have is because you plan to pick a fight! David should have been delighting· in God, trusting in God, and keeping his eyes on God. Instead, he was leaning on his military and looking out toward the potential conquest of other nations.

David's census, when seen from this perspective, bears a tragic resemblance to Israel's apostasy at the start of 1 Samuel. They wanted a king other than God to be their security and treasure; now David wants an army to replace God as his security and treasure. When any of us delights in something other than God—be that an army, a king, a bank account, a healthy family, or a life of moral goodness—we can be assured that we are in the same predicament as David. The result for Israel, for David (as we will see), and for us is always disastrous.

The Deep Waters of Sovereignty

We come finally to the third question, mentioned previously: Why was God so indignant about this census when He initiated it? Was God here the author of evil? How can we call Him good if He orchestrates situations like this and then punishes people for His decision?

We are sailing out into deep waters with questions like these, but we cannot help but ask them. And here is a detail that makes the waters deeper still: in the parallel account of this story, Satan—not God— incited David to count his army (1 Chr 21:1). The author of Samuel says that God incited David, and the author of Chronicles says that Satan did. It is difficult to imagine a contradiction more significant than confusing God and Satan. So we must conclude that here we face one of the most obvious contradictions in all of Scripture.

Or do we? Biblical critics are quick to point to these two passages as hopelessly irreconcilable, one example of many they claim discredit the authority of Scripture. They are right to point to these verses as significant. They are wrong, however, to assume that the biblical authors are so desperately confused that they cannot spot the difference between God and His greatest enemy. What we find in 2 Samuel 24:1 is a case study in a complex but not irrational subject—God's sovereignty.

The Bible teaches that God sometimes allows us to fall prey to the temptations of Satan or our own evil desires. So in one sense God is not the one doing this. Satan is tempting us. Our flesh is inciting us. We are choosing to sin. But in another sense God remains sovereign over that process because He could have interrupted it if He so desired. He allows us to pursue evil not because He delights in it but in a way that even these evil decisions become part of His greater plan.

Seen this way, the statements in both 1 Chronicles and 2 Samuel are correct. The author of Chronicles looks at the scene from the ground level, so to speak, and rightly says that Satan was the one prodding David. The author of Samuel looks at the same scene from a different perspective and acknowledges that God had a sovereign purpose even in Satan's acts. Nothing is outside God's control. He works all things—even the horrendous and the seemingly pointless—according to His plan. Does this mean He approves of evil acts? Absolutely not! The sinful acts we commit are not God's fault but are an exercise of the legitimate moral freedom God has granted us. And we are responsible for the decisions we make and the actions we carry out. Still, even these do not subvert God's plan.

This is, admittedly, a mind-boggling mystery. God takes our free decisions, even the most malicious intentions of humanity and demonic forces, and uses those decisions for a perfect plan. We cannot speculate *how* He does it. But we must confess *that* He does it. Remember: God's wisdom is infinitely higher than ours. If we could understand all His ways, that would only prove His wisdom is nothing better than ours. If our God does not sometimes confuse and confound us, then we are not dealing with a God that is worthy of our worship. We are, instead, worshiping a version of ourselves. Let us examine our hearts and put a little less confidence in our own ability to understand, and let us stop trying to make God as facile and one-dimensional as we are.

God's Response and Ours

When the prophet Gad comes to give David the word from God, it probably made David wish Nathan had gotten the assignment instead. The word is patently harsh, and while David is given a choice, the options before him are all horrific (v. 13). He chooses divine pestilence over military rout and famine, and in the course of three days, 70,000 men are dead (v. 15). David had been dreaming of numbers for nearly ten months—but not this one. What began as a show of strength ends in weakness, blood, and tears.

This segment of the narrative raises more uncomfortable questions for the contemporary reader. We are prone to view God's response as an overreaction (at best) or as morally despicable (at worst). Let us take each of those possibilities in turn and show why God was neither over-reacting nor exhibiting moral wickedness.

First, while the text certainly majors on David's sin, that does not therefore exonerate the rest of Israel. God is not responding to one solitary person's sin by doling out punishment on 70,000 other unsus-pecting and otherwise unaware individuals. The judgment comes to the *nation* of Israel because David had led the *nation* of Israel to sin.

Throughout the Old Testament, when God brings judgment on a society, He does so because the society has grown violent and depraved. The flood in Noah's day was precipitated because God knew that "every scheme [humanity's] mind thought of was nothing but evil all the time" (Gen 6:5). Sodom and Gomorrah, two towns obliterated by God's wrath, are condemned because they oppressed the poor (Ezek 16:49). When Jonah was sent to proclaim judgment to Nineveh, it was a result of Nineveh's brutal violence toward surrounding nations.

God does not delight in pouring out His wrath. As He told Moses, He is "slow to anger" (Exod 34:6), meaning that while He does become angry, it is not His first response. Yet God's patience is not endless, and when a society reaches a certain threshold, God steps in to say, "Enough." He will not allow the poor, vulnerable, and weak to sit under the thumb of oppression forever.

How does this connect to Israel? The census was, we recall, patently military in its scope. Israel was beginning to become a nation like its neighbors, looking to dominate and conquer. They were on the road to becoming a nation that, if left unchecked, would become characterized by violence, one God would be forced to oppose. So God stretches out His arm—not completely, as in previous judgments, but just enough to stem the tide.

In one sense, then, this judgment is actually a show of mercy. Had God not interrupted Israel's trajectory, a future judgment would have been must worse. Seventy thousand slain is extreme, but it saved them from a much more devastating judgment later.

God still works like this in our lives today. When He sees us ruining our lives with sin, He cares too much about us simply to let us follow that course. So periodically He sends pain our way to protect us from a much worse judgment later on. We think when a husband, for instance, is caught in the middle of an affair that he is experiencing God's wrath. But it is more appropriate to see that as God's severe mercy. Wrath would be allowing the man to get away with it, continuing down the trajectory of sin.

This individual example, however, raises the second half of our question. "For the sake of argument," you say, "I'll allow that God wasn't overreacting. But wasn't the punishment a bit erratic? What about the innocent who died during this plague?"

Human suffering has always made people ask questions like this. Whether the context is 2 Samuel 24 or a tragic current event, in a thousand different forms the question arises: Why do bad things happen to good people?

In this particular context, as we have argued, Israel does not exactly qualify. The nation as a whole was implicated not only in the military expansion represented by the census but in other rebellious acts. Many of them had rebelled against David—God's anointed king—first under David's son Absalom, then again under a rebel by the name of Sheba. These were not "good people."

A similar principle applies when it comes to evil in our lives today. We generally find pain and tragedy foreign in our lives because we assume we are innocent and good. We think we deserve good things. But Scripture paints a different picture. The human race is not a helpless and hapless group standing under the wrath of a capricious god. We are a rebellious and crooked bunch who repeatedly spurn the goodness of our Maker. We are not good. We do not deserve good things. These are uncomfortable truths, but they are truths we must accept if life is to make any sense at all. Every one of us deserves judgment.

The 70,000 who fell during this plague were not any different—cosmically speaking—than the millions who survived. If we understand the depth and the breadth of our depravity, what will surprise us is not God's judgment but His mercy. After all, even on the eve of God's judgment, David does not accuse God of injustice. Instead, he says, "Please, let us fall into the LORD's hands because His mercies are great" (v. 14). Faced with the imminent death of tens of thousands, David was not frustrated with God's wrath. He was confident in God's mercy.

If we react against the idea of God's wrath generally, it may be because we feel that we ourselves are not worthy of it specifically. The more we are persuaded of our own righteousness, the more the question of God's justice troubles us. However, the more we sense the noose of God's judgment rightly around our own necks, the more we will grow amazed at the greatness of God's mercy and not the severity of His justice.

The Gospel According to David

There is a pernicious idea present in the church today that the Old Testament God is full of wrath and judgment but that by the time of the New Testament, He had matured. So instead of fire and brimstone, we get Jesus, meek and mild. Not only does this severely truncate the ministry of Jesus, but it also distorts the Old Testament image of God. As David learned at the threshing floor of Araunah, the Old Testament God was more merciful than we could ever hope.

Note the verb used of God in verse 16—*relented*. Some translations say that God "changed His mind" or "regretted" what He was about to do. We must be careful here. When we humans experience regret or change our minds, it is nearly always a result of having made some mistake. But as Numbers reminds us, "God is not a man who lies, or a son of man who changes His mind" (Num 23:19). Whatever else this word means, it cannot mean that God suddenly realized He had taken a wrong turn. His relenting was not a course correction. Instead, it was the overflow of His great pity on His people.

God had every right to flex His arm and demolish Jerusalem. But as so often happens throughout Scripture—as so often happens in our lives—God relents. His heart is grieved not because He has made a mistake but because His compassion for us is boundless. And so, on a day that could have been marked solely by death and disaster, God draws back His hand. At the spot God's wrath subsided, God commands David to buy the field and build an altar there (v. 18).

What we do not see in 2 Samuel is that the threshing floor was atop Mount Moriah (2 Chr 3:1). This was the same place Abraham had offered the attempted sacrifice of Isaac, where God had stopped him and told him to offer a lamb instead. This threshing floor would later be the place where David's son Solomon would build the temple, where Israel would come to offer sacrifices for their sins. All three of these scenes, occurring years apart at the same place, point to the same reality: one day there would come a sacrifice who would satisfy God's wrath and take away sin forever—Jesus, the ultimate Lamb of God.

Jesus would accomplish what no previous sacrifice, no previous king could have accomplished. When Isaac's spot on the altar was replaced by a ram, it meant the deliverance of Isaac—for a time. But Isaac would still one day die. When the lambs were sacrificed in Solomon's temple, it meant the deliverance of Israel—for a time. But the sacrifices had to be made every day, every week, every year. And when David cried out to

God, "I am the one who has done wrong. But these sheep, what have they done? Please, let Your hand be against me and my father's family" (v. 17), he was offering himself as a sacrifice. David could never be that sacrifice. Yet David looked down at that field, and through history, and saw the Shepherd who really would be smitten for His wayward sheep.

Throughout 1–2 Samuel, as with most books in the Old Testament, we are left with a sense of disappointment. David was Israel's great hope, but he was not the king Israel needed. Nor is this unique to 1–2 Samuel. Moses, the lawgiver, cannot go into the promised land because he broke the law. David, Israel's greatest king, is a sinner who cannot save his people. He wishes he could die for them, but he cannot. Nehemiah, the rebuilder of Jerusalem, constructs a city that makes people weep in shame when compared to its former glory.

What we need is a Lawgiver who can both keep the law and redeem us when we break it, a Builder of a glorious kingdom that can never be shaken, a Shepherd who will not abuse His sheep but will die for them, a Father who will not neglect His children but will pursue them to the point of death and lay down His life for them, a King who will not sin against His people but will die in their place. That role could never be filled by Moses or David or Nehemiah. It was filled, once and for all, by Jesus Christ, God's Son.

From first to last, David's life is meant to point us to Christ. In Christ we find not only an example but a Savior, someone who both humbles us in times of strength and gives us hope in times of weakness. Jesus Christ is the only King who, if we receive Him, will satisfy us and, if we fail Him, will die for us. This is our King, and there is none like Him.

Reflect and Discuss

1. How does this passage help you understand God?
2. How does this passage of Scripture exalt Jesus?
3. How does this passage once again transition the story toward David's failure as king?
4. Why is it once again important to recognize that David is not the perfect king?
5. How do you handle it when you do not understand God or why God has done something?
6. Do you have a general negative perception of the wrath of God? Why or why not? Write down your thoughts.

7. In what ways do you think God's wrath and God's mercy relate to each other?
8. How does Jesus beautifully picture both the wrath and the mercy of God?
9. Why does David command the military census?
10. Are there times in your life where you can identify the same kind of pride David experienced? When was it, and why did you exhibit such pride?

WORKS CITED

Anderson, Bernhard W. *Contours of Old Testament Theology*. Minneapolis, MN: Fortress, 1999.

Barth, Karl. *Church Dogmatics*. III/1: *The Doctrine of Creation*. London: T&T Clark, 1958.

Becker, Ernest. *The Denial of Death*. New York: The Free Press, 1973.

Bennetts, Neil. "Beauty for Ashes." © 2000 Daybreak Music Ltd. TS641.

Boda, Mark J. *After God's Own Heart: The Gospel According to David*. Phillipsburg, NJ: Presbyterian and Reformed, 2007.

Bonhoeffer, Dietrich. *Ethics*. Translated by N. H. Smith. New York: Macmillan, 1965.

———. *Temptation*. New York: Macmillan, 1953.

Borowski, Oded. *Daily Life in Biblical Times*. Archaeology and Biblical Studies, 5. Edited by Andrew G. Vaughn. Atlanta: Society of Biblical Literature, 2003.

Brodie, Thomas L. *The Crucial Bridge: The Elijah-Elisha Narrative as an Interpretative Synthesis of Genesis–Kings and a Literary Model for the Gospels*. Collegeville, MN: The Liturgical Press, 2000.

Brueggemann, Walter. *David's Truth: In Israel's Imagination and Memory*. Minneapolis, MN: Fortress, 1985.

———. *First and Second Samuel*. Interpretation. Louisville, KY: John Knox, 1990.

———. *Genesis*. Interpretation. Louisville, KY: John Knox, 1982.

Chalmers, Aaron. *Exploring the Religion of Ancient Israel: Prophet, Priest, Sage and People*. Downers Grove, IL: IVP Academic, 2012.

Day, Peggy L. "Concubines." In *Eerdmans Dictionary of the Bible*. Edited by David Noel Freedman. Grand Rapids, MI: Eerdmans, 2000.

Doorly, William J. *The Religion of Israel: A Short History*. New York: Paulist, 1997.

Drinkard, Joel F., Jr., and Dan R. Dick. *The God of Hope: A One-Volume Commentary on God's Promises*. Nashville, TN: Thomas Nelson, 2013.

Dumbrell, William J. *Covenant and Creation: An Old Testament Covenant Theology*. Revised and enlarged edition. Milton Keynes, UK: Paternoster, 2013.

Ellis, E. Earle. *The Gospel of Luke.* New Century Bible Commentary. London: Marshall, Morgan & Scott, 1974.

Firth, David G. *1 & 2 Samuel.* Apollos Old Testament Commentary. Nottingham, UK: Apollos, 2009.

Goheen, Michael W. *A Light to the Nations: The Missional Church and the Biblical Story.* Grand Rapids, MI: Baker Academic, 2011.

Goldingay, John. *Men Behaving Badly.* Carlisle, UK: Paternoster, 2000.

Gordon, Robert P. *I & II Samuel: A Commentary.* Library of Biblical Interpretation. Grand Rapids, MI: Regency Reference Library, 1986.

Greear, J. D. *Gospel: Recovering the Power that Made Christianity Revolutionary.* Nashville, TN: B&H, 2011.

Green, Joel B. *The Gospel of Luke.* New International Commentary on the New Testament. Grand Rapids, MI: Eerdmans, 1997.

Greidanus, Sidney. *Preaching Christ from the Old Testament: A Contemporary Hermeneutical Model.* Grand Rapids, MI: Eerdmans, 1999.

Hahn, Scott W. *The Kingdom of God as Liturgical Empire: A Theological Commentary on 1–2 Chronicles.* Grand Rapids, MI: Baker Academic, 2012.

———. *Kinship by Covenant: A Canonical Approach to the Fulfillment of God's Saving Promises.* New Haven, CT: Yale University Press, 2009.

Hines, Nico. "Sunday Assembly Is the Hot New Atheist Church." *The Daily Beast* (2013). Accessible at http://www.thedailybeast.com/articles/2013/09/21/sunday-assembly-is-the-hot-new-atheist-church.html. Accessed August 7, 2016.

Hoerth, Alfred J., Gerald L. Mattingly, and Edwin M. Yamauchi, eds. *Peoples of the Old Testament World.* Foreword by Alan Millard. Cambridge, UK: Lutterworth/Grand Rapids, MI: Baker, 1998.

Howard, David M., Jr. "David." In *The Anchor Bible Dictionary: D–G.* Volume 2. Edited by David Noel Freedman. New York: Doubleday, 1992.

Hurtado, Larry W. *How on Earth Did Jesus Become a God? Historical Questions about the Earliest Devotion to Jesus.* Grand Rapids, MI: William B. Eerdmans, 2005.

———. *Lord Jesus Christ: Devotion to Jesus in Earliest Christianity.* Grand Rapids, MI: Eerdmans, 2003.

Johnson, Allen W., and Timothy Earle. *The Evolution of Human Societies: From Foraging Group to Agrarian State.* 2nd ed. Stanford, CA: Stanford University Press, 2000.

Keller, Tim. "The Prayer for David." MP3. Sermon delivered December 7, 2003.

———. *The Reason for God: Belief in an Age of Skepticism.* New York: Riverhead, 2008.

King, Philip J., and Lawrence E. Stager. *Life in Biblical Israel.* Library of Ancient Israel. Louisville, KY: Westminster John Knox, 2001.

Lamb, David T. *Prostitutes and Polygamists: A Look at Love, Old Testament Style.* Grand Rapids, MI: Zondervan, 2015.

Leithart, Peter J. *A Son to Me: An Exposition of 1 & 2 Samuel.* Moscow, ID: Canon, 2003.

Lewis, C. S. *The Four Loves.* Orlando, FL: Harcourt, 1960.

———. *Mere Christianity.* New York: HarperCollins, 2001.

Longman, Tremper, III, and Daniel G. Reid, *God Is a Warrior.* Studies in Old Testament Biblical Theology. Grand Rapids, MI: Zondervan, 1995.

Matthews, Victor H., and Don C. Benjamin. *Social World of Ancient Israel, 1250–587 BCE.* Peabody, MA: Hendrickson, 1993.

McCann, J. Clinton, Jr. *A Theological Introduction to the Book of Psalms: The Psalms as Torah.* Nashville, TN: Abingdon, 1993.

McCarter, P. Kyle. *II Samuel.* Anchor Bible Commentary. Volume 9. Garden City, NY: Doubleday, 1984.

Morris, Leon. *The Gospel According to Luke.* Tyndale New Testament Commentary. Grand Rapids, MI: Eerdmans, 1975.

Neusner, Jacob, ed. S.v. "David." In *Dictionary of Judaism in the Biblical Period: 450 B.C.E. to 600 B.C.E.* Volume 1. New York: MacMillan Library Reference, 1996.

Nouwen, Henri. *In the Name of Jesus: Reflections on Christian Leadership.* New York: Crossroad, 1992.

———. "Journey to L'Arche." Chicago Sunday Evening Club. Program 3301. First Air Date 1 October 1989. Transcript accessible at: http://www.csec.org/index.php/archives/23-member-archives/354-henri -nouwen-program-3301. Accessed October 12, 2014.

Owens, J. J. *Analytical Key to the Old Testament.* Grand Rapids, MI: Baker, 1989.

Peck, M. Scott. *People of the Lie: The Hope for Healing Human Evil.* New York: Simon and Schuster, 1983.

Peterson, Eugene H. *Eat This Book: A Conversation in the Art of Spiritual Reading.* Grand Rapids, MI: Eerdmans, 2006.

————. *First and Second Samuel.* Westminster Bible Commentary. Louisville, KY: Westminster John Knox, 1999.

————. *A Long Obedience in the Same Direction: Discipleship in an Instant Society.* 2nd ed. Downers Grove, IL: InterVarsity, 2000.

Pitre, Brant. "Jesus, the Messianic Banquet, and the Kingdom of God." *Letter & Spirit* 5 (2009): 145–66.

Sherman, Amy L. *Kingdom Calling: Vocational Stewardship for the Common Good.* Downers Grove, IL: InterVarsity, 2011.

Swindoll, Chuck. *David: A Man of Passion and Destiny.* Great Lives from God's Word. Volume 1. Nashville, TN: Thomas Nelson, 2000.

Thomas, Heath A. *Faith Amid the Ruins: The Book of Habakkuk.* Bellingham, WA: Lexham, 2016.

————. "The Old Testament, 'Holy War,' and Christian Morality." Pages 22–25 in *How and Why We Should Read the Old Testament for Public Life Today.* Comment Magazine Special Series. Edited by Ryan P. O'Dowd. Hamilton, Canada: Cardus, 2011. Online version: http://www.cardus.ca/comment/article/2991. Accessed August 7, 2016.

Thomas, Heath A., Paul Copan, and Jeremy Evans, eds. *Holy War in the Bible: Christian Morality and an Old Testament Problem.* Downers Grove, IL: IVP Academic, 2013.

Tsumara, David Toshio. *The First Book of Samuel.* New International Commentary on the Old Testament. Grand Rapids, MI: Eerdmans, 2007.

Wenham, Gordon J. *The Psalter Reclaimed: Praying and Praising with the Psalms.* Wheaton, IL: Crossway, 2013.

Wiersbe, Warren. *Be Successful (1 Samuel): Attaining the Wealth That Money Can't Buy.* Wheaton, IL: Victor, 2001.

Wigoder, Geoffrey, ed. S.v. "Barrenness." In *The New Encyclopedia of Judaism.* New York: NYU Press, 2002.

Witherington, Ben C., III. *Jesus the Seer: The Progress of Prophecy.* Minneapolis, MN: Fortress, 2014.

Wright, Christopher J. H. *The Mission of God: Unlocking the Bible's Grand Narrative.* Downers Grove, IL: IVP Academic, 2006.

Zimmerli, Walther. *Man and His Hope in the Old Testament.* Studies in Biblical Theology, 20. London: SCM, 1971.

SCRIPTURE INDEX

24:8-15 *154*
25 *161–62, 164, 166*
25:1-44 *16*
25:3 *162–63*
25:4-9 *162*
25:10-12 *162*
25:13 *163*
25:16 *162*
25:22 *163*
25:25 *163*
25:29 *163*
25:39 164
26 *161, 251*
26:8-25 *15*
26:9-10 *161*
26:9-23 *197*
26:10-11 *164*
27 *168*
27:12 *168*
27–31 *167*
28:1–31:13 *10, 34*
28:3-6 *168*
28:3-25 *14*
28:5 *168*
28:6 *169*
28:7-10 *169*
28:10 *169*
28:11 *169*
28:12 *170*
28:15 *170*
28:18 *170*
28:19 *170*
31 *179*
31:1-10 *172*

2 Samuel
1 *167, 179*
1:1-27 *34*
1–4 *12*

1:14-15 *164*
1:19-27 *11*
1–24 *9*
1:27 *10*
2 *28*
2:1–4:12 *10*
2–4 *15*
2:4 *179*
2:5-7 *179*
2–6 *178*
3 *180*
3:1 *180*
4 *180*
4:11 *181*
4:12 *164*
5 *28*
5:1-5 *96*
5:1–9:13 *10*
5:6-10 *181*
5–9 *211*
5:11-12 *181*
5:13 *17*
5:22-25 *182*
5–24 *12*
6 *178*
6:1-10 *182*
6:2 *22*
6:11-13 *186*
6:14 *188*
6:14-23 *188*
6:19 *190*
6:20 *188*
6:21-22 *188*
6:23 *17, 190*
7 *11, 23, 25, 28, 31, 37, 194, 197, 230, 233, 253*
7:1 *193, 207*
7:2 *193, 195*
7:4-11 *194*